SCIENTIFIC KNOWLEDGE IN CONTROVERSY

SUNY Series in Science, Technology, and Society
Sal Restivo, Editor

Scientific Knowledge in Controversy

The Social Dynamics of the Fluoridation Debate

BRIAN MARTIN

with a commentary by Edward Groth III

STATE UNIVERSITY OF NEW YORK PRESS

Published by
State University of New York Press, Albany

©1991 State University of New York

For information, address State University of New York
Press, State University Plaza, Albany, N.Y., 12246

Production by E. Moore
Marketing by Theresa A. Swierzowski

Library of Congress Cataloging-in-Publication Data
Martin, Brian, 1947–
    Scientific knowledge in controversy : the social dynamics of the
fluoridation debate / Brian Martin.
        p.   cm. — (SUNY series in science, technology, and society)
    ISBN 0-7914-0538-9.   —   ISBN 0-7914-0539-7 (pbk.)
    1. Water—Fluoridation—Social aspects. 2. Dental caries–
–Prevention—Social aspects. 3. Dental public health—Social
aspects.   I. Title.   II. Series.
    RA591.7.M37   1991
    306.4'61—dc20   90-34740
                                                                          CIP

10   9   8   7   6   5   4   3   2   1

CONTENTS

ACKNOWLEDGMENTS

Albert Burgstahler, Edith Waldbott, and many others (too numerous to mention) plied me with valuable information through correspondence. Gay Antonopoulos obtained copies of many publications for me through interlibrary loans. I thank the individuals listed in chapter 3 for their generosity in being interviewed. Discussions with Mark Diesendorf and Evelleen Richards provided me with insights. I received a large number of valuable corrections and comments on the earlier drafts from Albert Burgstahler, Brian Burt, John Colquhoun, Mark Diesendorf, Edward Groth III, Michael A. Lennon, Pam Scott, John Small, Donald Taves, and several anonymous reviewers. I especially thank Edward Groth III for his mammoth correspondence and for writing the commentary.

1

Introduction

The 1 August 1988 issue of *Chemical & Engineering News* contained an article that caused a sensation in the long-running controversy over fluoridation. "Fluoridation of Water," a special report written by associate editor Bette Hileman,[1] surveyed the arguments both for and against the measure.

Fluoridation is the addition of the element fluorine—called "fluoride" when in an ionized form—to public water supplies as a measure to help prevent tooth decay in children. Hileman's article outlined the standard view that fluoridation greatly reduces tooth decay, but also presented criticisms of this view. It described evidence both for and against claims that fluoridation may be involved in health problems, such as kidney disease, hypersensitive reactions, and cancer. It also recounted some of the methods used in the ardent promotion of fluoridation.

Hileman had not been involved in the fluoridation debate which has raged for decades. In writing the article, she studied the issue and consulted both supporters and opponents of fluoridation.

The ideas in her article were not new, and most of the evidence had been canvassed repeatedly in other forums. Why, then, did it cause such an impact? The reason is that never before had such a major scientific publication presented both sides to the debate in such an extensive treatment. In particular, never before in recent decades had a major professional association, such as the American Chemical Society which publishes *Chemical & Engineering News*, given the scientific criticisms of fluoridation such credibility.[2]

In the English-speaking countries at least, fluoridation has long been virtually untouchable for "serious scientists." Opponents of fluoridation have been categorized as cranks, usually right-wing, and akin to those who think the earth is flat.[3] In most dental, medical, and scientific journals, the arguments against fluoridation are given little space and little credence.

The *Chemical & Engineering News* article represented a dramatic contrast to the usual dismissal of antifluoridation views. The article generated news stories around the country and overseas, and led to a large volume of correspondence in later issues. Not surprisingly, opponents of fluoridation were delighted with the article; supporters were dismayed. More significantly, many correspondents congratulated Bette Hileman and *Chemical & Engineering News* for raising both sides of the issue for public discussion.

A BRIEF HISTORY

The use of fluoride to prevent tooth decay was promoted by various individuals in Europe in the 1800s.[4] But the key events on the road to fluoridation occurred later and in the United States.

Frederick McKay, a dentist, first noticed staining of teeth in his Colorado patients in 1901. The colors ranged from white, yellow, and brown to black. In serious cases, there was also pitting of the enamel. Unlike most others who had noticed this mottling, McKay was intrigued by it and, over the next three decades, he pursued its origins. He noticed that, whereas people who had lived in a particular community from birth had stained teeth, newcomers to the district did not. Further investigation convinced McKay that water supplies were responsible.

It was not until 1931 that chemical analysis provided an answer to what was causing the discoloration: fluoride. H. V. Churchill, chief chemist at the Aluminum Company of America, supervised tests on water samples and, with McKay's help, established a connection between fluoride in drinking water and mottled teeth. At about the same time, researchers M. C. Smith, E. M. Lantz, and H. V. Smith in Arizona were able to produce mottling in the teeth of rats by feeding them fluoride. Also in the same year, H. Velu reported the fluoride-mottling link based on work in Morocco and Tunisia.

McKay had long observed that mottled teeth, although unsightly, seemed to be more resistant to decay. Discovery of the fluoride connection finally stimulated the United States Public Health Service (USPHS) to investigate the issue. Led by H. Trendley Dean, USPHS scientists (mainly dentists) carried out surveys of decay in towns with different fluoride levels and also carried out experiments with animals.

A range of levels of fluoride led to the severe mottling observed by McKay and others. Severe mottling was widespread at five parts per million (ppm) and above, but less common at lower concentrations.[5] Investigators looked to see if there was a concentration which avoided most mottling while providing the benefits of reduced tooth decay. The level judged to be optimal in this regard was 1.0 ppm.

Only a small fraction of water supplies have high levels of fluoride naturally. Most have less than 0.2 ppm, a concentration too small to provide much impact on decay. In 1939, it was first proposed to add fluoride to waters which naturally have low fluoride levels. Fluoride would be added to bring the concentration to about 1.0 ppm.

The proposal struck a chord with a small number of dentists and public health officials in the United States who began campaigning vigorously for fluoridation. Many others were more cautious, including national health administrators and USPHS scientists who were still studying the dental effects of fluoride. In 1945, the first of a number of trials was begun. In these studies, two cities with similar characteristics were selected. Both had low natural levels of fluoride in the water. One city had fluoride added to its water supply, while the other's water remained unfluoridated. Rates of tooth decay in the cities were monitored by periodic examination of children's teeth.

The first study involved Grand Rapids, Michigan, where water was fluoridated in 1945. The water supply in control city, Muskegon, also in Michigan, remained unfluoridated. In the same year and in New York State, Newburgh's water was fluoridated, while Kingston served as the control. Other important early studies involved fluoridation of the water supplies in Evanston, Illinois, and Brantford, Ontario. Oak Park, Illinois, and Sarnia, Ontario, served as the respective controls.

At the time, it was thought that fluoride acted by being incorporated into the growing enamel of children's teeth. Hence, it would take quite a few years to see the full effect of fluoridation. The trials were planned to last ten or fifteen years. But after only a few years, the reported reductions in tooth decay were quite striking.

The proponents of fluoridation—in particular, a few enthusiastic advocates such as Wisconsin dentist John G. Frisch and Wisconsin dental administrator Francis Bull—were impatient with delay. Their lobbying was aimed especially at administrators in the USPHS, the most influential body in the public health field. H. Trendley Dean, whose work helped lay the ground for fluoridation, was not a supporter of rapid implementation, preferring to wait for the full results of the fluoridation trials. Along with others, his view was influential in maintaining the USPHS's cautious stand throughout the 1940s.

The high-pressure tactics of Frisch, Bull, and others eventually won out. The top administrators of the USPHS apparently overruled Dean,[6] and, in 1950, the USPHS endorsed fluoridation. Shortly afterward, two key professional bodies—the American Dental Association (ADA) and the American Medical Association (AMA)—also expressed support.

In the United States, however, decisions concerning public water supplies are made at the level of states, cities, or towns. The USPHS endorsement did not force any community to fluoridate, but it did provide vital authoritative backing for local individuals and groups that pushed for it.

The endorsements by the USPHS, ADA, and AMA were based on the claim that fluoridation resulted in massive reductions in tooth decay, typically quoted as 50 to 60 percent, with no associated health risks, and at little cost to the community. At the time, dental decay was widespread, and many dentists felt unable to cope with it. Many people had all their teeth removed at an early age due to decay. In this environment, fluoridation was an attractive proposition. During the 1950s, a large number of communities moved to fluoridate their waters.

But almost as soon as the push for fluoridation began in the 1940s, a vocal and persistent opposition arose. In many communities where fluoridation was proposed, there were local individuals and groups that claimed that it was dangerous. The opponents typically claimed that it caused certain health problems in some people, and that it was "compulsory mass medication" and, therefore, unethical as well as an abuse of government power.

This basic configuration of proponents and opponents has persisted from the 1940s until today. The arguments on each side have remained essentially the same. The proponents assert that fluoridation massively reduces tooth decay rates, has no proven adverse consequences for health (except negligible mottling of teeth, which is only of cosmetic concern), and is the cheapest and most effective way of getting fluoride to all members of the population. The opponents say that the benefits are overrated, that there are a variety of proven or possible adverse health consequences (including skeletal fluorosis, intolerance reactions, and cancer), and that fluoridation is unethical because it is compulsory medication with an uncontrolled individual dosage.

Although the arguments have remained much the same, the fortunes of fluoridation have waxed and waned. The population drinking fluoridated water in the United States greatly expanded during the 1950s, but the opposition caused local reverses and stopped many proposals. Since the 1960s, the fraction of the U.S. population served by water supplies with added fluoride has increased only gradually, and now hovers at about one half.[7]

From the United States, the message about fluoridation was sent around the industrialized world. Dental and medical authorities, after investigation, usually endorsed the measure. In several countries—especially Australia, Canada, Ireland, and New Zealand—the pattern has been similar to that of the United States: there has been widespread adoption of fluoridation in the face of strenuous opposition. On the other hand, in Britain, only one in ten people drinks fluoridated water. In continental Western Europe, the measure was greeted even more cautiously by government bodies, and fluoridation is found in only a few localities. Only in the Netherlands did a sizable fraction of the population ever receive fluoridated water, and that program was terminated in the 1970s. By contrast, several Eastern European governments have introduced fluoridation on a more substantial scale, although it is far from universal.

In nonindustrialized societies, fluoridation is not usually a feasible proposition. In some countries, tooth decay was not much of a problem as long as the diet remained sufficiently traditional. But as the diet became Westernized, with large amounts of refined and sugary foods, tooth decay became a serious problem. The main obstacle to fluoridation in nonindustrialized countries is a lack of centralized public water supplies. Often, water is obtained from private wells which are not suitable for fluoridation. There are some exceptions, such as urban Singapore which is entirely fluoridated.[8]

Table 1
Percentage of the Population Served by Water Supplies with Added Fluoride in Selected Countries in the Late 1980s.[a]

66	Australia	0	Lebanon
0*	Austria	0	Netherlands
0	Belgium	50	New Zealand
21	Brazil	0	Norway
36	Canada	7	Papua New Guinea
10	Chile	0*	Philippines
21	Czechoslovakia	3	Poland
0	Denmark	0*	Portugal
10	Fiji	0	Romania
2	Finland	100	Singapore
0	France	0	South Africa
20	East Germany	0	Sweden
0	West Germany	3	Switzerland
0	Greece	0	Thailand
0	India	0	Turkey
0	Iran	15?	U.S.S.R.
66	Ireland	9	United Kingdom
20	Israel	49	United States
0	Japan	0	Zimbabwe

*Greater than zero but less than 0.5 percent.
[a]For details see the appendix.

The proponent case has had no dramatic developments since 1950. The early promoters of fluoridation—including prominent figures such as H. Trendley Dean, John G. Frisch, and Francis Bull—have been followed by many others, such as Frank J. Mc-Clure, Ernest Newbrun, Herschel S. Horowitz, and Brian Burt. Other countries have their own lists of prominent proponents, including Douglas Jackson, John J. Murray, and Andrew J. Rugg-Gunn in Britain, and Noel Martin, Lloyd Carr, and Graham Craig in Australia.

The proponents refer to an accumulating body of data supporting the efficacy of fluoride in preventing tooth decay. They have also produced critiques on claims of hazards.

Compared to the proponents, it is easier to single out opponents among scientists around the world. George Waldbott was undoubtedly the most prestigious opponent in the United States from the 1950s until his death in 1982. Others have been Frederick Exner, Albert Burgstahler, and John Lee. These critics have concentrated on the health hazards of fluoridation, including allergic and intolerance reactions.

In the mid 1970s, John Yiamouyiannis and Dean Burk joined the debate when they made dramatic claims about a link between fluoridation and cancer, and, since then, this issue has been a continuing and contentious one. Yiamouyiannis is the most prominent opponent who is a scientist in the United States today.

Another side to the opponents' case is a critique of the evidence that fluoridation enormously reduces tooth decay. Waldbott, Exner, and others introduced this point, but the earliest comprehensive critique was presented by Philip Sutton, an Australian dental researcher, in 1959. In the 1980s, the critique of the size of benefits was taken up by John Colquhoun in New Zealand; Mark Diesendorf, Australia; John Yiamouyiannis, United States; and Rudolf Ziegelbecker, Austria. These individuals rank among the world's leading opponents of fluoridation who are scientists.[9]

The fluoridation debate has been such a bitter one that it is virtually impossible to say anything on the topic which cannot be questioned by one side or the other, or both. This applies to the history of fluoridation as much as to anything else. The abbreviated account I have given is largely the picture as presented by the proponents of fluoridation[10]. Some opponents have emphasized other events in the history, and given a different complexion to the whole account. I will have occasion to return to some events which have been the subject of debate. Suffice it to say that the selection of historical events as significant and the interpretation of motives are influenced by the stance of those making the selections and interpretations.

ANALYZING THE FLUORIDATION CONTROVERSY

The confrontation between expert proponents and opponents of fluoridation is a central focus in this book. By contrast, most social scientists have treated fluoridation as scientifically beyond dispute and have ignored natural scientists who are opponents.

These social scientists have focused on the popular opposition to fluoridation and tried to explain it by factors such as ignorance, political conservatism, alienation, and confusion. This approach exempts the scientific aspects of fluoridation from scrutiny. The resulting analyses of the controversy are one-sided, usually serving the proponents by implicitly denigrating the opponents.

To analyze the fluoridation controversy, I prefer to use instead what can be characterized as a power picture of science.[11] Instead of treating science solely as a search for truth, science is analyzed as is any other social activity, such as advertising or transportation. In this picture, science is something which people do which serves some interests in society more than others, epecially the interests of scientists themselves and of other groups with money and power enough to fund research and apply results.

Power is involved in all aspects of the practice of science, even in the daily processes by which scientists make decisions about what is valid knowledge. What is counted as knowledge depends on getting agreement from other scientists, and this may involve funding, status, or persuasive ability.

Fluoridation is a good topic in which to examine the dynamics of science and power because the opposition, while far from entirely successful, has not been totally submerged. The profluoridationists have been largely successful in maintaining their views as dominant among key groups in English-speaking countries, and this helps reveal the processes by which orthodoxy is established and perpetuated. But this insight is made possible by the persistence of a minority opposition, which ensures that the exercise of power in science is, to some extent, brought out into the open.

Furthermore, the issue has been a public one, and this means that many of the arguments for and against fluoridation have been spelled out with exceptional clarity. Internal disputes within the scientific community about theories of chemical catalysis, for example, do not generate very much accessible material for analysis. Finally, fluoridation combines technical, political, and ethical dimensions in a potent mixture.

In using the power picture of science to analyze fluoridation, I employ a variety of concepts and approaches. One is the idea of a "resource" or "tool." Various elements—including slogans, claims of scientific knowledge, publications (Hileman's article, for example), professional prestige, authoritative endorsements, community organizations, governments, and the mass media—have been used as resources in the struggle over fluoridation.

Another important concept is interest. For example, scientists have an interest in obtaining publishable results, establishing a good reputation, and having a good job. Corporate executives have an interest in increasing sales and profits, and also in protecting their executive status and privileges.

The idea of "social structure" or "social institution" is also valuable. For example, capitalism is a way of organizing work based on private property and the purchase of labor power. This results in patterned sets of relationships between people, such as the employer-employee relationship.

Rather than try to analyze fluoridation by using a single unified theoretical picture, I prefer to approach it at a series of different levels, using the concepts already mentioned where appropriate. I have selected parts of the controversy which highlight the interacting roles of knowledge and power.

Chapters 2 through 6 can be seen as a series of examinations of the fluoridation debate, and each shows the exercise of power on a successively larger scale. Each chapter reveals a power dynamic which casts a different light on the preceding chapters.

In chapter 2, I examine the arguments raised by scientists who support or oppose fluoridation in relation to benefits, risks, individual rights, and decision making. This can be considered to be an analysis at the level of intellectual debate, although, even here, the role played by other factors can be observed. In detailing the arguments, chapter 2 also sets the stage for the later analysis.

Proponents and opponents line up in an almost completely predictable fashion on the entire range of arguments, from science to ethics. Chapter 3 probes this remarkable coherency of viewpoints, which can be explained as a product of the polarizing nature of the fluoridation debate itself: the partisans develop their coherent views in order to make a solid case in the "rough-and-tumble" of public debates and campaigns. This analysis at the level of social psychology suggests that the scientific arguments outlined in chapter 2 have been shaped, directly or indirectly, by the requirements of public fluoridation debates.

Chapter 4 turns to the struggle for credibility, which involves obtaining authoritative backing and attacking the credibility of those on the other side. This means going far beyond attacking the credibility of scientific statements, which would constitute part of an intellectual dispute. Rather, the attack is on the credibility of individuals as scientists and as honest, sensible, and upstanding citizens. This is a level involving every possible use of rhetoric against the reputations of individuals as a tool in a struggle for authority. The existence of systematic attempts to undermine the credibility of individuals as people—rather than the credibility of their arguments, and to gain support on the basis of authority—shows the limitations of dealing only with arguments and views as in chapters 2 and 3.

Another exercise of power has been control over publication, research funding, and professional accreditation. In all these areas there are examples of the overt use of the power of the dental profession against antifluoridationists. Chapter 5 examines this side of the controversy by placing it in the context of the dental profession's support for fluoridation. This analysis at the level of professional power shows that the debate over scientific knowledge about fluoridation has involved more than language. It is not solely an intellectual dispute, nor a verbal duel for authority and credibility, as treated in chapters 2 to 4. Rather, the material basis for scientific communication, scientific research, and professional advancement—namely, publications, research grants, and accreditation—have been used as tools in the struggle.

Moving beyond a focus on individual researchers and partisans, chapter 6 looks at the role of industrial corporations, whose interests may have shaped the context of the fluoridation debate. This analysis, at the level of corporate power, suggests that the issue of fluoridation might not have arisen in the form that it took—or even become an issue at all—had the historical configuration of corporate interests and the dental profession been different.

Proceeding from chapter 2 through to chapter 6, the focus changes from the exercise of power at the level of individuals and arguments to the role of power at the large scale of social structures. All levels are required for a full picture. The large-scale, structural perspectives provide the context for detailed disputation; without these wider contexts, the debate might be imagined to be proceeding on the basis of fact and logic alone. But the structural perspectives do not tell the story by themselves. Rather, they provide a framework for and an influence on debate. Even so, only a detailed examination can tell what arguments are actually developed and deployed.

In chapter 7, I attempt to draw out some implications of the analysis. How *should* the debate be resolved? *Can* the debate be resolved? In retrospect, how could the proponents and the opponents have improved their strategies? I conclude that there is no simple answer to any of these questions. In confronting the fluoridation debate, one also confronts—implicitly or explicitly—basic issues about the organization of society.

A basic theme in my analysis is that it is impossible to separate the scientific and power dimensions of the fluoridation issue. In order to assess the scientific work on fluoridation, it is necessary to understand the wider social context—the careers of key individuals, the commitment of the USPHS and the ADA, and the potential of corporate support or hostility. All of these can influence what scientific research is done or not done, the predisposition of researchers to obtain particular types of results, and the assessment of contrary findings. The body of research relating to fluoridation, and the common evaluations made of it, cannot be separated from the wider power dimensions of the controversy.

Conversely, it is impossible to understand fully the power dimensions of the controversy without assessing the scientific issues. The common view that fluoridation is scientifically beyond question, as well as the minority view that it is scientifically indefensible, eliminate the possibility of understanding how scientific knowledge claims are embedded in power struggles. Assessing the struggles over scientific knowledge is essential to a full understanding of wider power dimensions.

It is not my task in this analysis to either support or oppose fluoridation. So far as I am concerned, that is a side issue. My interest is in the analysis of scientific knowledge as it is used and shaped in the course of a bitter public dispute. In developing my analysis, I have benefitted greatly from a handful of writers who have analyzed the issue without assuming that fluoridation is scientifically correct.[12]

Chapter 8 deals with the social analysis of the fluoridation controversy. I briefly describe standard approaches in previous studies, contrast my own approach with them, and defend my formal agnosticism about fluoridation. I also recount a potential difficulty encountered by those studying contemporary controversies: the involvement of the researcher, reluctant or otherwise, directly in the controversy.

In this book I present one way of looking at the issue of fluoridation. It is certainly not the only way. It is my hope that, in selecting some perspectives not often given attention previously, some will see this issue in a new light.

When I circulated the first draft of this book to a range of individuals for comment, I also invited them to write responses to my text. Edward Groth III took up this offer, and I am greatly pleased to have his insightful essay as part of this book. It deals with how to assess the scientific evidence on fluoridation. It is highly appropriate that Groth's views should be represented here, since his pioneering work on the fluoridation controversy has received insufficient attention.[13]

2

ARGUMENTS

The aim in fluoridation is to adjust the concentration of fluoride in public water supplies to the optimal level for dental health. The main beneficiaries are children up to the age of twelve or perhaps as old as sixteen. Benefits for adults are less certain.

The higher the concentration of fluoride in the water, the greater is the preventive effect against dental caries, commonly known as tooth decay. But as McKay discovered back in 1901, if the concentration is too high, staining and, in severe cases, pitting occurs. The optimal concentration of fluoride—considered to be about 1.0 parts per million (ppm)—is one which prevents tooth decay as much as possible without causing much mottling. In hotter climates where people drink more water, the concentration of fluoride is set lower, perhaps to 0.7 ppm. In cooler climates where people drink less water, the concentration is set higher, such as 1.2 ppm.

Fluoridation is not intended to provide a controlled dosage but rather to mimic naturally fluoridated water supplies which, as shown by H. Trendley Dean's studies in the 1930s, result in less tooth decay throughout the community. People who drink one liter of water with 1.0 ppm fluoride swallow exactly one milligram of fluoride. But different people drink different volumes of water.

Some, such as laborers and athletes, may drink several liters per day. Others may drink only milk or fruit juice and obtain no fluoride from the water supply. So, whereas the concentration of fluoride in the water can be specified and controlled, the dosage of fluoride to any individual is uncontrolled. ·

The most obvious way to ensure a precise dosage of fluoride is to take a tablet. Fluoride tablets have been advocated and used widely, especially in regions where water is not fluoridated or where there is no public water supply. The biggest problem with fluoride tablets is that most people find it a chore to take them. Children are expected to take them daily for the first 12 or so years of their life, and experiments show that few parents are able to instill the required habit.

By comparison, it requires no will power to reap the benefits of water fluoridation. Simply by virtue of drinking water, most people will obtain fluoride. This means that individuals who never go to a dentist, or those who have decay-producing diets due to poverty, ignorance, or preference, still obtain the benefits of fluoride. Admittedly, some children obtain less than the amount of fluoride specified as optimal. But water fluoridation still provides a wider cross section of benefits than do fluoride tablets, since more people drink some water than would persist in taking tablets.

Most promoters of fluoride to prevent tooth decay prefer water fluoridation over other methods of obtaining fluoride—so much so that the word "fluoridation" is normally taken to mean addition of fluoride to public water supplies. Water fluoridation gets to a larger fraction of the public and is also thought to be more effective than other approaches. It is also quite inexpensive on a per-capita basis, even when one considers that large volumes of fluoridated water are used in industry, to water lawns, and for other purposes. Only a tiny fraction of the water supply is actually consumed.

THE CASE FOR FLUORIDATION

The strength of the arguments in favor of fluoridation rests on the widely experienced pain of tooth decay, plus the claim that decay will be dramatically reduced by fluoridation and without any effort, harm, or much expense. A large segment of the population has experienced toothaches or seen their effects on family or friends. This set of experiences provides a powerful motivation to seek a way of reducing or eliminating this pain. Dentists in particular witness the problem regularly, and this helps explain why so many of them support fluoridation.

Fluoridation promises a solution which seems miraculous. Simply by adding a tiny concentration of a tasteless element to the water supply, tooth decay is supposed to be reduced by one-half or even more.

A limitation of the basic argument for fluoridation is that it only promises to prevent tooth decay. That doesn't help someone with a toothache *now*. If a fluoride tablet could positively cure decay, it would be much easier to sell. A quick cure is something that can be observed by anybody (although the *cause* of the cure may be debatable). Prevention is altogether harder to document and, therefore, harder to sell.

In their arguments for fluoridation, proponents most commonly refer to numerous scientific studies. The classic trials in Grand Rapids and Muskegon, Michigan; Newburgh and Kingston, New York; and other communities were designed to compare populations which were drinking fluoridated water against those drinking unfluoridated water. The researchers found that decay rates were greatly reduced in the fluoridated communities.

For example, John J. Murray and Andrew J. Rugg-Gunn refer to these studies in their authoritative book *Fluorides in Caries Prevention*. They conclude, "the strength of the experimental proof of the caries-inhibitory property of fluoride drinking water lies . . . in the fact that the three American studies, carried out by different investigators in different parts of the country, reached similar conclusions: addition of 1 ppm fluoride in the drinking water reduced caries experience by approximately 50 per cent."[1]

In surveying ninety-five studies from twenty countries on the effectiveness of fluoridation, Murray and Rugg-Gunn state that "The modal [most common] percentage caries reduction is 40-50 per cent for deciduous teeth and 50-60 per cent for permanent teeth—this is in agreement with the oft-quoted statement that 'water fluoridation reduces dental decay by half.' "[2]

In a briefer discussion of key clinical trials, prominent dental researcher Ernest Newbrun states that "the conclusion that fluoride is effective in reducing dental caries prevalence is based not only on clinical diagnosis of carious lesions but also on blind clinical and radiologic examination of children and on strictly objective criteria such as missing permanent first molars."[3] Similarly, Wesley O. Young, David F. Striffler, and Brian A. Burt, in a dental textbook, state that "Fluoridation is the most effective and efficient means of reducing dental caries on a community-wide basis. It reduces caries prevalence by 50 to 60 percent in the permanent dentition among children born and reared in a fluoridated community."[4]

These types of scientific findings are easy to use for promotional purposes. The results are presented typically to dentists, doctors, politicians, and the general public in the form of statements such as "More than 50 years of research and practical experience have proved beyond a reasonable doubt that fluoridation is effective in preventing tooth decay. Hundreds of studies have demonstrated reductions in tooth decay of 60-70% in communities with either natural or controlled fluoridation."[5]

Many antifluoridationists have left unchallenged the research results showing reductions in tooth decay by fluoridation. There are several reasons for this. First, there are many studies showing such reductions, as well as numerous studies of the microscopic processes in the mouth which explain how reductions can occur. It is hard to counter such a preponderance of research. Second, most of those who have done research on the effect of fluoridation on tooth decay have been supporters of fluoridation. There have been few inside this group of researchers to take up the antifluoridation cause. Finally, the arguments about health risks and individual rights are much more powerful tools for opposing fluoridation.

QUESTIONING THE BENEFITS

Nevertheless, there have been some criticisms of the claims for large benefits from fluoridation. The first thorough critique was by Philip R. N. Sutton, then a senior research fellow at the University of Melbourne Dental School. Sutton's monograph, *Fluoridation: Errors and Omissions in Experimental Trials*, was published in 1959 by Melbourne University Press. Sutton examined the five classic fluoridation trials, of which the comparison between Grand Rapids and Muskegon was the first. He began by stating that these trials constituted "the main experimental evidence which has led to the introduction of this process [fluoridation] as a public health measure."[6]

Sutton's work is a critique of the claims for massive benefits from fluoridation. He proceeds by scrutinizing the central research papers and exposing methodological flaws in them. For example, he points out the problem of examiner bias: if the dental examiners who count the number of decayed, missing, and filled teeth in children know whether a particular child is from the fluoridated or the unfluoridated community, this may unconsciously affect their evaluation. (Sutton points out elsewhere that assessment of whether a cavity is present depends on whether a dentist's probe encounters hard or soft material in the tooth, a process which involves a distinct evaluative element. Counting missing and filled teeth is a less contentious process.)

Sutton suggests that a proper blind procedure would involve bringing children from both fluoridated and unfluoridated communities to the examiners in such a way that they would not know which children were which. Because this was not done in any of the classic studies, they are all open to the criticism that examiners unconsciously found what they wanted or expected to find.

Sutton raises a large number of points in regard to the classic studies, including lack of sufficient baseline statistics prior to fluoridation, variations in sampling methods, examiner variability, and sampling error. In the Grand Rapids study, the results were limited by the fact that the control city, Muskegon, was fluoridated in 1951, six years after the beginning of the study.

The power of Sutton's critique is that it exposes the "soft underbelly" of scientific research, namely that scientists do not do everything the way they are supposed to in theory. But this does not in itself automatically lead to the conclusion that fluoridation doesn't work. A piece of research can come up with a valid conclusion even though the methods used are less than perfect.

Sutton himself did not carry out a proper controlled study of fluoridation. Nor did he prove that the studies he examined came to the wrong conclusion. He made a lesser claim: that the scientific methods used in the classic studies were inadequate, and, hence, these studies are not a good basis for proceeding with fluoridation. His assumption is that the onus of proof should lie with those promoting fluoridation to conclusively demonstrate its benefits.

After Sutton's monograph was published, the president of the Australian Dental Association sent copies to the scientists who had been in charge of the classic studies. As a result, several reviews were published, mainly in the *Australian Dental Journal*. In the second edition of his monograph, published in 1960, Sutton included four reviews and his replies to them.[7]

Several of the reviewers deal with technical points, either defending the studies against Sutton's criticism or criticizing Sutton's account. For example, Sutton had said that, in two of the control or unfluoridated cities, there were significant changes in tooth decay rates. This was contrary to the reports of the studies which claimed that these rates had stayed about the same.[8]

R. M. Grainger takes this up in one of fifteen specific points in his review. He said the important thing was that, in the control cities, the changes noted by Sutton "were upward trends or mere fluctuations" compared to the fluoridated city of Brantford where the change was "a highly significant continual downward trend."[9] Replying to Grainger, Sutton notes that the chance that fluctuations would be as great as noted was 1 in 370 and therefore these changes were significant rather than "mere fluctuations." Sutton also points out that the "highly significant continual downward trend" in decay rates in Brantford appeared only in children aged twelve to fourteen, and therefore Grainger's claim of a continual downward trend in Brantford is incorrect and misleading.[10]

This example is one of the more readily understandable points of technical disagreement between Sutton and his critics. It illustrates the small details involved. This technical attack and counterattack can be interpreted as a battle for credibility, in which showing even tiny mistakes in the other side's argument is important since it reflects on the soundness of their case.

If the first basic response to Sutton was to challenge him on technical points, the second response was to question whether his argument was relevant to fluoridation at all. Donald Galagan, the assistant chief of the Division of Dental Public Health, United States Public Health Service, made this point strongly. It is an important argument, since it has been used ever since then by pro-fluoridationists.

Galagan argues that the scientific basis of fluoridation had been solidly established *before* any of the classic control studies. The benefits of fluoride were shown by examination of children who drank naturally fluoridated water. "The fact is that the projects at Brantford, Grand Rapids, Newburgh and Evanston were designed primarily to evaluate the technical, financial and administrative problems associated with the controlled addition of fluorides to a municipal water supply, and, secondarily, to *demonstrate* the effectiveness of the procedure to the profession and the public."[11]

The basis of Sutton's monograph was the claim that "proposals to fluoridate domestic water are almost entirely based" on the results of experimental trials in these four cities.[12] Arguably, one reason why studies of naturally fluoridated communities cannot be used to draw ironclad conclusions about artificially fluoridated communities is that most waters that have high natural levels of fluoride also have high levels of other minerals such as calcium and magnesium, and also contain trace elements such as strontium and boron. It is difficult to rule out that the high mineral content of so-called hard water, which is usually associated with high natural fluoride levels, may contribute to the resistance of teeth to decay. The controlled studies were exactly the sort of test required to determine whether added fluoride alone, without the other elements, would reduce tooth decay.

Sutton's reply to Galagan does not rely so much on this sort of logic (which was implicit in Sutton's analysis) as on quotations from key researchers involved in the classic trials themselves. For example, he quotes one group of researchers involved in one of the two Brantford studies as saying in 1951, "It was recognized that fluorine in the public water supply was not a proven method for the prevention of dental caries, and that it might take ten years to prove or disprove its preventive value."[13] Through a series of quotations, Sutton attempts to show that, at the time, the controlled studies were seen as tests of the effectiveness of artificial fluoridation against tooth decay. In this way, Sutton asserts the relevance of his critique of methods used in those studies.

It is important to note that what is ostensibly a technical dispute about scientific experimentation actually involves a dispute about history: the history of fluoridation. Sutton interprets the history as one in which the controlled studies of matched communities were seen as a crucial test of the effectiveness of fluoridation. Many of the proponents of fluoridation interpret the history as one in which fluoridation was established scientifically in the 1930s through studies of naturally fluoridated communities and through animal studies, and in which the controlled studies of matched communities were demonstrations of the effectiveness of fluoridation.

A related response to Sutton is to point out that scientific understanding of the mechanism by which fluoride prevents tooth decay has changed. In the 1940s and 1950s, it was accepted that fluoride needed to be incorporated into the enamel of growing teeth. But in recent decades, the topical or surface effect of fluoride has been assessed to be of equal or greater significance. Fluoride in the saliva is thought to inhibit decay, for example, by promoting remineralization at the surface of the tooth. The classical studies and Sutton's critique do not allow for the topical effect of fluoride in drinking water, which could reduce tooth decay quickly.

Although Sutton's criticisms were met with a vehement response in the reviews published in 1960, little debate on this topic was carried out thereafter. Sutton did not pursue his challenge, and antifluoridationists, while sometimes citing his views, did not take them up as a central plank in their campaigning. The intricate technical points involved are not the best type of material for public campaigning. For their part, the proponents have assumed that the effectiveness of fluoridation has been established. Few texts or review papers on fluoride and tooth decay even mention the existence of a critique by Sutton or anyone else.[14]

This situation changed only in the 1980s when John Colquhoun, Mark Diesendorf, and Rudolf Ziegelbecker published critiques of the effectiveness of fluoridation. Diesendorf's approach is similar to Sutton's. He examines studies claiming to show that fluoridation reduces tooth decay to determine whether they conform to a rigorous methodological ideal in which a control is used, baseline data are available, examinations of cavity rates are carried out in a blind fashion, and there are no confounding factors. Even though there have been dozens of studies—almost all of them showing a reduction in tooth decay associated with fluoridation—Diesendorf argues that few, if any, are satisfactory statistically.[15]

Diesendorf has injected two important points into the fluoridation debate. First, he quotes studies and data showing significant declines in tooth decay in unfluoridated regions. Second, he quotes studies and data showing continued declines in tooth decay in fluoridated regions, long after the maximum effects should have been obtained.

For example, seven-year-old children should obtain maximum benefits if their communities' water supply has been fluoridated for seven years or more (although benefits may well occur in less than seven years). For a community fluoridated for twenty years, tooth decay rates for seven-year-olds should be stable for the last thirteen years, unless other factors are operating. Diesendorf refers to studies showing continued declines in tooth decay long after the maximum benefits from fluoridation should have occurred.

Diesendorf's argument is that fluoridation has never been conclusively demonstrated to be effective, and that other factors—such as changes in diet, immunity, and dental hygiene—are likely to be involved in declines in tooth decay.

Profluoridationists assume that fluoridation has long since been shown to reduce tooth decay. They see Diesendorf's criticisms as irrelevant, just as they dismissed Sutton's contentions of a quarter of a century earlier. They respond to the observed declines in tooth decay in unfluoridated regions by suggesting the importance of fluoride tablets, fluoride toothpastes, and topical fluoride treatments by dentists. Also, they reject the import of Diesendorf's criticisms of many of the studies. Although there may be some methodological shortcomings in some studies, these do not by themselves show that fluoridation is not effective.

Diesendorf and Colquhoun[16] have focused their criticisms on the controlled trials of fluoridation. As noted before, many proponents treat these trials as demonstrations, and consider the studies of naturally fluoridated communities in the 1930s and 1940s to be definitive proof of the effectiveness of fluoridation in preventing tooth decay. Yet these classic studies have also been criticized by antifluoridationists from the 1950s on.[17] Rudolf Ziegelbecker, in an often-cited 1981 paper, claimed that the classic work by H. Trendley Dean on the relationship between natural fluoride levels in public water supplies and the average rate of tooth decay in children relied on selecting a biased sample of twenty-one data points from the many hundreds available to him.[18] Ziegelbecker's analysis has, in turn, been criticized as incorrect.[19]

The criticisms of fluoridation trials by Sutton, Diesendorf, Colquhoun, and Ziegelbecker are one way in which opponents can try to undermine the case for fluoridation. This approach has the strength of challenging the scientific basis for fluoridation, but, by the same token, the disadvantage of turning the issue into a very technical debate. Arguments about the significance of figures for decayed, missing, and filled teeth in twelve-year-olds in Newburgh or Sarnia in 1950 are hardly the sort of thing to excite the public or even galvanize dentists.

NEITHER NECESSARY NOR SUFFICIENT

Another approach used to criticize fluoridation is more accessible. The argument here is to say that fluoride is neither necessary nor sufficient for good teeth. The terms "necessary" and "sufficient" are used here as in formal logic. If fluoride is not necessary, that means that a person can have good teeth without fluoride. This is a counter to the claim by proponents that fluoride is a missing ingredient in human nutrition and that fluoridation is essentially the "topping up" of water supplies to what nature would normally supply as optimal.

Opponents argue that many people did—and still do—have excellent teeth although their drinking water contains almost no fluoride and although they obtain no extra fluoride through toothpaste or other nondietary sources. (There are traces of fluoride in most foods, so, in practice, a completely fluoride-free diet is virtually impossible.)

The new conventional wisdom is that fluoride has a greater effect in the mouth, at the surface of the teeth, than it does incorporated into the growing teeth as a result of swallowing it. As noted, this knowledge has been used by proponents to explain rapid improvements in decay rates in the trials of fluoridation. But it also provides a new argument for antifluoridationists.

Why drink fluoridated water? Why not just rinse out one's mouth with fluoridated water, gaining most of the benefits, and then spit it out, avoiding most of the risks?[20] This can be seen as a modification of the argument that fluoride is not necessary for good teeth. It accepts that fluoride may be helpful in the mouth but, to obtain most of the benefits, it is not necessary to swallow it.

The other part of the argument is that fluoridation is not sufficient to prevent tooth decay because some people have many cavities in spite of drinking fluoridated water.

The opponents' argument is that tooth decay is not caused by a lack of fluoride, but rather by poor diet, in particular eating refined sugary foods. Those populations with excellent teeth in spite of little fluoride are ones whose diets are largely unprocessed and contain a preponderance of grains, fresh vegetables, and fruits. Those populations with many decayed teeth in spite of fluoridation typically eat highly processed foods containing considerable amounts of sugar. The brushing of teeth and practicing oral hygiene in general, may also be relevant in this context.

Some opponents of fluoridation argue that it is better to address the ultimate cause of tooth decay—namely diet with avoiding sugary foods as the main emphasis. They also point to the dietary role of other minerals besides fluoride in building strong teeth. These include calcium, of course, plus phosphorous, strontium, vanadium, and molybdenum.[21] Poor diet can also have consequences for dental health by affecting the gums. Periodontal disease is a more serius problem than decay, expecially in adults. This means of criticizing fluoridation does not impress the proponents, especially dentists. Some of them have been pushing for better diet for many decades. Typically the proponents simply say something like this: "We agree that sugary foods are a primary cause of tooth decay. But, in spite of major campaigns, most people will not change their diets—they prefer processed and sugary foods. Diet is something we can influence only a little. But we can control fluoride levels in the water supply, and, in this way, do something definitive against tooth decay."[22]

When the debate goes in this direction, it is apparent that it is no longer strictly about fluoridation, but deals with preventive dentistry in the broadest sense. In this area, there is actually considerable agreement between the proponents and opponents of fluoridation: both support better diet. But this has never been a basis for establishing harmonious relations. The opponents in particular have emphasized criticism of fluoridation rather than positive alternatives. For example, in *The American Fluoridation Experiment*, the most authoritative book which was critical of fluoridation and published in the 1950s, only a few of the more than two hundred pages are devoted to criticism of the claims about benefits of fluoridation, and fewer still deal with alternatives.[23]

HEALTH RISKS

Overall, the debate about the existence and size of benefits from fluoridation has been a sideline to the main arena, the risks involved. The debate here is straightforward. The opponents claim that fluoridation causes serious health problems in a fraction of the population. The proponents deny the existence of any such problems.

The apparent simplicity of these issues is part of their attraction. Everyone can understand a statement that fluoridation causes poisoning or cancer, or the claim that fluoridation is entirely safe. Statistical nuances do not intrude so obviously. Yet, in practice, the debate about hazards involves just as many scientific complexities as the debate about benefits.

There are many claims made about the adverse effects of fluoridation on human health. I will concentrate only on effects considered to be the most important by prominent critics of fluoridation, who are scientists, such as Albert Burgstahler, Dean Burk, Frederick Exner, John Lee, George Waldbott, and John Yiamouyiannis.[24] Three key areas are chronic fluoride toxicity, intolerance reactions, and genetic effects. Because these and other topics have received exhaustive treatments, only a few examples will be used to illustrate the ways in which the debate has proceeded.

"Chronic fluoride toxicity" refers to toxic effects caused by a long period of exposure to low levels of fluoride. Many fluoride compounds are poisonous. For example, a dosage of several grams of sodium fluoride can cause death in human adults. The effects from large doses are called "acute effects."[25] Because fluoridation involves the ingestion of tiny amounts of fluoride over many years, it is the possible long-term or chronic effects that are of greatest concern.

Opponents refer to mottling of teeth as a sign of chronic toxicity. They consider that it reflects an excessive intake of fluoride which may also be affecting other organs or functions of the body. Proponents see mottling as only a cosmetic problem which has no health implications. The different interpretations of mottling are representative of different approaches to the issue of toxicity. At least both sides agree that mottling does occur.

The only other consequence of fluoride on which there is much agreement is skeletal fluorosis, a bone disease caused by excessive fluoride intake which, in serious cases, can cause crippling deformities. It is agreed that skeletal fluorosis is found in some high-fluoride regions in India and several other countries, typically with 2.0 ppm to 10.0 ppm fluoride in the water. Occupational exposure to high levels of fluoride is also linked to skeletal fluorosis.

Opponents say that 1.0 ppm of fluoride in water can be enough to cause symptoms of skeletal fluorosis in some people. They point out that, in India and other countries with well-documented incidents of skeletal fluorosis, there are many more severe cases when the fluoride level in drinking water is very high at 5.0 to 10.0 ppm. But there are also some cases seen even at fluoride levels of 1.0 ppm or lower. Also of concern to opponents are subtle changes in the skeleton due to fluoride, which occur prior to the clinical symptoms of skeletal fluorosis.

Proponents say, to the contrary, that the margin between 1.0 ppm and the concentration required to cause skeletal fluorosis is sufficient. This divergence of opinion is possible because there have been very few reported cases of skeletal fluorosis in Western countries. Other factors, in addition to fluoride, may contribute to the high levels of skeletal fluorosis in some parts of India.

The opponents argue that the margin between the 1.0 ppm concentration used for fluoridation and the somewhat larger concentrations usually required to cause overt skeletal fluorosis and other symptoms of chronic fluoride toxicity is simply not great enough. They consider that a small fraction of the population may be experiencing some forms of chronic fluoride toxicity.

The proponents argue that there is no evidence in Western countries that fluoridation contributes to skeletal fluorosis. As one report puts it, "In non-tropical countries there has been no report of clinically symptomatic skeletal fluorosis in areas with drinking water less than 4 mg/litre [4.0 ppm]."[26] "Non-tropical countries" eliminates the evidence from India. "Clinically symptomatic skeletal fluorosis" excludes toxic effects which do not show up as overt or clinical symptoms. The 4.0 ppm figure puts fluoridation's 1.0 ppm in the safe range.

(Despite its qualifications, the foregoing statement can still be challenged. There are some reported cases of skeletal fluorosis in the United States and other "non-tropical countries" that contradict it.[27] To be more accurate, the statement would have to exclude cases where other factors contribute to skeletal fluorosis, such as kidney failure and excessive thirst.)

Each side puts the onus of proof on the other. The proponents cite a scarcity of reports of "clinically symptomatic skeletal fluorosis" as a refutation of the danger. In other words, it is up to the opponents to come up with studies showing significant effects at water fluoridation's level of 1.0 ppm. The opponents, on the other hand, claim that the margin of safety is too small, leaving it to the proponents to demonstrate that 1.0 ppm does not cause problems for, at least, some people.

This divergent interpretation of evidence reflects a theme in the debate which goes back to the original studies. What constitutes a sufficient examination of the health consequences of fluoridation? The proponents repeatedly assert that there is no evidence of risk from fluoride at the dosages involved with water fluoridation.

Newbrun summarizes some of the early investigations showing the safety of fluoridation. "Very thorough medical examinations of the children accompanied both the Newburgh-Kingston and the Grand Rapids-Muskegon fluoridation studies. No significant differences in health or in growth and development were found between children in study and control cities. The Newburgh examination was very detailed and included tonsillectomy rates, height and weight, onset of menstruation, bone density by X-ray examination of hands and knees, skeletal maturation, hemoglobin level, erythrocyte count, leukocyte count, urinalysis, and skin moisture, texture, color, and eruptions. The conclusion of this long-term pediatric study was that, aside from the reduction in caries, there was no indication of any systemic effects, adverse or otherwise, from the use of fluoridated water."[28]

A typical overall conclusion is that of Murray and Rugg-Gunn. "The effect of water fluoridation on general health has been thoroughly investigated in a series of population studies. There is no evidence that the consumption of water containing approximately 1 ppm F (in a temperate climate) is associated with any harmful effect."[29]

One way to challenge these findings is to demonstrate individuals who react adversely to fluoridation. If only a small fraction of individuals react this way, the effect may not readily show up in statistical studies of populations, especially if the adverse reaction can result from other causes as well as fluoride.

For many years, the leading U.S. opponent of fluoridation who was a scientist was George L. Waldbott, an allergist and researcher who campaigned against the measure from the mid–1950s until his death in 1982. Waldbott published many articles in which he documented adverse reactions by particular individuals to fluoride, often in amounts associated with water fluoridation.[30]

Supporters of fluoridation—with a few exceptions[31]—have ignored or dismissed Waldbott's findings. For example, H. C. Hodge in his "Evaluation of some objections to water fluoridation," says "Reports of 'fluoride allergy' have come principally from the late Doctor George Waldbott." After describing one of Waldbott's cases, Hodge comments, "Competent immunologists do not accept Waldbott's case histories as evidence that fluoride allergy exists."

Hodge then quotes the executive committee of the American Academy of Allergy which stated, in 1971, "There is no evidence of allergy or intolerance to fluorides as used in fluoridation of community water supplies."[32] Hodge does not refute Waldbott's extensive evidence, but uses an argument from authority. Certainly the executive committee of the American Academy of Allergy provided no scientific refutation of Waldbott's findings. Furthermore, Waldbott interpreted most of his cases in terms of intolerance reactions, not allergy as implied by Hodge.

At least Hodge did go to the trouble of briefly describing Waldbott's findings. In Murray and Rugg-Gunn's key book, *Fluorides in Caries Prevention*, Waldbott's studies are not mentioned at all.[33] This is the more common pattern.[34]

One of the arguments used against claims of fluoride toxicity in individuals is that studies must be double blind: that is, the reaction of the "subject" to drinking water or tablets should be investigated using an experimental procedure in which neither the investigator nor the subject knows which samples contain fluoride and which do not. This is important, since knowledge on the part of investigators or subjects could result in false responses. An example would be if subjects reacted physically simply on being told they had ingested fluoride. If the subject reacts to a placebo (no fluoride), this shows the lack of a physical basis for the reaction.

Many of Waldbott's patients who showed reactions to fluoride were not tested in blind conditions. This allows critics to be skeptical. But *some* of his patients *were* tested in blind conditions.

Some of Waldbott's critics also suggest that his claims have not received independent verification.[35] Admittedly, Waldbott did not allow outsiders access to his files on his patients, making it impossible for his unpublished documentation to be inspected or his patients to be tested by other doctors.[36] But there have been quite a number of other blind and double-blind studies which provide support for Waldbott.[37]

The profluoridationists seem to demand a high standard of proof before they will accept claims about the effects of fluoridated water on individuals. Even if particular individuals react adversely to small administered dosages of fluoride, this does not show that fluoride in water at 1.0 ppm causes the same effect. They note that fluoride is widespread in the environment—for example, it is contained in many foods—and therefore tracing adverse reactions to the fluoride in water supplies is difficult. The profluoridationists seem to require a set of definitive experiments, but few of them make clear what these definitive experiments would be.[38]

The antifluoridationsts see the studies by Waldbott and others as showing that fluoridation cannot be judged safe. They put the burden of proof on the other side. They say that profluoridationists have not conducted careful double-blind trials in an attempt to determine whether water fluoridation is causing intolerance or other adverse reactions.

The relevance of double-blind trials depends on what assumption is made about the onus of proof. The profluoridationists argue that such trials are necessary to avoid bias by those who may have falsely accused fluoridation of causing problems. The antifluoridationists argue that documented cases of allergy, intolerance reactions, or hypersensitivity are strong evidence against fluoridation until it can be proved that fluoridation is not responsible. Remember that Sutton, in criticizing the classic fluoridation trials, pointed to the lack of blind examinations of children's teeth; in the case of intolerance reactions, it is the proponents who complain about the lack of definitive double-blind trials.

Within the medical research community, clinical randomized double-blind trials are commonly considered to be the ultimate scientific arbiter of the objective effects of a substance on humans. But such trials are not the end of the matter. Any given trial and result can be criticized and dismissed in various ways, such as by alleging shortcomings in methods used, by suggesting that the researchers are biased, by reinterpreting the findings, or by rejecting the results as incompatible with standard findings or theories.[39] Clinical double-blind trials certainly have not been treated as definitive in establishing allergic, intolerance, or hypersensitivity reactions to fluoride at the level involved in water fluoridation.

Another area of contention is mutations and cancer, which can be called genetic effects. There have been several claims, all of which have been rejected by supporters of fluoridation, that fluoride is responsible for genetic effects.

In the 1950s, Alfred Taylor at the University of Texas reported that cancer-prone mice drinking fluoridated water developed tumors at an earlier age than mice drinking distilled water. Ionel F. Rapaport at the University of Wisconsin in the 1950s concluded that fluoride was associated with the birth defect called mongolism, or Down's Syndrome. Ever since the 1970s, Dean Burk and John Yiamouyiannis have claimed that fluoridation is linked to increased cancer death rates in U.S. cities.[40] The response to the claims by Burk and Yiamouyiannis illustrates the way in which the issue of genetic effects has been dealt with.

Burk and Yiamouyiannis collected figures on cancer death rates in a series of large U.S. cities, both fluoridated and unfluoridated. They claimed that the cancer death rates averaged over the group of cities were the same before fluoridation but diverged afterwards, with the fluoridated group showing a 20-percent greater cancer death rate. According to Burk and Yiamouyiannis, fluoridation appears to be responsible for many thousands of extra deaths in the United States.

Unlike the issue of allergic and intolerance reactions in which individual patients can be tested, the controversy over cancer and fluoride is concerned mainly with statistics. Critics of Burk and Yiamouyiannis have said that they did not make corrections for the distribution of the population by age and sex. Alternative analyses of the cancer death rate statistics were carried out, showing no correlation with fluoridation.[41]

Burk and Yiamouyiannis countered by saying that, contrary to their critics, they *had* corrected for age and sex. They criticized a contrary study by saying that it had omitted 90 percent of the data. The proponents argued, in turn, that Burk and Yiamouyiannis had not corrected their data sufficiently. As in every other area of the dispute, entirely different interpretations of evidence have been made, with no concessions to the other side.

The argument about genetic effects also takes place at the level of mechanisms. The antifluoridationists cite laboratory studies which show that fluoride can cause mutations in tissue cultures of human cells at low concentrations. Mutagens are often carcinogens or cocarcinogens. In other words, these studies suggest that a plausible mechanism exists by which water fluoridation could be associated with cancer and genetic defects. The profluoridationists counter by criticizing the relevance of the laboratory studies of mutagenic effects. They say that the concentrations of fluoride in the experiments are too high, or that they do not replicate the effect of fluoride in water supplies.

There is a curious inversion of stances in the way the debate on benefits and the debate on genetic effects has proceeded. In the case of the benefits, the proponents bring forward statistical evidence of declines in tooth decay backed by experimental work showing the microscopic processes by which fluoride can inhibit decay. The opponents have challenged this position by criticizing the statistical studies on methodological grounds, while setting the experimental work aside as irrelevant unless effects can conclusively be shown for populations.

Quite the opposite set of stances is taken on genetic effects (although often by different figures in the debate). The opponents Burk and Yiamouyiannis bring forward statistical evidence of in-

creases in cancer death rates backed by experimental work showing the microscopic processes by which fluoride can induce mutations. The proponents have challenged this position by criticizing
the validity of the statistical studies, while setting the experimental
work aside as irrelevant unless effects can conclusively be shown
for populations.[42]

The critics of the benefits, such as Sutton and Diesendorf,
believe that the evidence of risks is sufficiently strong to warrant
questioning about fluoridation. Therefore, unless fluoridation can
be conclusively proven to be as effective as claimed, it cannot be
justified. Their implicit conclusions about risks provide a basis for
their assumption about the burden of proof on the benefits.

The proponents adopt an opposite perspecitive. So far as they
are concerned, the existence of risks has not been demonstrated.
Therefore criticisms of the benefits must be conclusively proved
before fluoridation can be rejected. Also, they believe that the effectiveness of fluoridation has been proved beyond any doubt, in
which case a high standard of proof about hazards is required
before rejecting fluoridation and its benefits.

INDIVIDUAL RIGHTS

Along with arguments about risks of fluoridation, the other
staple argument in the antifluoridation case concerns individual
rights. Once fluoride is introduced into the public water supply, it
is very difficult to avoid ingesting it. Filters are available, but they
are not cheap and, if not replaced regularly, can lead to sudden big
doses of fluoride. In effect, most people are forced to have fluoride
whether they need it or want it. Those who are toothless or who
work in fluoride-contaminated occupations (such as aluminum
smelting) drink the fluoridated water just the same as the children
whose teeth are to be protected.

The individual-rights argument has been a vital one, especially in the United States where the ideology of individualism is
powerful. It is an ethical and political objection, but it cannot be
separated easily from what are called scientific issues.

A number of public health measures are compulsory, such as
certain vaccinations and isolation of individuals with highly con-
tagious diseases. Opponents argue that these instances do not provide a precedent for fluoridation because tooth decay is not life-
threatening. Proponents then refer to laws requiring the use of seat
belts in cars. Sometimes, seat belts can cause death, as in the case

of fire or a car falling into water. But, so the argument goes, seat belts save many more lives than they put at risk. Hence, legislation requiring people to wear them is legitimate.

Associated with the individual-rights argument is the argument that fluoridation is unethical because the dosage to individuals is not controlled. It depends on how much fluoridated water an individual drinks. To force people to ingest an uncontrolled dosage of a substance to reduce the incidence of a nonlethal disease is seen as unacceptable by opponents.

The individual rights argument is powerful because it appeals to the concept of purity—that is, the purity of water.[43] Water is seen by many people as something that should be pure and unadulterated especially, perhaps, in an age when colorings, flavorings, preservatives, and the like are added to so many foods and drinks.

The obvious and frequent response to this is that public water supplies are not pure but are chemically treated in a number of ways. Chlorination—the process by which chlorine gas is bubbled through water in order to kill bacteria—is the most well-known method of treatment. (Perhaps because the words are similar, chlorination and fluoridation are often confused.)

Opponents respond by saying that chlorination is designed to treat the *water*, whereas fluoridation is designed to treat the *person* drinking it. These opponents draw analogies with putting contraceptives or sedatives into the water supply—ideas which are generally considered to be ethically unacceptable—to illustrate the social danger of allowing water supplies to be used for dosing the population.

The individual-rights argument also draws strength from the existence of many alternative methods of dispensing fluoride, most of which are voluntary (see table 2.1). For example, adding fluorides to salt or sugar allows the marketing of both fluoridated and unfluoridated varieties, and, unlike water fluoridation, offers consumers a choice.

The individual-rights argument is a powerful one because many people are mobilized by it. In terms of logic alone, it is not automatically a weapon for the antifluoridationists. There are various ways for proponents to reply.

One response to the individual-rights argument is to say that water fluoridation is not really compulsory because people can choose to drink unfluoridated bottled water. Fluoridation, in this view, does not force people to drink fluoridated water, but im-

Table 2.1
Compulsion and Control over Dosage Associated with
Several Ways of Getting Fluoride to People's Teeth.

Fluoride vehicle[a]	Dosage	Compulsion
Public water supplies	Uncontrolled	Compulsory
School water supplies	Uncontrolled	Compulsory for school children
Table salt[b]	Uncontrolled	Voluntary**
Sugar[c]	Uncontrolled	Voluntary**
Milk	Uncontrolled	Voluntary**
Topical application by dentist	Not ingested*	Voluntary**
Toothpaste	Not ingested*	Voluntary**
Mouthwash	Not ingested*	Voluntary**
Bottled water	Controlled if desired	Voluntary**
Tablets	Controlled	Voluntary**

*Except inadvertently, which does occur.
**When parents choose any method to get fluoride to the teeth of their young children, the child is seldom in a position to provide informed consent.
[a]For a discussion of different fluoride vehicles see for example J. J. Murray (ed.), *Appropriate Use of Fluorides for Human Health*, Geneva: World Health Organization (1986).
[b]Th. Marthaler, "Practical Aspects of Salt Fluoridation," *Helvetica Odontologica Acta*, vol. 27, no. 3 (1983): 39–56, in *Schweizer Monatsschrift für Zahnmedizin*, vol. 93, no. 12 (1983): 1197–1214.
[c]H. Luoma, "Fluoride in Sugar," *International Dental Journal*, vol. 35, no. 1 (1985): 43–49.

poses upon them inconvenience and financial costs if they wish to avoid it. An analogy to the financial penalty on those who choose to pay for unfluoridated bottled water is the taxation of childless people to support public schools.[44]

Another response is to accept the premise that there is some violation of individual rights, but that this must be weighed against the benefits from fluoride. Various analogies are used in this contention. People in a modern society must accede to some constraints on their freedoms in order to serve the general good. People accept that, in driving a car, they must stay on the correct side of the road and stop at stop lights. This may be a violation of "individual rights" to drive where and how one likes, but people accept that such "violations" are necessary for the common good.

Proponents are critical of fluoride tablets, table salt, and topical treatments for various reasons, but one important reason is that these methods of dispensing fluoride do not provide benefits to the whole community. An *individual's* right not to ingest fluoride may be protected, but it is at the cost of the social rights of *people in general* to enjoy the benefits of fluoride. Thus, the rights argument is reversed: people should have the right to good teeth through fluoridation, and other approaches besides water fluoridation do not provide this right or benefit to everyone in the population.

The conception of "rights" has been the subject of struggle in the fluoridation debate. Although the antifluoridationists have used the rights argument much more than have the proponents, this is not necessarily because the argument over rights by logic alone supports the opponents. It may be because the proponents have kept mainly to the scientific arguments about benefit and risk, an area in which they have a near monopoly on authoritative support. The issue of individual rights and social welfare is more obviously an ethical and political issue, one which the opponents can use even if they have relatively few scientists supporting them on the issues of risks and benefits.

Another means by which proponents have responded to the individual-rights argument is to say, contrary to the opponents, that fluoridation is replication of a natural process. Instead of seeing floridation as "artificial," water supplies without fluoride are described as depleted. Fluoridation is simply the process of "topping up" water supplies which are "deficient" in fluoride. Large-scale water supplies for urban areas are seen by some profluoridationists as what is artificial, not the presence of fluoride.[45] They portray water with fluoride—whether it is added or not—as healthy and natural. (While superficially plausible, I know of no actual studies of the impact of urbanization on fluoride levels to back up this argument.)

For their part, antifluoridationists consider water with added fluoride to be unnatural. They also point out that mother's milk is normally very low in fluoride, even when the mother drinks fluoridated water. Therefore, they say, if nature knows best, fluoride for infants is inappropriate.

Thus, each side in the debate has attempted to define the concept of "natural." This is because the wider community looks favorably on that which is "natural" and "pure." But whether fluoridated or unfluoridated water is "natural" cannot be determined solely by reference to "nature," which provides no unambiguous evidence. Instead, the meaning of "natural" becomes an essential part of what the fluoridation controversy has been about.

DECISION MAKING

A key "bone of contention" in the fluoridation issue has concerned how decisions should be made about fluoridation of public water supplies. This is overtly a political issue, but the role of expert knowledge about fluoridation is crucially involved. There are, in principle, a large number of different ways in which decisions about fluoridation could be made.

- Experts make a decision based on their assessments of the benefits and risks, and they have the power to implement that decision directly.
- Experts make a recommendation to a statutory authority or semiautonomous government organization which, in turn, makes a decision and implements it.
- Elected officials make a decision based on hearing evidence and arguments on scientific, ethical, and individual-rights aspects, and implement it.
- A commission of inquiry accepts submissions from all interested parties and, on the basis of these, makes a recommendation to elected officials who, in turn, make a decision and implement it.
- Elected officials make a decision, based on results of a referendum of the affected population, and implement it.
- A binding referendum is held and the result implemented.

These are only a few of the possible decision-making models. The actual reality of fluoridation decision making is usually much messier. Typically, an elected government—whether national or local—is pressured by profluoridation or antifluoridation groups to either start or stop fluoridating. Various interest groups try to exert their powers. Experts make submissions, government bodies apply pressure, and community groups and individuals write letters to newspapers. The situation becomes further confused by visiting experts, legal challenges, bans by trade unions, advertising campaigns, public meetings, and debates. If the conflicting demands are too sensitive to confront directly, the government may diffuse the responsibility by instituting an inquiry or a referendum. But the result of any formal assessment of opinion—whether an expert's submission, a public inquiry, or a referendum—is seldom the final word. There is always room for further contention.

The method by which fluoridation decisions are made is crucial to the struggle, and, indeed, part of the struggle has been between proponents and opponents each trying to ensure that the actual decision-making procedure is one that gives them an advantage.

Because the proponents have had the support of most of the acknowledged dental experts in the field, they almost always favor a decision-making method that gives these particular experts a key role. For example, most proponents would be happy with governments making decisions based on advice from authoritative bodies of dental researchers. This means that their persuasive efforts could be directed at one specific body of experts. They oppose referendums.[46]

The opponents have been more successful in generating support among the general public. Therefore they tend to favor decision-making methods which allow public participation, such as referendums.

Unlike the debate over the benefits and risks of fluoridation, differences involving preferred methods of decision-making are not clearly articulated in most written material about the issue. Proponents often say or imply that fluoridation is a scientific issue—in other words, the decision should be made on scientific grounds alone—but they also realize that they must, nevertheless, wage a political struggle and win the support of the general public as well as politicians. Opponents are suspicious of giving experts too much power, but they are quite willing to call upon their own experts—such as Waldbott or Yiamouyiannis.

CONCLUSION

The benefits of fluoridation, the risks of fluoridation, individual rights, and decision making: these have been the key areas of the debate. In this chapter, I have presented the arguments as if they are issues of science, logic, and assessment of human welfare by rational means. This is a narrow and inadequate framework from which to analyze the issue, as later chapters will show. But, even within this framework, it is possible to see that "arguments" do not stand outside society. They rely on a variety of rhetorical devices,[47] and are embedded in systems of belief and everyday practices.

It is convenient to conceptualize arguments about benefits and risks as "tools" or "resources" which partisans can use to support their cases. For example, the reported results of the classical fluoridation trials have been a powerful resource used by the proponents. The opponents have tried to counter this with methodological criticisms. The opponents have used claims about individual rights as a tool to oppose fluoridation of community water supplies. Proponents have responded with arguments about community welfare and lack of any dangers.

Arguably, the prominence of particular lines of argument in the debate has depended on their usefulness in winning over relevant individuals—including dentists, politicians, and members of the public. Scientific details about the benefits of fluoridation have not, in the past, played a major role in the public debate, probably because the technical nature of epidemiological studies is not suited for communication to nonscientists. Issues of individual rights and community welfare are easily comprehended by nonspecialists, and so these have played a prominent role in the debate.

In each case, the arguments have been tied to wider constellations of ideas. Individual rights connotes a link to freedom of speech and religion. Community welfare may suggest a link to widely supported amenities such as clean air and national parks.

What makes a good argument is not logically coherent or socially important factors in some abstract sense, but logically and socially relevant realities tied to deeply felt problems and beliefs.

It is important to note that an analysis of the arguments about fluoridation, as presented in this chapter, is insufficient to promote understanding of much of the dynamics of the fluoridation controversy. Many questions remain unanswered.

How are different arguments used in relation to each other? What further resources have been used in the struggle over fluoridation? Why have most dental authorities supported fluoridation? Why has the debate been about fluoridation rather than some other facet of dental health? The following chapters will address these questions.

3

COHERENT VIEWPOINTS

The benefits of fluoridation, the risks of fluoridation, individual rights versus community welfare, decision making about fluoridation—these are four key areas involved in the fluoridation issue.

Considering these areas separately, it might seem that there is no necessary connection between conclusions reached on each one. But, when one looks at leading proponents and opponents of fluoridation, they turn out to have remarkably coherent views. That is, they either take positions supporting fluoridation in relation to benefits, risks, individual rights, and decision making, or they take positions opposing fluoridation in all these areas. If these partisans support or oppose fluoridation, they do so on all possible grounds rather than as a balance of advantages and disadvantages.

To understand the fluoridation controversy, it is necessary to go beyond an examination of the arguments, such as presented in the previous chapter, which implicitly assumes that evaluations are based solely on scientific evidence, logic, and human welfare. The coherency of viewpoints is an indication of the passionate commitments commonly found on this issue. These commitments, either for or against fluoridation, help explain the nature and style of argumentation on the issue, as well as the behaviors described in following chapters.

Coherency of viewpoints is apparent in most of the writings on fluoridation, which are easy to divide into "pro" and "anti" camps. But rather than present a detailed exegesis of written views, I will describe in this chapter my interviews in Australia with leading proponents and opponents of fluoridation who are scientists.

In Australia, as in other English-speaking countries, the fluoridation issue has been a major public controversy for several decades. The National Health and Medical Research Council, an advisory body made up of ad hoc expert committees, has made recommendations in favor of fluoridation since 1952.[1] Following the early recommendations, the idea was studied by dental and health bodies in different parts of the country. Because of Australia's federal structure, there has never been an attempt to introduce fluoridation nationally. Decisions have been made at the state level and, more frequently, at the level of individual cities and towns.

Mainly due to the initiative of individuals, a few Australian towns were fluoridated in the 1950s. Most capital cities have also fluoridated their water supplies, including: Canberra (1964), Hobart (1964), Sydney (1968), Perth (1968), Adelaide (1971), Darwin (1972), and Melbourne (1977). The only capital city remaining unfluoridated is Brisbane. Thus, about two-thirds of Australians drink water with added fluoride.

The decision-making process involved varied considerably, ranging from administrative decision to extensive political maneuvering and public debate. In most cases, public debate about fluoridation was minimal in any given area in the years after a decision, whether it was pro or con. But the issue is kept on the boil by new proposals to fluoridate various towns, such as Geelong in Victoria in the mid 1980s. Similarly, decisions by the newly established self-government in Canberra in 1989 to stop and then restart fluoridation triggered an enormous public debate.

There have been many people involved in the fluoridation issue in Australia, including dentists, politicians, government bureaucrats, and "members of the public." I set out to examine the views of knowledgeable professionals who have played an important role in the debate, with "professionals" referring mainly to scientists, dentists, and doctors. The number of such individuals who have played an important promotional or oppositional role is quite small, and has been depleted by deaths. Those interviewed are listed in Table 3.1.

Table 3.1
Fluoridation Partisans Interviewed, Plus Their Positions
at the Time of Interview.

Proponents

LLOYD CARR, special advisor (Dental), Commonwealth Department of Health, Canberra; and chairman, National Health and Medical Research Council (NHMRC) Working Party on Fluorides in the Control of Dental Caries.

GRAHAM CRAIG, associate professor, Department of Preventive Dentistry, University of Sydney; and member, NHMRC Working Party on Fluorides in the Control of Dental Caries.

JEAN CURRIE, School Dental Section, Australian Capital Territory Health Authority, Canberra.

GERALD DICKINSON, orthodontist, Melbourne; and former chairman, Australian Dental Association (Victorian Branch) Fluoridation Committee.

BRUCE LEVANT, dentist, Melbourne; and former chairman, Australian Dental Association (Victorian Branch) Fluoridation Committee.

JACK MARTIN, Professor of Medicine, University of Melbourne; and NHMRC Working Party on Fluorides in the Control of Dental Caries.

NOEL MARTIN, professor, Department of Preventive Dentistry; and Dean, Faculty of Dentistry, University of Sydney.

GAVAN OAKLEY, dentist, Melbourne; and former chairman, Australian Dental Association (Victorian Branch) Fluoridation Committee.

ELSDON STOREY, Professor of Child Dental Health, Department of Preventive and Community Dentistry, University of Melbourne.

DAVID THORNTON TAYLOR, orthodontist, Canberra; and former chairman, Australian Dental Association (ACT Branch).

KEITH TRAYNOR, dentist, Canberra.

Opponents

MARK DIESENDORF, Visiting Fellow, Human Sciences Program, Australian National University; and former principal research scientist, Division of Mathematics and Statistics, Commonwealth Scientific and Industrial Research Organization, Canberra.

LESLIE KAUSMAN, retired pharmaceutical chemist, Melbourne; and former secretary, Antifluoridation Association of Victoria.

JOHN POLYA, retired associate professor, Department of Chemistry, University of Tasmania.

GEOFFREY SMITH, dental researcher and consultant with experience in general practice, Melbourne.

PHILIP R. N. SUTTON, retired as senior lecturer, School of Dentistry, University of Melbourne; and author of *Fluoridation: Errors and Omissions in Experimental Trials*. Melbourne: Melbourne University Press (Second edition, 1960).

GLEN WALKER, chairman, Antifluoridation Association of Victoria; chairman, Freedom from Fluoridation Federation of Australia; former owner and then chairman of directors of a metal finishing supply company; and author of *Fluoridation: Poison on Tap*, Melbourne: Glen Walker (1982).

(Note that Jack Martin and Noel Martin are not related to the author of this book.)

I planned to interview the most important figures in the fluoridation debate in the cities of Canberra and Melbourne, plus those from other localities if convenient. Fluoridation was introduced in Canberra (Australian Capital Territory) in 1964 by administrative decision with little public debate, whereas Melbourne (Victoria) was not fluoridated until 1977 and after two decades of political struggle. I hoped to uncover any divergence of opinion due to the divergent political contexts of the introduction of fluoridation in these two cities.[2]

To select potential interviewees, I initially contacted some well-known figures in the debates as well as state health departments and branches of the Australian Dental Association. At the end of each interview, I asked the interviewee to name others who were prominent in the debate and who should be interviewed. It soon became apparent that I had attained almost complete coverage of the leading figures in the fluoridation controversy in Canberra and Melbourne.

Only two other individuals from these two cities are obvious candidates for the list of opponents: Arthur Amies, the former Dean of the Melbourne University Dental School and now deceased; and Edward Dunlop, a surgeon in Melbourne who declined to be interviewed. Indeed, the short list of opponents whom I interviewed constitutes an almost complete coverage of scientists, dentists, doctors, and other technical workers who have been prominent in the debate in major cities throughout Australia.

A similar near-complete coverage of leading proponents in Canberra and Melbourne was obtained. There are no widely recognized leading figures in these cities whom I did not interview; on the other hand, there was a greater number of people recommended to me for interview on the proponent side, but I did not contact every one of them. Because of the long and active struggle over fluoridation in Melbourne, there seems to be a high density of partisans there. Those knowledgeable about campaigns in other states informed me that there were relatively few to contact in Perth, Adelaide, or Brisbane.

Of the individuals listed in Table 3.1, only one—David Thornton Taylor—said he did not play an important role in the decision making or debate on fluoridation. Several—most notably Gavan Oakley and Glen Walker—are inveterate campaigners.

The interviews were carried out between September 1986 and February 1987. Bruce Levant, Leslie Kausman, and Geoffrey Smith were interviewed by telephone. The others were contacted face-to-face. The interviews lasted for 30 minutes to three hours, with the median length being one hour.

Using an interview schedule, I asked questions about the introduction of fluoridation in the relevant state, reasons for fluoridation, assessment of alternatives to water fluoridation, reasons for opposition to fluoridation, why there is little fluoridation in Europe, and appropriate decision-making procedures concerning fluoridaton.

COHERENT VIEWPOINTS

The viewpoints of every person interviewed were highly coherent, and indeed mobilized, either in total support or total opposition to fluoridation. This included both technical issues (concerning the benefits and risks of fluoridation), as well as ethical and political issues.

The proponents were unanimous in crediting fluoridation with massive reductions in tooth decay. While figures on the order of 50 percent reduction are standard in the technical literature, two dental practitioners volunteered that the reduction in decay which they had personally observed in children's teeth would be on the order of 90 percent, if both the number and seriousness of cavities were taken into account. By contrast, only one of the opponents accepted that any reductions had been conclusively shown to be due to water fluoridation. (None ruled out that water fluoridation *may* have resulted in reductions in tooth decay.) They pointed to flaws in the experimental trials, and also pointed to the decline in tooth decay in unfluoridated cities, such as Brisbane.

The opponents argued that there are health hazards from fluoridation, such as intolerance reactions, for at least a small fraction of the population. They said that the possibility that fluoridation increased the cancer death rate could not be ruled out, although, as yet, the evidence was not fully conclusive. In complete contrast, the proponents denied that there was adequate evidence to demonstrate a hazard to a single individual from fluoridation. The studies which purported to show such hazards were dismissed as unsubstantiated, poorly done, or biased.

Concessions from these monolithic perspectives were so infrequent that they are worth itemizing. Smith, an opponent, said that an optimal intake of fluoride as a decay preventive has been well established.[3] John Polya, another opponent, said that fluoride *may* play some useful role in preventing decay, via individual doses for those who are not sensitive. Taylor, a supporter though not a leading proponent, noted that there is only a factor of three between 1 parts per million (ppm) of fluoride in water which is optimal and 3 ppm which he said can cause unacceptable mottling of teeth, and that this factor of three is small compared to the usual factor of 100 between recommended use and harmful effects. These were the only conspicuous concessions toward the opposition's views on benefits and risks which were raised in all the interviews.

One feature of the coherency of the viewpoints of proponents was a total dismissal of alternatives to the policy endorsed. One of my questions was "To what degree and why was water fluoridation promoted in preference to major campaigns for widespread use of fluoride tablets; fluoride in school water supplies; fluoride in table salt; topical applications of fluoride; improved oral hygiene; and better diet?"

Almost without exception the proponents dismissed each of these alternatives as impractical, ineffective, or even undesirable. It was said, typically, that fluoride tablets work but few people persist in giving them to their children; that school water supplies do not provide a full coverage and miss preschool children in particular; that excessive intake of salt is undesirable for health reasons; that topical applications are too expensive and do not reach the entire community; that improved oral hygiene is of limited importance for tooth decay although it benefits gums; and that achieving better diet, while desirable, is very unlikely to occur.

The reasons stated against these alternatives were not surprising, since objections have been raised to each of them in the literature. What was striking was the total rejection of all alternatives coupled with the total endorsement of water fluoridation.

For example, fluoride tablets were rejected as not providing the coverage of the community that water fluoridation offers. But, since some communities reject water fluoridation, it might be thought that tablets would be appropriate in these places, since they avoid the objection of compulsion. Again, fluoride in table salt avoids compulsion, and has been effectively implemented in Switzerland. Yet, the advantages of the alternatives in overcoming some of the primary objections to fluoridation were never mentioned by proponents.

The proponents agreed that strong efforts had been made to improve oral hygiene and diet. There were divergent opinions about whether diet had actually improved, but agreement that little could be done to dramatically alter the decay-producing aspects of Western diets and agreement that fluoridation was still necessary.

The actual words used by proponents and opponents to describe their positions are revealing. Studies have shown that scientists typically express different evaluations of evidence and knowledge through the use of different types of language. When claims about knowledge are accepted, they are typically referred to as having been derived from objective examination of material reality. The language used here is called the "constitutive" or "empiricist" repertoire.[4] An example would be, "The early studies showed that fluoride in water significantly reduces tooth decay."

When claims about knowledge are challenged, it is common for the human aspects of the claims to be exposed. The language here is called the "contingent" repertoire. For example, "The early investigators selected their figures in a way which favored fluoridation, while, actually, some towns with high fluoride levels had higher decay."

I expected that advocates on each side would use the constitutive repertoire when describing their own positions and the contingent repertoire when describing the other side. As shown in the following paragraphs, this did occur regularly; but, in addition, the contingent repertoire was often used by proponents and opponents in describing views and behavior on *both* sides. This seems to be a product of the intensely political nature of the debate, which means that the operation of "political" factors is more overt and recognized on both sides.

Most interviewees claimed their stand was based on the scientific evidence, while denying that there was any rational basis for a contrary view. The proponents regularly described the opponents as a fringe minority. Lloyd Carr said that opponents, such as Amies and Sutton, were in the corner of a field, and that credence should be given to those in the center, including the World Health Organization, health authorities, and parliaments. When asked to account for the opposition of particular prominent figures—I specifically mentioned Amies and Dunlop—several proponents simply said they couldn't understand it and that they never had understood what motivated antifluoridationists.

Arthur Amies was the most prominent opponent of fluoridation in Victoria for many years before his death. In view of his position as Dean of the Dental School at the University of Melbourne, both proponents and opponents said that Amies was responsible for greatly delaying the introduction of fluoridation in Melbourne where nearly one-fifth of all Australians live. The frequency and variety of contingent explanations for Amies' stand were fascinating. It was explained to me by different proponents that Amies' views were colored by his wife's diabetes; that he was strongly opposed to dentistry in the United States and saw fluoridation as American in origin; and that he had a philosophical preference for treating the individual rather than using mass treatment.[5] By contrast, Kausman and Philip R. N. Sutton, opponents who knew Amies, attributed his opposition to knowledge.

Although the participants interviewed always attributed their own stands to knowledge (the constitutive repertoire), most of them were quite open in describing why they had become involved with the topic, and, in most cases, this explanation relied on the contingent repertoire. This difference is understandable in terms of a distinction between arguments for or against fluoridation and reasons for being involved in the debate. The arguments—both for or against—were seen by most interviewees as scientific, whereas involvement in the debate was seen as political, which legitimately may be described by using the contingent repertoire.

Most proponents, without being asked, explained their own support for fluoridation and their involvement in the debate as being a result of their experience with massive decay problems, most commonly in the 1950s and as dentists or dental researchers. The dentists recounted their experiences in extracting numerous teeth—and sometimes the entire dentition—from child after child under general anesthesia, and with tears from the child, the parents, and even the dentist. It was their experience of the human suffering of tooth decay that led to their support for a preventive measure.

The opponents expressed a much more varied set of motivations. Mark Diesendorf had previously been involved in campaigns on a number of environmental and health issues. Sutton said he became involved after Amies asked him to look at figures on fluoridation trials. Walker had come across fluoride in his metal finishing supply company and found it to be highly dangerous.

Contingent explanations came into their own in responses to the question "How do you account for the failure to fluoridate in some other countries, especially in Europe?" Detailed information about the reasons for lack of fluoridation in Europe is not readily available (see appendix), and so this question provided a type of

Rorschach ink-blot test on which interviewees could supply speculations about the lack of fluoridation. Two respondents mentioned some sources for their information, which was mostly about Scandinavia. On the other hand, a number of respondents admitted their comments were speculative.

Explanations offered by proponents were uniform in insisting that health concerns were not the reason for lack of fluoridation. Political factors—specifically the organized efforts of antifluoridationists—were most commonly mentioned. For example, Carr said that countries have not avoided fluoridation on the basis of health, and therefore, by exclusion, there must be political reasons.

Other reasons suggested were legal obstacles, popular opposition to centralized measures (due to the experience of fascism); the low status of European dental professionals; the use of other methods to prevent tooth decay (such as fortnightly treatment of people showing a tendency towards decay); a lower level of decay; and higher natural levels of fluoride in the water. It was mentioned by a couple of respondents that the parliamentary vote against fluoridation in the Netherlands had immediately followed a claim on television by an American antifluoridationist that fluoride causes cancer.[6] In this context Oakley said "It is nothing to do with science—it's all politics." This was a common view.

Opponents in their explanations gave much more weight to the rational consideration of evidence by European authorities. Kausman said that European countries had been guided by scientific advisors. Walker said that the failure to fluoridate in Europe was because their scientific communities were better educated, more inquiring, and objective. But most opponents put rational considerations in the context of contingent factors. Polya and Diesendorf each suggested that medical and scientific bodies in some countries may have been more cautious, especially of an American-based idea.

In describing the introduction of fluoridation in Australia, many of those interviewed had a great deal of information, and both proponents and opponents gave detailed accounts which usually included a strong component of contingent factors. In this chapter, I only give a few examples of how a "fact" raised on one side can be undercut by the other side.

Oakley mentioned that a local newspaper had published an antifluoridation article which said that there had been a 63 percent increase in hospital admissions for kidney problems, which the author attributed to fluoride.[7] Oakley was writing a response; he had checked with the hospital and found that the reason for the so-called increase was that there were more dialysis machines available.

In a letter to the Melbourne *Age* Elsdon Storey criticized Sutton's opposition to fluoridation.[8] Storey noted that the judge in the Strathclyde (Scotland) court case on fluoridation had said that Sutton had made no criticism of the important Tiel-Culemborg (Netherlands) study. Sutton and Walker each spontaneously brought up this issue, noting that Sutton, in his testimony, had only been asked whether the Tiel-Culemborg study was an important one. He had replied "yes," but had not been asked anything further about the study. In other words, he had not been asked if he had any criticisms, which he did have.

To an outsider, these may seem like minor points, and not really affecting the major issues at stake. But to those involved, small errors or alleged misrepresentations by the other side reflected the general inadequacy of those against whom they were debating.

While a few interviewees recollected the satisfaction of disputing a technical point raised by the other side, the more common experience was the intensely political nature of the debate. This was generally regarded as undesirable, and certainly seen as frustrating by nearly everyone concerned, since they believed that there was a "truth" which favored their position.

Gerald Dickinson said he would have respect for opponents if they raised constructive criticisms. But this was not the case, and, eventually, he dropped out of the issue because of the emotionalism involved. Polya was unique in being openly derogatory of nonscientist partisans involved on both sides. He characterized the proponents as having latched onto the idea of fluoridation and then being tied to it with religious fervor, whereas many of the opponents were Luddites, often with fundamentalist connections. Polya thought that there was no real science involved in the debate since there was no peer group for scientific argument, and he believed that he had joined a political rather than a scientific debate.

It is common in controversial issues for partisans to attempt to associate their causes with favorable images. In this debate, the proponents regularly refer to "controlled fluoridation"—so called because the concentration of fluoride in the water supply is controlled—while opponents refer to "artificial fluoridation," noting that the dosage of fluoride to people who drink fluoridated water is not controlled. The claim that fluoridation is artificial or unnatural is a staple of the antifluoridation repertoire.

What was striking in the interviews was the number of proponents who, without prompting, described water with added fluoride as more natural than its previous unfluoridated state. Graham Craig said that water fluoridation is chosen to mimic nature and to supplement depleted water. Jean Currie said that water reservoirs for urban areas are overpurified compared to natural water supplies, and contended that fluoridation is not really adding anything, but bringing the level up to natural levels. This seemed to be a common perception of fluoridation by proponents, and not just an argument of convenience. The disagreement about what is called "natural" shows that this concept is one which can be challenged as well as struggled for. "Naturalness" does not spring unambiguously from "nature."

Perhaps the most dramatic evidence of the coherency of viewpoints came with views expressed about ethics. The objection to fluoridation that it is a violation of individual rights as compulsory mass medication for a nonlethal disease had been central to the opposition. It shapes the scientific claims of both sides.

Proponents regularly deny that there has been a single documented and authenticated case of damage to an individual's health from water fluoridation. If it were acknowledged that, for example, fluoridation caused harmful effects in even just one of a million people, then this would have to be weighed against benefits in the form of reduced tooth decay. The argument would then become one of health costs versus health benefits.

But if there are no health costs, the argument is shifted to a different ground. There is then, no apparent reason to object, and opposition seems irrational. Craig, for example, admitted that some value judgements—which he left unspecified—are involved in the fluoridation issue, but said that, concerning the issue of relative risks, there are no demonstrated risks.

Some opponents think the individual-rights argument is so important that they would oppose fluoridation even if there were no health risks. The attitude of proponents to the individual-rights argument is vastly different.

Keith Traynor said that fluoridation, like chlorination, is a health measure which is beneficial to the community, and individuals cannot do anything about it. Oakley took the measured view that liberties are not absolute, and that people should submit to reasonable laws for overall benefit, provided that safety is assured. Dickinson said that it is ethical to have fluoridation, citing that when there is widespread disease causing pain and cost, there is a need for community health measures; an appropriate analogy is seat-belt legislation. Thus the rights issue, a key one to most opponents, carried little weight with proponents or was actually turned to their advantage.

A key question in the interviews was "What do you think is an appropriate decision-making procedure on fluoridation?" Here the views of proponents and opponents diverged again, along lines congruent with their stance on fluoridation.

In Australia, the 1968 Tasmanian Royal Commission[9] and the 1980 Victorian Committee of Inquiry[10] have been the two most important public inquiries into the issue. Both strongly endorsed fluoridation.

With some notable exceptions, most overseas commissions and inquiries have also supported fluoridation. Opposition to fluoridation—in the United States, at least—has been more effectively expressed in referendums. When the public has been given an opportunity to express opinions on fluoridation—for example, in public debates involving meetings, petitions, and letters to newspapers—opponents are frequently much more successful than they are in formal inquiries.

Without exception, proponents favored paths in which expert bodies played a major role, advising a government which then took action and implemented the specialists' and experts' advice. They opposed referendums and were uniformly reluctant to support any direct public involvement in decision making, except that which is implicit in the election of representative government.

For example, Carr said that government—which is the voice of the people—should decide, and that the government should not make a decision without consulting the experts, such as health authorities, the National Health and Medical Research Council, and university professors. Traynor said there should never be a referendum on a public health issue because the public is not qualified to offer an opinion. Levant opposed referendums but favored a public education campaign before or after the decision to tell the public what had been done and why.

The views of proponents on decision making about fluoridation are compatible with their own situations and conclusions. Most expert bodies have favored fluoridation. They (the proponents) favor it, and many of them are the very experts whom they consider should be relied upon to play a major role.

The opponents[11] supported community participation, usually by referendum, in decision making on fluoridation. Walker said that experts can put their cases to the people before the vote. Polya said that people should be free to choose their own medicine and health, provided that the choice does not disadvantage others. He suggested that, even with support in a referendum, fluoridation should not proceed, drawing the analogy that there should not be a referendum on religion, even though one religion may be best for the community.

The opponents still left an important role for science and expert opinion. But, contrary to the proponents, they thought that a full range of experts would not necessarily support fluoridation.

For example, Diesendorf saw value in specialists' knowledge, but opposed a technocratic elite making decisions for the public. He contended that community decision making was necessary since political and ethical issues were involved. Sutton favored referendums in practice, but thought that, in an ideal world, fluoridation would be a scientific issue decided by appropriate scientists, including statisticians. Smith did not mention referendums, but commented that it is dangerous to legislate to enforce something that is supposed to be a scientific issue. He added that politicians should understand that no scientist has the ultimate truth.

The more diverse range of views of the opponents concerning decision making can be interpreted as reflecting two conflicting tendencies. On the one hand, they are likely to favor referendums because this has been an effective way by which fluoridation has been stopped. On the other hand, most of them hesitate to rule out the role of experts, since that is where their own role in the issue lies.

Rounding out the picture was the regularity with which both proponents and opponents criticized the decision-making approach favored by the other side. Proponents dismissed referendums, claiming that antifluoridationists would win because it is easy to scare people with allegations about poison and cancer and, anyway, people usually vote "no" in any referendum.

Two of the opponents denigrated formal inquiries. Sutton commented that judges are predisposed for judging the law and are not equipped for judging science. He also contended that they rely on the opinions of advisors and witnesses whose credibility depends partly on reputation. Polya said simply that inquiries are set up, not for science, but to keep people quiet.[12] In each case, the decision-making procedure favored by the other side was undermined by using the contingent repertoire.

SOURCES OF COHERENCY

The views of partisans who are knowledgeable about the technical issues involved in the fluoridation debate show a remarkable coherency which cuts across the common division between scientific and nonscientific issues. The topic may be the benefits of fluoride, the hazards of fluoride, alternatives to water fluoridation, reasons for the lack of fluoridation in Europe, the naturalness of fluoride in water, the ethics of fluoridation, or the most desirable methods of decision making on technical issues. Regardless, the partisans line up on opposite sides of the fence in a completely predictable fashion.

One possible explanation for this coherency of viewpoints is that the partisans held, prior to encountering the fluoridation issue, a set of attitudes about health risks and benefits, ethics, and decision making which they have applied to the fluoridation issue and expressed in the course of the debate. This explanation is both implausible and virtually untestable.

Probing this explanation, it may be asked: Why are there no individuals prominent in the debate who have studied the issue carefully and decided that the benefits of fluoridation are large and the hazards are negligible, but have, nevertheless, concluded that, on ethical grounds, the measure should be opposed? Why have no prominent fluoridation partisans found that the benefits are overestimated and the hazards are of concern but, nevertheless, concluded that the benefits outweigh the costs and that the decision should be made via expert committees? If knowledgeable individuals with these or other such mixtures of views do exist, they have not become prominent in the Australian fluoridation debate.

In the current and recent social climate—and speaking very generally—concern about the hazards of trace substances is characteristic of environmentalists. Support for individual rights over collective benefits is characteristic of the political right, and support for direct citizen participation in decision making is characteristic of the libertarian left. It seems most unlikely that antifluoridation partisans would have originally come to the issue with this mixture of orientations and that profluoridation partisans would have had precisely the opposite orientations. In short, it is implausible that prior sets of attitudes explain the observed coherency of views.

It may be asked: Why not test this point by asking partisans their views on seat-belt legislation, compulsory AIDS testing, nationalized health insurance, and a variety of other issues? The trouble is that for most of the partisans, the issue of fluoridation is much more significant in their lives—in some cases it is the central social issue—than the other areas to which it might be compared. As a result, personal stands on fluoridation will tend to shape views on related issues, in order to reduce cognitive dissonance.[13] For example, views on individual rights linked to the fluoridation issue are more likely to influence views about seat-belt legislation than the reverse process.

In order to test whether views on fluoridation reflect prior sets of attitudes, one would have had to examine attitudes on a range of issues prior to an individual's exposure to the fluoridation debate. This implies examining virtually everyone—in some cases, before the fluoridation debate even arose, since some partisans were involved with the issue from the beginning. Thus, this explanation for coherency of viewpoints is virtually untestable—at least for the case of fluoridation.

A more plausible explanation of coherency of viewpoints is the influence of the fluoridation debate itself on the partisans.[14] Because there has been an intense public debate on fluoridation, any person with claims to expertise who speaks publicly on the issue comes under strong pressure to support one side or the other. Because most authorities—at least in English-speaking countries—favor fluoridation, any expert who voices even moderate criticism tends to be taken up by opponents as "supporting their cause." Anyone who conspicuously spurns partisanship is unlikely to find professional or emotional support from either side. This seems likely to create pressures to join one side or the other, or to drop out of the issue.

In the camps of both proponents and opponents, there are processes which encourage the coherency of viewpoints. In the fluoridation committees of the Australian Dental Association, the explicit and sole aim is to promote fluoridation. Those actively involved in such committees scour the literature to find relevant evidence and arguments, and, in their speaking engagements, they quickly learn the most effective responses to various questions. Anyone who has debated an issue in public knows that it is difficult to stick to only a portion of the issue, especially the technical part. Other issues are raised in questions and, if the cause is to be promoted, effective answers must be provided.

The intense and all-consuming nature of the campaign for many of those involved is seldom apparent to people on the outside. For activists on both sides,[15] there are talks to be given to public meetings, community groups, and the media; enquiries from the public to be answered; letters to write to newspapers; and submissions to make to politicians.

Oakley, of the proponents, and Walker, of the opponents, seemed among the most persistent and indefatigable of partisans. Interestingly, each one expressed the view that the activists, on their side, were an embattled few, with little money and insufficient people willing to take an open stand.[16] It is precisely this self-image of a small group of partisans making enormous efforts in the face of perceived apathy that helps mold a coherent overall perspective. Some of the scientists involved were not so heavily involved in the day-to-day struggle. Nevertheless, their views were no less coherently organized around the issue, so far as can be seen from the limited sample.

With two exceptions, the proponents reported that they had given fluoride tablets to their children. In the exceptions, the community water was fluoridated, and they supplemented this with topical fluoride treatments. Such parental action is likely to solidify belief in the benefits of fluoridation, since it would be difficult to admit to doing the wrong thing for one's children. By contrast, the opponents had not given fluoride tablets to their children, similarly making it more difficult to admit that they were wrong in their beliefs.

Another factor promoting uniformity of viewpoints is the reliance on material from overseas by both proponents and opponents. Certainly, endorsements by dental and medical associations from other countries are regularly cited by proponents, while critical work is cited by opponents. But it is not clear how much the use of this material actually influences the coherency of positions. Obviously, not all overseas material is used, and what *is* used must be adapted for Australian conditions and audiences.

One factor which reflects the coherency phenomenon as well as maintains it is the lack of informal personal contact between proponents and opponents. It would seem that the most regular contact between those on opposite sides occurs during hearings or debates on fluoridation—for example, before local councils. There seems to be little free discussion of the issues. Symptomatic of this is the comment by Sutton that no one in the Melbourne University School of Dentistry approached him to talk about fluoridation during his ten years there, although the school included many supporters of fluoridation, including the prominent proponent, Storey.

While contact between partisans on opposite sides is uncommon, interaction between those on the same side is frequent and can be intense. Consultation can occur to check facts, prepare arguments, coordinate talks, or compose letters to newspapers and journals, and so forth. It is not surprising that interaction between sympathizers is common. Some of the opponents reported receiving considerable correspondence from around the world. Naturally, most of it is from other opponents.[17]

In organizing speakers for public meetings, preparing testimony for formal hearings, or arranging publicity material for the media, each side promotes those individuals who are most effective in supporting the overall case. Those with intermediate, complex, or ambivalent positions receive little encouragement to take leading roles. In Edward Groth's words, there is a "natural selection for extremist leadership."[18] Only those tough enough and committed enough to stand up to abusive attacks and to suppress self-doubts are likely to stay in the campaign.

Another factor is the lack of criticism by people on one's own side. Pro- and antifluoridation scientists have seldom openly criticized the inaccuracies, exaggerations, and simplifications made by activists on their own sides, although they may privately deplore these shortcomings. Usually, they try to maintain scientific integrity by attacking mistakes made by those on the other side, while presenting their own cases in as persuasive a manner as possible yet compatible with their assessments of the evidence. Peer-group pressure restrains individuals from criticizing others on the same side and, thus, "breaking ranks" since, in the context of the controversy, this would, indeed, seem to help the other side—at least in the short term.

Does it make sense to analyze separately the views of partisans on science, ethics, and politics? My conclusion, based on interviews with Australian fluoridation partisans, is that it does not. The coherency of viewpoints most plausibly derives from engagement in a public debate on an issue with both scientific and political dimensions. To resist pressures for coherency within the debate would mean, not so much individual cognitive dissonance, but rather social dissonance—attacks from both sides and pressures to take a stand.[19] For the technically knowledgeable partisans discussed in this chapter, it makes little sense to isolate views on the benefits or hazards from opinions on individual rights, because beliefs on the whole array of issues are made coherent by the debate itself.

The partisans themselves often distinguish between science and politics, usually in a way which aids their own argument. The distinctions which they make can be described as being "socially constructed." For the purposes of social analysis of partisan viewpoints, it seems much more useful to set aside their usual distinctions between science and politics and to analyze their viewpoints on a whole range of topics. In this way there is less illusion that views are separately formed on the merits of the case, whether in science, ethics, or politics. Rather, what seems to happen is that individuals make a global judgment about fluoridation in the context of the polarized debate. Then, their stance for or against fluoridation promotes a coherency of views on the separate arguments, cutting across the line of distinction between scientific and nonscientific factors.

FLUORIDATION PARADIGMS?

The coherency of viewpoints is compatible with the idea that thought and behavior on the fluoridation issue is guided by two contrary paradigms.[20] The concept of "paradigm" here is a liberal adaptation of Thomas Kuhn's notion of paradigm as a complex of ideas and practices which guide the routine performance of scientific research within specified areas, such as the paradigm of Ptolemaic or earth-centered cosmology which was superseded by the paradigm of Copernican or sun-centered astronomy.[21]

To speak of two paradigms in a single area is to imply a situation of conflict or crisis. The profluoridation paradigm is basically that water fluoridation is highly beneficial and competely safe and, hence, socially desirable. The antifluoridation paradigm is essentially that fluoridation is harmful to some people, unethical, and possibly not proven to be especially beneficial and, hence, socially undesirable.

Using this picture, partisans collect and interpret evidence starting from the presuppositions of their own paradigm, and mobilize arguments to support it. Whether one calls it a paradigm, an examplar, a world view, or a coherent position, the value of this concept is that one can predict with considerable accuracy the arguments of a partisan by knowing the answer to a single question: "Are you for or against fluoridation?"

4

THE STRUGGLE OVER CREDIBILITY

Only to a limited extent has debate on fluoridation proceeded on the basis of pure discussion of claims about knowledge. Almost always salient has been *who* has made the claims. If a doctor or dentist makes a statement about tooth decay it is given more credence than exactly the same statement made by a layperson. If a professional body, such as the American Dental Association, makes a statement, it is given more credence than exactly the same statement made by a single dentist or even a group of dentists.

Endorsements

Authoritative backing has been a key to the debate on fluoridation. In the 1940s in the United States, the most influential relevant bodies—the United States Public Health Service (USPHS), the American Dental Association (ADA), and the American Medical Association (AMA)—had not endorsed fluoridation. The promoters of fluoridation devoted much of their efforts towards convincing the key people in these bodies of the value and need for early endorsement.

In the late 1940s, the USPHS adopted a policy of delay: it would not endorse fluoridation on the basis of information then available. This stand by the premier authority provided valuable support for opponents of fluoridation. As historian Donald McNeil said, "Recommendations for delay by the national organizations became potent weapons in the hands of local opponents of fluoridation."[1] The opponents could justify their stand by pointing to caution by the USPHS and the ADA. This added authority, but not extra evidence or arguments, to the opponents' position.

John J. Frisch, Francis Bull, and other leading proponents of fluoridation kept heavy pressure on the top figures in the USPHS throughout the late 1940s. Finally the USPHS acquiesced. In May 1950, it announced its support for fluoridation. This is generally acknowledged as a turning point in the struggle. With the USPHS taking a stand, the ADA added its support. It, too, had been the subject of intense lobbying and pressure for some years.

Although the evidence about the risks and benefits of fluoridation was essentially the same before and after the endorsements by the USPHS, the ADA, and the AMA, the resources available to the proponents and opponents were vastly changed. The opponents, previously able to cite the stands of these organizations to justify their reservations, now had to confront proponents backed by their endorsements.

Prior to the endorsements, the proponents were overtly political in their approach. Frisch "was often impatient with his professional colleagues who felt the battle should be waged on a factual and dignified level."[2] He believed that political campaigning methods were needed on this political issue. The intense and unrelenting campaign by Frisch and his colleagues was important in obtaining the endorsements for fluoridation. But, once the endorsements were obtained, the style of the confrontation changed. Now, it was the turn of the opponents to be overtly political while the proponents portrayed themselves as strictly scientific and following the best expert advice.

Ever since 1950, the weight of authoritative backing has strongly favored fluoridation. Professional endorsements have been used repeatedly as a prime argument for fluoridation, as is apparent from perusing just about any piece of promotional literature. In this situation, it is the opponents who appear overtly political. In order to promote their case, they have to challenge the "authorities."

Frank J. McClure's book *Water Fluoridation: The Search and the Victory* illustrates the heavy use of endorsements. In the chapter on "Approval," he quoted some of the early statements for fluoridation made in the 1940s. After outlining the early endorsements by professional organizations in the early 1950s, Mc-Clure stated, "Fluoridation has been given official approval by virtually all national and international health and professional organizations."[3] He proceeded to quote statements from ADA, AMA, the American Association for the Advancement of Science (AAAS), the American Federation of Labor and Congress of Industrial Organizations, the American Water Works Association (AWWA), and the American Institute of Nutrition (AIN). He then listed thirty-four American and fifteen British organizations approving fluoridation. He quoted from the Canadian Dental Association (CDA), and quoted "additional statements" from eight individuals or organizations.[4] This section of McClure's book is testimony to the importance which he placed on endorsements.

Such endorsements often are used as a general recommendation of fluoridation. They serve as a shorthand. Instead of giving a detailed account of the arguments for and against the measure, the endorsements are cited as evidence of the conclusion of "those who should know." This is a usual procedure in many areas of health and technology: professional endorsements of safety are taken to indicate that experts have investigated a product or practice and found it safe.

For the opponents of fluoridation, the extensive endorsements are a major stumbling block. There are several ways in which they have responded. One is to find individuals or groups who openly criticize fluoridation, or who refuse to make endorsements. The work of opponent scientists—such as George Waldbott and John Yiamouyiannis—is repeatedly cited.

Another way to criticize endorsements is to try to undermine the process of endorsement itself. One line of argument is that the great number of endorsements do not represent independent evaluations of the important issues. Bodies such as the AIN did not carry out their own research or comprehensive assessments of the research literature. Instead, most of the endorsements have been made on the basis of earlier endorsements by a few key organizations, in particular the USPHS and the ADA.

At best, endorsing bodies relied on advice from a small number of experts, almost all of whom were committed promoters of fluoridation.[5] Furthermore, opponents alleged that key pro-moters applied pressure on professional societies for rapid—and hence, less carefully considered—endorsement. One such pro-moter was H. Trendley Dean in the case of the AAAS, of which he was a former president.[6] The opponents saw a "bandwagon" or "snowballing" process, in which organizations concluded that, if the "real" authorities were for it, it must be all right.

Opponents also alleged that some endorsements have been "pushed through" without proper concern for due process, not to mention the arguments. Concerning the endorsement of fluorida-tion by the World Health Organization in 1969, Waldbott, Albert W. Burgstahler, and H. Lewis McKinney stated that "during the final hours of the session, when only 55 to 60 of the 1,000 delegates from 131 countries were still present, all bills that had not been ac-cepted were collected into one and voted upon, including a state-ment on fluoridation."[7] (The profluoridationists could complain of a similar lack of due process in some of their defeats, such as the Swedish Parliament's repeal of the Water Fluoridation Act in November 1971.)[8]

There remains the further problem that the World Health Organization has reendorsed its profluoridation stand, a fact seldom mentioned by antifluoridationists. One response would be to say that it is much easier to reendorse a stand than to reverse it.

While the argument about "snowballing" and contrived en-dorsements may undercut the persuasiveness of the great number of endorsements, it does not explain away the important early en-dorsements. The opponents have two lines of attack here.

First, they argue that these endorsements were pushed through by a small number of profluoridation activists, and do not represent the opinion of all the members of the organization. Sec-ond, they assert that the endorsements are not based on original research by the endorsing bodies. They are simply statements by groups who claim that the research points to a particular policy.

This second line of argument leads to the conclusion that peo-ple should be looking at the evidence rather than at endorsements, and this is precisely the approach favored by the opponents. They usually prefer to deal directly in the arguments about benefits, risks, and individual rights, whereas the proponents often refer to endorsements.

This difference does not arise because opponents, by the nature of their stand, have some special commitment to informing the public about the actual issues (although some opponents do have a commitment to this). Rather, the opponents cannot use the resource of endorsements because so few prestigious bodies oppose fluoridation. If dental associations opposed fluoridation, most opponents would use endorsements as readily as do the proponents. This is clear from the regular reference by opponents to those few professional bodies which do openly oppose fluoridation.

Widespread authoritative endorsement allows some proponents to go a step further and deny that there is any legitimate scientific debate at all. For example, Conrad A. Naleway of the ADA wrote in 1988 that "there is no scientific case to support the antifluoridation position."[9] In denying the existence of scientific debate, proponents are implicitly stating that all knowledgeable people support fluoridation and that anyone who opposes fluoridation must, therefore, be uninformed, politically motivated, or in some other way "unscientific."

In 1978, the magazine *Consumer Reports* ran a two-part article attacking opponents of fluoridation. The article concluded with the statement that "The simple truth is that there's no 'scientific controversy' over the safety of fluoridation. The practice is safe, economical, and beneficial. The survival of this fake controversy represents, in CU's [Consumers Union] opinion, one of the major triumphs of quackery over science in our generation."[10] What is only implication in other statements is spelled out here: there is no scientific debate; therefore, opponents are quacks.

It is revealing that the claim that all experts support fluoridation and that there is no scientific debate became routine only after the endorsements by professional bodies in the early 1950s. These endorsements did not change the scientific evidence then available, but they did eliminate a major resource used by the opponents—namely, that authoritative bodies had not endorsed the measure.

To Debate or Not to Debate

In the struggles over fluoridation, there have been many opportunities for the issues to be debated—for example, in public meetings, in local government meetings, and before community groups. Profluoridationists often have refused to openly debate antifluoridationists in such settings when they consider that debating will hurt their campaign. The reason they give for this is that there are no valid grounds for opposing fluoridation, and, therefore, any debate can only give credibility to the opponents by acknowledging that there is something worthy of debate. Refusing to debate can be interpreted as an attempt by those with a near monopoly on credibility—in this case scientific or professional credibility—to deny any of it to the opponents.

In 1952, Charles Eliot Perkins, a biochemist and physiologist opposed to fluoridation, described how proponents refused to appear on a radio forum in Washington, D.C. shortly after the city's water supply had been fluoridated. Perkins concluded that "The professonal proponents of fluoridation, as a rule, refuse to discuss the subject in public meetings or debate fluoridation with anyone who opposes it in public forums."[11] This has remained the pattern ever since.

In 1979, the Society for Social Responsibility in Science in Canberra, Australia, organized a debate on fluoridation and cancer between fluoridation supporter Roland Thorp and fluoridation opponent John Yiamouyiannis. Afterward, Dr. Peter Cooper, chairman of the Australian Capital Territory Cancer Society, wrote an article and letters for the *Canberra Times* denying any link between fluoridation and cancer, and calling fluoridation a "nonissue."[12] When challenged by Mark Diesendorf to a public scientific debate on the issue, Cooper replied that Disendorf "doth rant and rave, and mightily stir to keep the fluoridation pot aboiling." Then, he declined to debate.[13]

Robert Isman, in an often-cited article, "Fluoridation: Strategies for Success," which was published in 1981 in the *American Journal of Public Health*, commented: "Several authors have recommended that debates be avoided and I concur with this recommendation. This is little to gain and much to lose from debating an emotional issue like fluoridation. A debate simply serves to give more credibility to fluoridation opponents."[14] Prominent proponent Ernest Newbrun concurs. He says that he normally refuses to debate because "it is my policy not to give credibility to antifluoridationists."[15]

In 1985, Michael W. Easley commented similarly in an article "The New Antifluoridationists" in the *Journal of Public Health Dentistry*. He wrote, "Armed with volumes of scientific literature and lists of endorsements, eager proponents of fluoridation too often are trapped into consenting to public debates on this sociopolitical controversy. Almost nothing can be gained by debating. Regardless of which side is successful in presenting the best argument, the mere fact that the debate even took place conveys to the public that a legitimate scientific controversy exists."[16]

This does not mean that the proponents do not campaign at all. They conceptualize the issue as being in two parts: a scientific part, and a political part. The scientific part, they believe, consists of scientific findings which contain no basis for opposing fluoridation. This is the foundation for the claim that there is no scientific debate. The political part of the issue arises from the existence of opponents who are motivated for nonscientific reasons. This political opposition must be countered, and thus many of the proponents counsel the waging of a political struggle for fluoridation.

Easley concluded, "Foremost is the need to recognize and accept the realization that fluoridation is no longer strictly a scientific or legal issue, but that it has become predominantly a political issue."[17] Part of the political struggle is the refusal to debate, thereby denying the opponents any credibility.[18]

Unfortunately for the profluoridationists, refusal to debate can raise problems. Ernest Newbrun commented that "Whether or not to participate in radio or TV talk shows or debates on fluoridation poses a real dilemma for the dental researcher." Participating in and responding to antifluoridation arguments can give them legitimacy, whereas "by refusing to appear on such programs, there is always the risk of permitting the antifluoridationists free rein."[19]

Another problem is that, when supporters of fluoridation refuse an open invitation to debate, this often is seen by citizens as arrogance. As analyzed by Raulet, professionals such as dentists and physicians promoting fluoridation can take either the role of experts or partisans. Many have attempted to fill both roles, and this sometimes leads to difficulties. As experts, they can act as authoritative sources of information but are open to the charge of arrogance in refusing to debate. But if they enter the debate as open promoters, the role of expert knowledge in support of fluoridation is undercut.[20]

To be an authoritative source of information while not openly promoting fluoridation means taking a low-visibility role. The scientist who publishes technical papers in specialized journals or the dentist who answers questions from patients falls into this category. This stance draws its strength from the image of the objective and socially concerned professional who has no apparent vested interest in a particular course of action. It is precisely from *not* being openly partisan that the role of the objective professional draws its strength. Ideally (for those who support fluoridation), this would be all that is required to create a climate which leads to the implementation of fluoridation.

While this stance is possible for some supporters of fluoridation, it has seldom been adequate to introduce and sustain the measure. The opponents of fluoridation have been open and vociferous in their campaigning. A low-key stance is not enough to counter such opponents. Consequently, *some* supporters of fluoridation have had to be openly political as well, and this has included many dentists, doctors, and scientists.

Partisans have been involved in lobbying fellow professionals and politicians, speaking at community groups, writing letters to newspapers and journals, writing general interest articles, speaking on radio and television, debating, fundraising, passing out leaflets, and a host of other activities. Dentists, doctors, and scientists supporting fluoridation as partisans can be effective via their activism, but, at the same time, many of them rely on their professional role to give status to their views beyond that of a lay partisan. But their activism can undercut the advantages of professional status to some extent, since many of the methods of campaigning are widely perceived to be incompatible with objectivity.

Note that the two "roles" of expert and partisan are only perceived to be divergent. It is quite possible for an "objective source of information" to be an effective proponent—for example, by publishing scientific papers or teaching dental students in ways which favor a particular conclusion. Likewise, it is possible for an active partisan to be extremely careful with the evidence and arguments, more so than those who are not partisans.

In each case, the role of expert and partisan is not inherent in the knowledge or social role, but depends on the interaction of behaviors and beliefs. The social construction of an expert or partisan depends to a great extent on the ways, or lack of ways, in which opponents can attack.

For example, it is very difficult for the opponents to criticize those who make contributions only in specialized scientific journals. Such criticism tends to be highly technical—as in the case of Sutton's critique of the classic fluoridation trials—and, hence, is not very useful for public campaigning. By contrast, those who make the same points in newspapers or on radio are much more vulnerable to attack. When translated out of the technical context, the "same points" are subject to criticism in a way which would not be permissible in a scientific journal.

It is also important that partisans can be attacked *because they are partisans.* The opponents can claim, with apparent justification, that fluoridation is not just a scientific matter, but is being promoted because of various vested interests. The partisan promotion of fluoridation—made necessary by the partisan opposition—thus must be masked as much as possible. This is because the rhetoric of promotion sounds incompatible with the language of objective science, and opponents can use this ostensible incompatibility to attack the proponents.

Promoting Fluoridation

An early and revealing example of this dynamic centers around a talk given by fluoridation proponent Francis Bull in 1951, at the Fourth Annual Conference of State Dental Directors with the USPHS and the Children's Bureau, in Washington, D.C. Remember that Bull was one of the leading figures behind the push for fluoridation in the 1940s, a push which led to the key endorsements in 1950 and 1951. In his talk titled "Promotion and Application of Water Fluoridation,"[21] Bull was essentially telling new supporters how to sell fluoridation.

Bull was quite candid in his talk. Unknown to him, there was a stenographer present making a complete record of the proceedings. Later, antifluoridationists obtained a copy, and, ever after, they have been quoting Bull out of context in order to damn the promotion of fluoridation.[22]

Bull spent considerable time describing how to answer objections to fluoridation.

> I think the first one [objection] that is brought up is: "Isn't fluoride the thing that causes mottled enamel or fluorosis? Are you trying to sell us on the idea of putting that sort of thing in the water?" What is your answer? You have got to have an answer, and it had better be good. You know, in all public health work it seems to be quite easy to take the negative. They have you on the defensive all the time, and you have to be ready with answers. Now, we tell them this, that at one part per million dental fluorosis brings about the most beautiful looking teeth that anyone ever had. And we show them some pictures of such teeth. We don't try to say that there is no such thing as fluorosis, even at 1.2 parts per million, which we are recommending. But you have got to have an answer. Maybe you have a better one.[23]

Bull's comments suggested to many opponents of fluoridation that the proponents were trying to hoodwink people about the problem of fluorosis by calling mottled teeth "beautiful looking teeth."

Waldbott certainly took this view, saying "Bull instructed his colleagues to describe mottled teeth to the public and to the profession as 'egg-shell white' and 'the most beautiful looking teeth that anyone ever had,' even though these teeth are known to turn brown and brittle in later years."[24]

The context of Bull's talk was his confidence in data which showed that fluoridation is highly beneficial and harmless. For Bull, fluoridation, unlike all previous public health measures, "has absolutely no bad connected with it."[25] Therefore, the issue was how to promote it. Language and images are important, and part of this is the language used to describe mottled teeth.

Bull continued by dealing with another perception of fluoridation.

> And, incidentally, we never use the term 'artificial fluoridation.' There is something about that term that means a phony. The public associates artificial pearls or artificial this or artificial that with things that are not real or genuine. We call it 'controlled fluoridation.'[26]

To this day, a fairly reliable test of a person's stance on fluoridation is whether they call it "controlled" fluoridation, as do the proponents, or "artificial" fluoridation, an expression favored by the opponents. The choice of language is a crucial part of the debate.

Bull continued:

> Incidentally, we never had any 'experiments' in Wisconsin. To take a city of 100,000 and say, 'We are going to experiment on you, and if you survive we will learn something'—that is kind of rough treatment on the public. In Wisconsin, we set up demonstrations. They weren't experiments.[27]

Bull's advice has been taken up by proponents ever since. Sutton in his critique of the "classic trials" argued that they were experiments. Sutton's critics argued that fluoridation had already been proved, and that the trials were demonstrations. Here is a case in which Bull's advice on promoting fluoridation (and that of others) entered into the "scientific" area of disputes over the validity of the trials.

The next quote from Bull shows how much difference context makes.

> . . . this toxicity question is a difficult one. I can't give you the answer on it. After all, you know fluoridated water isn't toxic, but when the other fellow says it is, it is difficult to answer him. I can prove to you we don't know the answer to that one, because we had a city of 18,000 people which was fluoridating its water for six or eight months. Then a campaign was started by organized opposition on the grounds of toxicity. It ended up in a referendum and they threw out fluoridation. So I would hate to give you any advice on that deal [Laughter]. It's tough.[28]

It is easy, and tempting for opponents, to take this statement out of context—especially the part about "this toxicity question is a difficult one. I can't give you the answer on it"—and conclude that Bull was admitting that the proponents, at least in 1951, didn't know for sure whether fluoridation might have toxic effects.

But this is not what Bull was saying. He stated, after all, that "you know fluoridated water isn't toxic." Bull was concerned about promoting fluoridation, and he was raising the problem that there was no good argument or turn of phrase to counter claims of toxicity. When he said that "we don't know the answer to that one," he meant that there was no answer that was effective for public campaigning, rather than no answer at all. He was seeking an answer, such as calling mottled teeth "beautiful" or referring to controlled fluoridation.

The point is that promotion assumes—or sometimes ignores—the validity of what is to be promoted. In an honest and open talk, a promoter describes the good and bad ways of going about the promotion. But "honest and open talk" is dangerous if it gets into the wrong hands.

Bull also said, "Now, why should we do a pre-fluoridation survey? Is it to find out if fluoridation works? No. We have told the public it works, so we can't go back on that. Then why do we want a pre-fluoridation survey?"[29]

This quote seems to be the most damning yet. Bull appeared to be saying that the promoters cannot go back on their claims that fluoridation works. But the context gives a different story.

Bull advocates making prefluoridation surveys of tooth decay, and says that the fluoridation committee of the state dental society can assist in doing this. After the previously quoted passage, he went on to say that the point of a prefluoridation survey would be to show, later on, the effectiveness of fluoridation in preventing tooth decay as insurance against possible future campaigns to stop fluoridation.

Once again, Bull was assuming that fluoridation is a good thing, and was simply presenting his views as to how it could best be promoted. He was advocating prefluoridation surveys as insurance against subsequent attempts to stop fluoridation. In this quote, he was telling others not to fall into the trap of thinking—or saying—that a prefluoridation survey is intended to find out if fluoridation works. If anyone said that, it could be used against them by opponents.

It is clear from this example why statements about how to promote fluoridation are better left out of the public eye, just as the candid discussions of the designers of advertising copy would be damaging to the product concerned.

Bull's talk is part of the large literature on how to promote fluoridation. Annabelle Bender Motz, in a 1971 review article published in a collection entitled *Social Sciences and Dentistry*, outlined some of the recommendations stemming from this literature.[30] First, the community to which fluoridation is to be introduced should be studied closely, noting demographic characteristics, the political system, and so forth—all in an effort to plan an effective strategy.

Second, fluoridation should, if possible, be introduced through legislation or administrative action since popular participation, for example through a referendum, often leads to the rejection of fluoridation.

Third, if popular involvement cannot be avoided, grassroots support for fluoridation should be developed through community groups and locally influential people. This might involve Rotary clubs, mothers' groups, health associations, trade unions, and many other organizations.

Fourth, "confrontations whether in the form of panel discussions, public debates, or referenda" should be avoided. Here, Motz referred to several social-science studies. For example, "[H.] Nathan and [S.] Scott have shown that confrontations give the anti-fluoridationists the stamp of legitimacy on a par with that of the recognized community leaders and organizations."[31]

Fifth and last, the role of the "health publicist" should be developed. Such people would, for example, use knowledge about a community to plan a program to introduce fluoridation or some other health measure. By being neither a scientist nor a medical practitioner, the "health publicist" may be able to avoid being typecast as an arrogant professional.

The large body of social-science research which suggests how to best promote fluoridation is based on the proponent claims that fluoridation is a scientific issue and that there is no scientifically credible opposition to it. The idea of creation of the "health publicist" assumes that the professional experts will decide what is best for the community, and then this will be "sold" to the community by using the best selling techniques that social science can provide.

From the point of view of the opponents—especially those who are scientists—the refusal to debate is a denial of all that is proper.

Part ii: responding to scientist opponents

Without endorsements by the major professional bodies, the best that the opponents have been able to do is cite a few organizations which have opposed fluoridation and a number of individual professionals who are critical of fluoridation. Although the number of these individuals is very small compared to the total number of dentists and doctors formally represented by pro-fluoridation professional bodies, their critical perspectives are vitally important because they challenge what would otherwise appear to be unanimous professional support for fluoridation.

The opposition to fluoridation has included a large number of "extremists." In the 1950s in the United States, the John Birch Society was involved, as were some other right-wing and anti-Communist groups. The opposition has also included members of some religious groups—such as Christian Scientists—as well as naturopaths, chiropractors, and others considered by the medical profession to be fringe practitioners or "quacks." In other words, "reputable" bodies—such as the ADA—supported fluoridation, while "fringe" bodies and individuals opposed it.

This, at least, was the picture painted by the proponents. It is a picture quite favorable to the proponents, since it suggests that rational and respectable people support fluoridation, whereas opponents are found only among "fringe" groups. The rhetoric of many fluoridation opponents often helps to confirm this view.

Nonscientists who are opponents frequently sound extreme—but so, also, do some of the scientists.

Charles Eliot Perkins in his 1952 booklet, *The Truth About Water Fluoridation*, included numerous scientific arguments, but these are interspersed with political commentary with extreme-sounding claims. Perkins concluded that "It is common knowledge that artificial water fluoridation is a technique in mass control through mass medication, which is an integral part of Communist philosophy."[32]

Frederick B. Exner, a medical doctor and leading opponent of fluoridation in the 1950s, wrote that, in convincing people that fluoridation is completely safe, "the primary tools have been equivocation and prevarication. Outright lies are rarely used except when so tightly cornered under cross-examination that there is no other way out."[33] Exner referred to the promotion of fluoridation as "an incredible story of chicanery and malfeasance."[34] He attributed fluoridation to a totalitarian philosophy, both in those "who sincerely believe in the *Führer* principle" and "'do-gooders' who promote totalitarianism through good-intentions-gone-crosswise."[35]

Philip E. Zanfagna, a doctor and coauthor of a book opposing fluoridation published in 1974, wrote that "While the fluoridation travesty is in progress, Americans are ingesting more poisonous fluorides (and other dangerous chemicals) with their food, water and from polluted air than any other people on earth. Related to this consumption, the national incidence of heart attacks, cancer, crippling arthritis, infant deaths, and enzyme-deficiency diseases continues to rise."[36]

Zanfagna's coauthor, writer and activist Gladys Caldwell, used more colorful language, describing fluoridation as "the most disastrous and costly consumer fraud of this polluted century. Hundreds of millions of tax dollars have been spent to programme an entire generation to salivate like Pavlov's dogs when the word fluoridation is mentioned."[37]

Glen Walker, a leading Australian antifluoridationist, concluded his long and vehement book on the topic with the statement that "Yes fluoridation is a hoax!"[38]

Robert Mick, a New Jersey dentist and researcher, and highly visible opponent, said that "Hitler was a Boy Scout compared with the United States Public Health Service . . . To be selected by the United States Public Health Service for an experiment is a

CRIMINAL CONSPIRACY surpassing acts of those Nazis who were hung for selecting humans for experiments."[39]

Other statements similar to these would be easy to list. In each case, undoubtedly, those making the statements would argue that they are being perfectly accurate. But others may be repelled by the intemperate-sounding language, and be drawn to the proponents' categorization of all opponents as "cranks."

This picture has always been complicated by the presence of some orthodox, mild-spoken, and otherwise respectable professionals—dentists, doctors, and scientists—who are critical of fluoridation. While some of them—such as Exner and Mick—on occasion used extreme-sounding language, others, such as Albert Burgstahler and John Colquhoun, have been more restrained.

The very existence of such individuals undermines any suggestion of professional unanimity. Proponent Sheldon Rovin recognized the problem: "There are increasing numbers of 'credentialed opponents' lurking about in fluoridation matters. One or two dentists or physicians coupled with a few scientists who are opposed to fluoridation can stymie even the best organized and conducted fluoridation campaign."[40]

The promoters of fluoridation have responded to these critics in various ways. One response has been to criticize their arguments, as described in chapter 2. But a response of logical and cautious criticism is not always enough to undermine an opponent's credibility.

Further—or different—measures have been taken in many cases. Rovin said, "Ways to neutralize these people are limited. The choices are to ignore them, assail their motivations, or drown them out by enlisting large numbers of dentists and physicians on behalf of the issue in a manner highly visible to the public. Of these, the third is obviously the best choice."[41]

But, quite often, methods other than Rovin's "best choice" have been used.

Ignoring the Critics

One potent response has been simply to ignore the critics. Sutton's detailed criticisms of the classic fluoridation trials are not even mentioned in most discussions of the case for fluoridation. Likewise, Waldbott's reports of toxic effects of fluoride are not referred to at all in many treatments.

Because the critics have been ignored, a number of technical disputes concerning the risks and benefits of fluoridation cannot be said to have been resolved scientifically. There has been no process of engagement with the arguments of the critics, allowing for a continual revision, refinement, and testing of claims. Often the antifluoridation material is simply assumed to be wrong or irrelevant and not worth refuting, and then just ignored. In other cases there is a response at first, as in the initial reviews of Sutton's 1959 monograph, but no follow-through. Sutton's second edition of 1960, including replies to his critics, was ignored.

This type of response can be successful only when the overwhelming weight of professional credibility and endorsement is on one side. If the critics are ignored, this seems to say that their views are not worth bothering with.

So far as most profluoridationists are concerned,[42] the issues are closed and dead and not worth raising again. Antifluoridationists prefer a different interpretation. For them, the proponents ignore criticisms because a thorough examination of them might support the claims of the critics. If the opponents can persuade people that this is the real explanation for proponents' silence, then ignoring the critics can be counterproductive.[43]

Attacking in General Terms

A related approach is to attack the antifluoridationists in general terms, without mentioning any names or sources. For example, Dr. Russell B. Scobie, a pediatrician who "helped pioneer the drive in 1944 to have Newburgh selected for the now classic Newburgh-Kingston Fluoridation Study" and who has given lectures around the world on fluoridation, wrote "the opposition rely on innuendo, half-truths and deliberate untruths to support their position. They never ask for information, although they are always willing to provide instruction. They know the answer with a religious fervor and they are obviously not susceptible to educational efforts."[44]

Donald R. McNeil, in a 1969 booklet, *Fluoridation: For Your Community and Your State*, published by the ADA on how to promote fluoridation, described some of the arguments of the opponents but gave no names or references. He said, "Despite thousands of scientific studies on fluoridation and nearly unanimous agreement by scientists that it is safe, effective and worthwhile, fluoridation remains under attack. Few scientifically proven public health measures have been the object of such falsehood, distortion and deceit."[45]

Dental researcher Herschel Horowitz, a leading proponent in the United States, wrote in a mostly technical paper in the *British Dental Journal* that "It is truly unfortunate that a public health measure with these impressive attributes, on occasion, generates so much public controversy."[46] Horowitz gave no reference to scientists among the critics of fluoridation.

Ronald J. Hunt, in an article about fluoridation in small Iowa towns, referred to the arguments of the opponents in only a couple of sentences: "opponents of the measure have found that it is much easier to create confusion and fear than it is to educate people. The fluoridation issue increases in complexity when antifluoridationists cause controversy by continuing to claim that fluoridation causes cancer and has been linked to other diseases, even though these claims have repeatedly been scientifically refuted."[47] Hunt gave no references to scientific work on either side of the controversy.

A book called *Appropriate Use of Fluorides for Human Health*, published by the World Health Organization in 1986 and edited by J. J. Murray, a leading proponent of fluoridation, includes discussions of implementation of fluoridation, safety, legal aspects, and referendums, plus a mention of "the often misguided opposition to community fluoridation programmes,"[48] without giving a single reference to scientific criticisms.

A variant of this technique is found in a compilation called *Classification and Appraisal of Objections to Fluoridation* by Kenneth R. Elwell and Kenneth A. Easlick. More than 100 separate objections are listed, followed by responses including numerous references. What is evident on inspection is that, whereas the profluoridation arguments are well documented, the objections are not. The names of people making the objections are seldom mentioned, and their publications are seldom cited. For example, Alfred Taylor's research on fluoride and cancer in mice is mentioned, but his publications on this topic are not cited; whereas, responses to Taylor's work *are* cited. Waldbott is not named but, instead, is alluded to as "a physician." His publications are not cited.[49]

Edward Groth III, after examining a wealth of scientific literature on fluoridation, concluded that virtually all sources "are tainted by detectable political bias." He noted that the bias in antifluoridation reviews of the scientific literature is often overt, whereas in profluoridation sources, it can be less obvious. In the latter, "Reports of the effectiveness and safety of fluoridation are extensively discussed, but the numerous studies which have suggested contradictory conclusions, or which contain critiques of the validity of the evidence presented, are often neither quoted nor listed in the bibliography. Such reports may mention allegations of harm from fluoridated water, and attempt to refute such allegations; but in doing so, the specific evidence that supports claims of potential harm is rarely discussed."[50]

This method of not giving the opponents the status of a name or an argument has been used frequently—for example, in numerous editorials and notices in the *Journal of the American Dental Association* over the years.[51] Attacking the other side in unspecific terms can be done by anyone from any position, but it is especially useful for those who have more status, since they avoid giving recognition to the other side.

Circulating Unpublished Critiques

Another technique for attacking credibility is the unpublished critique. For example, after Mark Diesendorf's *Nature* paper was published,[52] a critique was written by Australian proponent Graham Craig and circulated to government health departments and editors of newspapers and journals. (Diesendorf eventually obtained a copy.)[53] Craig's critique was not designed to be published. In fact, in a cover letter to the editor of *Nature*, Craig stated that his letter and critique were *not* for publication.[54]

This technique avoids putting the criticisms in the open scientific literature where they can, in turn, be criticized. Hence this denies the criticized paper the status of being taken seriously in a prestigious open forum, but profluoridationists are able to use the unpublished critique when preparing responses for local debates.

Diesendorf found it difficult to respond to this. He prepared a reply, but it seems unusual to publish in a journal a response to unpublished material. But there was no obvious way to circulate his reply—or even notice of its existence—to all those who would have received the unpublished critique.

Another critique of Diesendorf's *Nature* paper, by leading British proponents Murray and Andrew Rugg-Gunn, was "issued" by the British Fluoridation Society.[55] Again, as the critique did not appear in the open scientific literature, Diesendorf had the same problems in replying.

Colquhoun has encountered similar difficulties. After the appearance of his two-part article in *American Laboratory*,[56] a letter criticizing his research was circulated by the director of the Division of Dental Health's head office in Wellington, New Zealand. The letter was written by Peter Hunter, principal dental officer for research. It alleged mistakes in Colquhoun's calculations of decay rates in New Zealand school children. The letter was the basis for a statement circulated to local water supply authorities in New Zealand from the Director-General of Health, stating that Colquhoun's data contained a serious error in at least one instance. Later, the Centers for Disease Control, part of the USPHS, reproduced the letter as part of one of their publications. At no time was Colqhoun sent a copy of the letter. When Colquhoun found out about the letter, he wrote to the Director-General of Health asking for access to the data to assess the alleged error, but this was denied.[57]

An article by Colquhoun and Robert Mann criticizing the study of the effect of fluoridation in Hastings, New Zealand, appeared in the December 1986 issue of *The Ecologist*.[58] The authors claimed that the Hastings results were wrong because the diagnostic criteria for tooth decay were changed in Hastings but not in the control town Napier. In 1988, they obtained by indirect means an unpublished critique of their paper by Peter Hunter and Elsdon Storey. This critique had been circulated to the general manager of the City of Hastings, among others, but not directly to Colquhoun and Mann. They responded by circulating a booklet reprinting the Hunter-Storey critique and accompanied by comments of their own in reply.[59]

The unpublished critique seems to be a common way to attack the credibility of opponents. For example, Ionel Rapaport's studies of the link between fluoridation and mongoloid births were the subject of a critique by A. L. Russell, who did research supposedly refuting Rapaport. Russell's research has never been published, but a letter of Russell's about this research has been widely cited by profluoridationists.[60]

Edward Groth III's 1973 doctoral dissertation was seen as critical of fluoridation by many proponents. Leading proponent Ernest Newbrun wrote an attack on the dissertation which was circulated by the USPHS for years. Groth did not learn of its existence for about ten years.[61]

In one sense, the unpublished critique is a curious tactic, as the proponents undoubtedly have greater opportunities for publishing in dental journals. The advantage of the unpublished critique is that nothing about the issue being contested appears in dental journals at all, and so the issues are not raised to the status of being worthy of professional debate.

Prestigious dental journals generally do not publish antifluoridation articles.[62] Nor do they often publish careful refutations of antifluoridation scientific work. Thus the antifluoridation scientists are not given recognition—not even the negative recognition of criticism—in the crucial journals. Responses remain in the domain of unpublished, informally circulated manuscripts.

This point was articulated well by leading proponent David B. Ast at the 1951 conference of dental directors where Francis Bull spoke. In commenting on how to respond to an "alleged rumor" about fluoridation and cancer, Ast said:

> If a refutation is published it will reach a very much larger number of persons. I wonder if it would not be preferable for a refutation to be prepared at the University of Texas and made available to those who make inquiry for it, and for the dental directors to write to the University of Texas for that information. So if the question comes up in their community they will be well heeled with information to answer the question rather than to publicize this rumored information.[63]

In exceptional cases, the work of opponents has sufficient impact to lead to refutations being published in scientific and dental journals. The claims of Yiamouyiannis and Burk on fluoridation and cancer stimulated replies by several scientists in medical and scientific journals.[64] More recently, the studies by Diesendorf and Colquhoun in nondental journals, such as *Nature* and *American Laboratory*, have triggered proponents to write refutations in the *Journal of Public Health Dentistry*[65] and the *New Zealand Dental Journal*.[66]

To me, the most reasonable explanation for why critiques are sometimes published and sometimes not published is campaigning effectiveness. As long as the research critical of fluoridation is not widely known, it is more effective to circulate unpublished critiques. But when the research gains widespread publicity, publication of critiques may be warranted.

Claims about fluoridation and cancer were made by Alfred Taylor in 1950s and by Yiamouyiannis and Burk in the 1970s. It is hard to argue that differences in scientific quality explain the differences in the form of the responses to their work. The key is that Yiamouyiannis and Burk obtained enormous publicity for their work; Taylor did not. Hence, Taylor could be dealt with by an unpublished critique, whereas Yiamouyiannis and Burk merited published refutations. Similarly, the initial responses to Colquhoun and Diesendorf were unpublished critiques, but, as their work continued to attract considerable attention, published responses were deemed warranted.[67]

This is not to say there is any conscious conspiracy to choose either publication or circulation of unpublished critiques. Rather, the struggle for credibility within the fluoridation controversy sets the general context in which the standing of various arguments and critics is assessed. Within this context, it then seems natural to choose a response which is more effective in the circumstances.

Attacking the Critics Personally

Yet another response to critics has been to attack them personally, rather than merely attacking their arguments. The aim here is to destroy personal credibility and authority.

In my interviews with fluoridation partisans, the scientific credibility of those on the other side was a key point in many comments. There were a number of statements undermining the status of those on the other side as scientific or scholarly. For example, one proponent told me that Geoffrey Smith was unable to get anything published in refereed scholarly journals, and could publish only via the unrefereed letters column of the *New Zealand Dental Journal*. (Smith told another story. Unable to get past the referees in the *Australian Dental Journal*, he had had no trouble getting his articles published in international scientific journals. He has sent me reprints of several such articles.)[68]

One proponent told me that Mark Diesendorf's article in the prestigious scientific journal *Nature* had not been refereed, and that this information had come to him via a contact in Britain. According to Diesendorf, the article *was* refereed. He sent me a copy of the referee's report and his correspondence with the editor of *Nature*.

The point here is that attempts were made to undermine the conventional scientific achievements of those on the other side. This was something that could be done more effectively by the proponents, since they have a near-monopoly over professional opinion and membership of key policy-making and advisory bodies.

A number of interviewees, both proponents and opponents, spontaneously mentioned the Briggs case. Michael Briggs had been a professor of human biology and dean of science at Deakin University in Geelong, not far from Melbourne. Allegations were raised in the early 1980s that Briggs had fabricated some of his research findings on oral contraceptives. Briggs denied any wrongdoing. In a drawn-out affair, the university had difficulties in initiating a formal inquiry into the allegations.

Eventually, Briggs resigned, and, not long afterward, died in Spain in 1986. A university investigation later concluded that data in at least some of Briggs' publications was partly fabricated. The continued publicity about the Briggs case made his name a symbol of fraud in Australian science.[69]

The way in which the Briggs case was mentioned by several proponents and opponents suggested that scientists on the *other side* could well be fraudulent. For example, one proponent noted, in relation to Diesendorf's antifluoridation article in *Nature*, that Briggs had published in *Nature*. The implication was that even fraudulent work could get into prestigious journals, and so the publication of an antifluoridation paper there did not mean it was scientific.

Some proponents and opponents interviewed made highly derogatory comments about each other, but only about those on the other side. Some or all of those on the other side were called "unscientific," "discredited," and occasionally much stronger things such as "liars" and "fools." Some very specific examples were offered to justify this sort of language. (Only some interviewees made such derogatory characterizations. They arose spontaneously in the interviews.)

Scientists—including leading scientists—commonly make derogatory and abusive comments about those with differing views, as is recognized by most people in the profession.[70] It is less common for such attacks to be made in print. The fluoridation controversy is somewhat unusual in that the professional literature contains quite a number of personal attacks.[71]

The Attack on Sutton. Donald Galagan's 1960 review of Philip Sutton's book contains some technical points, but also some personal attacks, including the following:

Although it is nothing new to see an accredited scientist mix fact and fancy, near truth with truth, and emotion with reason, it is always shocking to realise that an intelligent individual in a responsible position can so baldly misinterpret scientific data. . . . The contents of the monograph, therefore, represent no more than an exercise in semantic and scientific dilettantism designed to serve some other purpose. . . . I can only conclude that Dr Sutton has an intense and emotional drive to oppose fluoridation. Why he feels this way is not clear, but it seems likely to come from some motive other than a sincere concern for the statistical or scientific validity of the concept.[72]

There are several implications within these statements. Galagan accused Sutton of mixing "emotion with reason." The underlying assumption is that scientists should be concerned only with reason, and that emotion should not influence their judgements.

Galagan stated that Sutton was a dilettante or, in other words, not a "real" or professional scientist so far as this subject is concerned. Finally, Galagan concluded that Sutton was motivated to oppose fluoridation—with "motivated" suggesting some impulse other than truth or human welfare.

All of these implications serve to paint Sutton as other than scientific. The usual image of scientists is that they are rational, professional, and unmotivated by anything other than the search for truth. Galagan suggested that Sutton, in this piece of work, had not performed according to this scientific ideal.

This sort of attack shows again how the promoters of fluoridation have taken on the mantle of scientific orthodoxy. In the 1940s, it was the proponents who were political, emotional, and "motivated." John Frisch, according to McNeil, was "a man possessed" in his promotion of fluoridation: "Fluoridation became practically a religion with him."[73] Even after the endorsements, proponents were often evangelistic in their activities. The difference is that, because they were then backed by professional authorities, their promotional activities were taken as compatible with scientific objectivity.

Actually, there are no statements in Sutton's 1959 book suggesting emotionality or ulterior motivations. Sutton's language and style is dry and characteristic of formal scientific writing. Ironically, it is Galagan's review which contains emotional language—namely, his attacks on Sutton.

There is no paradox here. Galagan had assumed that Sutton was mixing reason with emotion precisely because Sutton was not wholeheartedly supporting fluoridation. Galagan had assumed that being critical of fluoridation is, itself, evidence of emotion and ulterior motives, whereas support for fluoridation is automatically rational and without ulterior motives.

The strategy implicit in Galagan's attack on Sutton—namely to categorize any opposition to fluoridation as irrational by that very fact—has been openly pursued by proponents of fluoridation. Because right-wing and other fringe groups were vocal opponents of fluoridation in early years in the United States, it was an obvious strategy to respond by denigrating the credentials of the opponents rather than their arguments. The next stage of this strategy was to include *anyone* who was prominent in opposing fluoridation in the same basket. This is the familiar process of "guilt by association."

The ADA Dossier. This process is most public in a dossier on opponents compiled by the Bureau of Public Information of the ADA since the mid 1950s.[74] Versions were published in the *Journal of the American Dental Association* in 1962 and 1965. Entitled "Comments on the Opponents of Fluoridation," the compilation begins, "The following pages contain excerpts from material concerning some of the individuals, organizations and publications opposed to the fluoridation of community water supplies. This material has been compiled for the general information of members of the dental profession and others interested in this public health measure."[75]

A large number of groups and individuals are listed, including right-wing groups, such as the John Birch Society and the Ku Klux Klan. The actual "comments" on these groups are almost entirely quotes from newspaper articles, journals, and letters. A large number of the quotes serve to classify the group or individual concerned as a "crank" or "quack." For example, Dr. Morris A. Bealle, who edited a newsletter called *American Capsule News*, is said to be opposed to the Salk vaccine and to claim that polio comes from consuming soft drinks and ice cream, which occurs more often during hot weather.

Others on the list are documented as having been patients in mental hospitals or convicted for criminal activity, such as practicing medicine without a license. The Ku Klux Klan is included, seemingly only to show that it opposes fluoridation. For example, the *Chicago Sun-Times* of 22 May 1961 is quoted as saying that Klan leader Robert M. Shelton "has been actively opposed to increased state appropriations for mental health and against fluoridation of drinking water, contending they have subversive aims."[76]

On the other hand, some of the information is not particularly damning in and of itself. For example, the only information on Ludwik Gross is taken from a memorandum of 24 September 1962 by the Division of Dental Public Health and Resources of the USPHS.

> Dr. Ludwik Gross, Chief of Cancer Research, for the Veterans Administration, states: "The plain fact that fluorine is an insidious poison, harmful, toxic and cumulative in its effect, even when injected in minimal amounts, will remain unchanged no matter how many times it will be repeated in print that fluoridation of the water supply is safe." He also opposed fluoridation on the grounds that the consumption of water varies greatly, that the margin of safety is narrow and that the engineering problems in large cities are formidable. The Veteran's Administration which employs Dr. Gross states: "Dr. Gross is free to offer his personal opinion in any relation he may desire. However, Dr. Gross does not speak for the Veteran's Administration on the subject of fluoridation. This agency is not opposed to the fluoridation of public water supplies."[77]

Two points are worth noting. First, the USPHS went out of its way to deny that Gross spoke for anyone but himself. Second, the ADA saw fit to include this statement about Gross in its "Comments on the Opponents of Fluoridation." By being included in a list with extreme right-wing groups, opponents of vaccination, other "health quacks," and people with criminal convictions and admissions to mental hospitals, Gross's opposition to fluoridation was implicitly categorized with these stigmatized groups.

The Attack on Waldbott. As mentioned before, George Waldbott was, for many years, the leading scientist in the United States who opposed fluoridation. As an internationally respected allergist and author of numerous publications, Waldbott's opposition to fluoridation was especially powerful. In addition, he was highly active in writing articles, giving talks, and presenting testimony against fluoridation. Any undermining of Waldbott's credibility, therefore, would have been important for the cause of fluoridation.

The ADA's dossier contains a large section on Waldbott. It begins with a statement by Dr. J. Roy Doty, secretary of the Council on Dental Therapeutics of the ADA, which criticized a circular by Waldbott on the grounds that Waldbott had not correctly reported certain items from the medical literature.[78] This is clearly an attempt to impugn Waldbott's claims to scientific status.

The second item is from a newspaper, the *Milwaukee Journal* of 8 November 1955. The item reports that Waldbott, as a witness against fluoridation, was challenged by Dr. E. R. Krumbiegel, the City of Milwaukee's health commissioner. The *Journal* quoted Waldbott as saying that he was "the first person to describe allergic pneumonia as a disease," and said that he was "the first to demonstrate the role of pollen in allergy." Krumbiegel challenged this by stating that "a Dr. Loeffler" first described allergic pneumonia, and that the role of pollen in allergy had been demonstrated long before Waldbott grew up.[79] Krumbiegel's statements seem to show that Waldbott had made false claims concerning his own scientific discoveries, thus undermining his credibility on fluoridation as well.

The *Journal*'s article went on to quote several other witnesses who were critical of Waldbott. One was Francis Bull, who was quoted as saying "It's astounding that we have to get a doctor from outside the state to tell us that people here are walking around half dead," and that people who opposed fluoridation were also opposed to nearly all public health measures.[80]

The *Journal*'s article also reported that Dr. Delbert P. Nachazel, identified as "chairman of the fluoridation committee of the dental association," said that, after studying "all the available scientific reports on fluoridation," he could find nothing written by Waldbott.[81] His comments suggested that, if Waldbott had not published anything on fluoridation, his views were not worth that much.

These comments are highly damaging to Waldbott's credibility as a scientist and, hence, as a critic of fluoridation. Waldbott was well aware of this, and wrote a letter to the ADA responding to a number of the claims. Unlike all other entries in the ADA dossier, the material on Waldbott includes a response by Waldbott. He wrote, "At no time have I stated that I was the first to discover the role of pollen in *allergy* as claimed. I stated that I was first to discover the role of pollen in *chronic perennial asthma*." He also states that allergic pneumonia, which he first described, had nothing to do with "Loeffler's Syndrome." The

ADA dossier also mentions that Waldbott, in another letter, said he had had "thirteen articles published in medical journals."[82]

Much of the material on Waldbott in the ADA dossier serves to damage Waldbott's credibility without responding to his arguments. Although Waldbott was able to reply to some of this in the published version of the dossier, material from the dossier was widely used in campaigning for fluoridation. A dossier on Waldbott was first issued by the ADA in 1955. Its effect is best described in his own words.

> This dossier accused me of intellectual dishonesty and incompetence. I was grouped with lay opponents, one of whom was alleged to have escaped from a mental institution, the other was claimed to be an imposter. Subsequently, wherever I raised my voice against fluoridation, this dossier always showed up like a steady companion. It was made available by the American Dental Association through local dentists and by the U.S.P.H.S. through local health officials. It was sent to fluoridation committees of district dental societies. It was handed to newspaper editors, physicians, dentists, medical editors, officials of medical societies, key lay persons, leaders of clubs and organizations, wherever and whenever there was a need for countering my data. It reached the desks of the Svenska Dagbladet, Stockholm, Sweden; the Berner Bund, Switzerland; the New Zealand Fluoridation Commission. It showed up in Germany, in Holland and in hundreds of communities in the U.S.A. from Jacksonville, Florida, to Boston, Mass.; from New York City to Seattle, Washington. Rarely, if ever, was I aware where it had appeared until it was too late to reply to the allegations.[83]

Frank J. McClure was a leading USPHS researcher whose work supported the promotion of fluoridation in the United States. His book, *Water Fluoridation: The Search and the Victory*, published in 1970, is a classic in the literature favoring fluoridation. In the final chapter, "Contest and Victory," McClure gave his version of the fluoridation debate and included a section on Waldbott. McClure's treatment of Waldbott is revealing in its focus on Waldbott's personal behavior in the debate, rather than on the findings which Waldbott reported in the medical literature.

McClure began by referring to the ADA dossier and mentioning some of the extremist groups opposed to fluoridation, naming the Ku Klux Klan, the John Birch Society, and the American Association for Medico-Physical Research. In the same paragraph he then discussed "two leading opponents of fluoridation," George L. Waldbott and Frederick B. Exner.

Referring to Waldbott's reports of fluoride poisoning from water fluoridation (citing Waldbott's book, *A Struggle with Titans*, but not any of his numerous research papers published on the topic), McClure said "This threat has been the theme of most [of] the antifluoridationists' efforts to discredit the findings of recognized scientists and health organizations."[84] McClure characterized Waldbott's research as "threats," and counterposed Waldbott's findings with those of "recognized scientists and health organizations," thus implying that Waldbott was not a "recognized scientist."

McClure next referred to an instance in which the City of Milwaukee's Health Department offered to test one of Waldbott's "cases of fluoride poisoning" (McClure's quotes) in a hospital. Waldbott declined. This suggests that Waldbott was afraid to let others replicate his clinical findings. This may well have been the case, but McClure did not mention that Waldbott might have had legitimate reasons to refuse.

McClure moves on to the visit to Waldbott by Dr. Heinrich Hornung, an "experienced public health officer" from Kassel-Wilhelmshoche, who was "dedicated to the promotion of dental health in Germany."[85] In a letter to the *Journal of the American Dental Association*, Hornung claimed that Waldbott had not personally investigated the cases of alleged poisoning caused by fluoridation. McClure quoted from Hornung's letter, concluding with this statement: "The American Dental Association and the public health authorities are fully justified in their contention that Dr. Waldbott presented no proof to substantiate his belief that chronic poisoning had been caused by water fluoridation, and those organizations, therefore, should proceed with their program."[86]

This is an excellent example of how to discredit a scientist's findings by exposing the human underside of published findings. Hornung's visit to Waldbott allowed him to see Waldbott's files and, later, to expose what he said was a lack of proper scientific investigation behind Waldbott's published claims. McClure used Hornung's statements to do the same.

Waldbott devoted several pages to the Hornung visit in his book, *A Struggle with Titans*. Hornung, according to Waldbott, was "one of Europe's most fanatical promoters" of fluoridation. Hornung came to the United States to study fluoridation, and made a stop at Waldbott's clinic near Detroit. Waldbott showed him around his farm and showed him data about fifty-two "cases of poisoning from fluoridated water, a report of which was about to appear in a leading European medical journal, *Acta Medica Scandinavica*."[87]

According to Waldbott, he had sent a questionnaire to individuals to see which ones were worthy of investigating more carefully. Waldbott said he used the questionnaire to decide whether to contact the family physician, and that he personally examined most of the fifty-two people.

Later, Hornung sent a letter to fluoride pioneer Frederick McKay, with a copy to Waldbott. This letter was also published in the *Journal of the American Dental Association*. It is the letter quoted by McClure. In it, Hornung said that "Dr. Waldbott distributed a questionnaire in which 'leading' questions were listed, and whenever a single one of these questions was answered positively by one of the recipients of the questionnaire (mostly elderly ladies), this was recorded as proof of poisoning by fluoridation."[88]

Waldbott mentioned other distortions in Hornung's letter, saying that Hornung "must have lifted out of context and attributed to me some of the patients' own descriptions in their replies to my questionnaire."[89] Essentially, Hornung used access to Waldbott's research files to discredit the research by exposing apparent inadequacies observable only to an insider.

As most researchers will admit, an examination of their day-to-day activities, including failed experiments, rejected hypotheses, and sloppiness, can give quite a different impression than their polished reports in scientific journals. Inside descriptions, even with the best intentions, can undermine claims to being objective and scholarly. With hostile aims, the results can be damning, indeed. To expose the limitations of the insider description, an alternative description of day-to-day procedures is usually required, and this can never appear to be as authoritative as a published account which gives an idealized reconstruction of research procedures.

For Hornung to write about his observations to a dentist and researcher, Frederick McKay, was one thing. For the account to be published in the central journal of the dental profession in the United States, the *Journal of the American Dental Association*, gave it much more visibility and credibility. The ADA made full use of the letter. According to Waldbott, it was the subject of a nationwide news release on 31 August 1956 and used heavily thereafter. He said, "The American Dental Association and the P.H.S. utilized this letter for all it was worth. . . . Whenever my name was mentioned in connection with fluoridation, the local promoting dentist or health official handed the story to the newspaper or the local fluoridation committee."[90]

Waldbott clearly made a mistake in allowing Hornung access to his files. He commented, "the thought would never have crossed my mind that a health official's motives could be political rather than scientific. His gift of roses to my wife had convinced me that he was a gentleman. It was perhaps my German background which made me assume that a scientist, a German, and a gentleman could only be interested in science and truth."[91]

Now, to return to McClure's abbreviated account of Hornung's encounter with Waldbott: after a brief resume and quotations from Hornung's letter, McClure gave Waldbott's side. "In *A Struggle with Titans* Waldbott accused Dr. Horning [sic] of quoting him erroneously in the letter to McKay."[92] McClure then turned to other comments on Waldbott and Exner. By giving no detail about Waldbott's response to Hornung, McClure left the impression that Waldbott did no more than "accuse" Hornung of quoting him erroneously and without further substantiation.

McClure concluded his few paragraphs on Waldbott and Exner with these comments:

> Neither of these men appears to have engaged personally in a constructive program of research on the dental or physiological effects of fluoridated water. Neither are dentists, and apparently have only limited interests in basic physiology and biochemistry, essential for clinical and epidemiological research. The charges of these physicians regarding health hazards of fluoridated water are lacking in substantial evidence and are rejected by the majority of physicians, scientists, and public health authorities.[93]

McClure first accused Waldbott and Exner of not being engaged in a "constructive program of research." Certainly, Waldbott was engaged on a program of research, but, presumably because he was opposed to fluoridation, this program was not considered to be "constructive" by McClure. The fact that

Waldbott was not a dentist appears to be held against Waldbott, although the relevance of being a dentist to studying fluoride toxicity is not clear. McClure's statement that claims by Waldbott and Exner on hazards of fluoridated water "are lacking in substantial evidence" sounds authoritative. It provides a striking contrast to McClure's lack of analysis of any of Waldbott's scientific papers and his concentration on criticisms of Waldbott's behavior.

McClure concluded by saying that the charges by Waldbott and Exner were "rejected by the majority of physicians, scientists, and public health authorities." This statement might suggest that this rejection was the result of scientific examination of the charges. The role of the ADA in promulgating Hornung's attack is not mentioned, although arguably, this played a major role in the "rejection" of Waldbott's work.

As noted in chapter 2, Waldbott's research findings are seldom mentioned in recent reviews by fluoridation supporters. The campaign against Waldbott by the profluoridationists, as supported by the USPHS and the ADA, served to discredit Waldbott in the eyes of most dentists and doctors. Perhaps it is not surprising that few scientists have made serious attempts to find and study cases of fluoride toxicity.[94]

The Attack on Yiamouyiannis. In the mid 1970s, biochemist John Yiamouyiannis argued that fluoridation was associated with increased cancer death rates, and quickly became a leading opponent of fluoridation. To argue a link between fluoridation and cancer is an especially potent challenge because cancer is symbolically a "dread disease," perceived as an especially horrible way to die. The claims by Yiamouyiannis and his collaborator, Dean Burk, have been repeatedly challenged in scientific forums. But in addition, Burk and Yiamouyiannis have been personally attacked on numerous occasions.

Setting the tone for the attack was an unsigned article in the prestigious American consumer magazine *Consumer Reports* in July 1978, entitled "Fluoridation: The Cancer Scare."[95] This article is of unusual importance since it is widely known to dentists and doctors and often provides the basis for their response to the claims by Burk and Yiamouyiannis. The article opens with Burk's appearance on Dutch television on 10 February 1976, an apperance which the *Consumer Reports* author credits with the repeal of fluoridation in the Netherlands, previously the most highly fluoridated country in Europe.[96]

The article gives a history of fluoridation, and then turns to the National Health Federation (NHF), which was set up in the mid–1950s by Fred J. Hart. Both Hart and the NHF were investigated by the federal Food and Drug Administration for making false medical claims. The FDA reported "From its inception, the federation has been a front for promoters of unproved remedies, eccentric theories and quackery."[97] Among its concerns, the Federation opposed fluoridation. According to *Consumer Reports*, "in 1974 the NHF decided to mount a new national campaign to 'break the back' of fluoridation efforts. It hired Dr. Yiamouyiannis to do the job."[98]

Yiamouyiannis did a study showing a positive correlation between fluoridation and cancer death rates in American cities. Setting a higher priority on campaigning than scientific publication, Yiamouyiannis first "published" his findings as a campaign leaflet for a referendum in Los Angeles. Only later did he seek publication in scientific journals.[99] Nevertheless, it is interesting to note the response to Yiamouyiannis.

Consumer Reports quotes Thomas Mack, a Los Angeles doctor, commenting on Yiamouyiannis's work: "All over the documents one finds . . . conclusions emblazoned essentially in the form of slogans, without cautious interpretation or restrictions . . . this bias is so pervasive and obvious, the mistaken logic so gross and naive, that the reader assumes the author to be, however competent in his Ph.D. field, totally unaware of the principles of epidemiology."[100]

Consumer Reports goes on to comment: "Most people are unfamiliar with the principles of epidemiology, however, and a Ph.D. degree can sometimes lend credibility even to claptrap. In Los Angeles it evidently did. The scare tactics of the NHF and other antifluoridationists scored a stunning victory over dental health."[101]

The article continues by describing the collaboration between Burk and Yiamouyiannis and their use of their findings to campaign against fluoridation in Britain and the United States.

The charges against Yiamouyiannis and Burk are fairly clear. Yiamouyiannis worked for an organization associated with medical quackery; their research was biased and uninformed, and was motivated by the aim of opposing fluoridation; and they have not published in the open scientific literature. These attacks are more effective against Yiamouyiannis, since he is the one who worked for the NHF. It is harder to attack Burk, a prominent biochemist who worked for the National Cancer Institute. *Consumer Reports* said "Like the National Health Federation, Dr. Burk is a leading advocate of the worthless cancer drug Laetrile . . . and he shares the NHF's aversion to fluoridation."[102] Thus, Burk is damned by his association with the causes of the NHF.

This same sort of guilt by association is used in a profluoridation article by Mary Bernhardt and Bob Sprague, entitled "The poisonmongers." After introducing Yiamouyiannis as the most active opponent in the United States, they commented that "Yiamouyiannis is often accompanied by Dean Burk, Ph.D., another biochemist. Burk is a retired employee of the National Cancer Institute, the highly respected branch of the U.S. Public Health Service which evaluates proposed cancer treatments to see if they work. But in recent years, Burk has been a major promoter of the worthless cancer remedy, laetrile."[103]

The damning of Burk by association with laetrile is intriguing. Support for laetrile is taken by the defenders of medical orthodoxy as a sign of being "beyond the pale," exactly as is opposition to fluoridation.[104] Supporters of "unorthodox" cancer treatments have been denigrated in a fashion similar to the response to antifluoridationists.[105]

Bernhardt and Sprague continue their discussion:

Yiamouyiannis and Burk claim that fluoridation causes cancer. But their claim is based upon a *misinterpretation* of certain government statistics. In true anti fashion, they compared cancer death rates in fluoridated and non-fluoridated cities. But they failed to consider various factors in each city (such as industrial pollution) which are known to raise the cancer death rate. When the National Cancer Institute did a *genuine* comparative study, it found *no* link between fluoridation and cancer. Undaunted, Yiamouyiannis and Burk charged NCI with a "cover-up." They were joined in this hoax by Congressman James Delaney, who is an anti of long standing.[106]

The most fascinating part of this quote is the implication that comparing cancer death rates in fluoridated and nonfluoridated cities is an "anti" way of studying the link between fluoridation and cancer. Bernhardt and Sprague suggest that being a "devout anti" is some sort of psychological problem. They say "It is important to realize that a devout anti cannot be dissuaded by facts," and they refer to an article suggesting unconscious drives in many of those opposed to fluoridation.

> Most damaging to the cause of fluoridation are the few antis who are physicians, dentists or others who presumably should be able to judge fluoridation on its merits. Some of them are simply misinformed. Others are alienated for reasons unconnected with fluoridation, but take this cause to get back at the scientific community which they feel has 'slighted' them.[107]

Here, Bernardt and Sprague spell out why opposition by scientists such as Yiamouyiannis and Burk is so important. Opponents who are not physicians, dentists, or scientists can be dismissed as ignorant of the facts. They do not fall into the category of those "who presumably should be able to judge fluoridation on its merits." Hence, it becomes especially important to undermine the credibility of Yiamouyiannis, Burk, and any other credentialed individuals who become prominent in the opposition.

The Bernhardt-Sprague attack on antifluoridationists has been widely used by proponents. An example is Yiamouyiannis's invitation to debate fluoridation in St. Charles, Mo. Dr. Michael Garvey, a local dentist, was invited to present the case for fluoridation, but he refused to participate. Instead, he released a press statement, which included the following:

> Yiamouyiannis is viewed in the bona fide scientific medical and dental community as a walking example of scientific fraud. The problem is, that he's so smooth in his presentation that the average person without scientific background will be snowed and is likely to believe his every word. This Yiamouyiannis is a "poisonmonger," according to experts in the bona fide scientific community.[108]

Garvey's view clearly is taken from the Bernhardt-Sprague article, which is entitled "The Poisonmongers," a term which refers to the opponents of fluoridation who spread "poison" into people's minds. According to Bernhardt and Sprague:

> The antis' basic technique is *the big lie*. Made infamous by Hitler, it is simple to use, yet surprisingly effective. It consists of claiming that fluoridation causes cancer, heart disease,

kidney disease and other serious ailments which people fear. The fact that there is no supporting evidence for such claims does not matter. The trick is to keep repeating them—because if something is said often enough, people tend to think there must be some truth to it.[109]

Antifluoridationists find this sort of attack especially aggravating, since, in their view, it is fluoride which is the poison. One way they could respond is to point out that neither of the authors of this article is a qualified expert in the field. Both Mary Bernhardt and Bob Sprague are listed as freelance journalists. Bernhardt was also secretary of the Council on Dental Health of the American Dental Association from 1968 to 1976.[110]

As noted earlier, there was also a serious scientific response to the work of Yiamouyiannis and Burk, even though their work was not published in high-status scientific journals. As I argued before, this phenomenon is best explained by the political effectiveness of their claims. Richard Doll and Leo Kinlen, who did one of the studies challenging Yiamouyiannis and Burk, commented that "The preparation of our paper was prompted by the concern aroused at the wide publicity that Burk and Yiamouyiannis had sought and obtained in Britain for their misleading use of crude cancer-mortality rates in fluoridated and non-fluoridated U.S. cities."[111] But the scientific response was not treated as sufficient. There was a concerted attack on the credibility of Yiamouyiannis as a person as well.

More than one can play the game of attacking the credentials, motivations, and honesty of those with opposite views. But the proponents have won this battle over reputation in an overwhelming fashion because they have the preponderance of professional support and especially the backing of professional societies and many ardent supporters who are willing to use their resources to the utmost.[112]

Conclusion

In chapter 2, I described the main arguments used in the struggle over fluoridation, presenting them as a form of intellectual struggle. But the "debate" has been more than intellectual. It has been a highly polarized confrontation in which evidence and arguments are deployed to win adherents, both expert and nonexpert. The polarization of debate helps to explain the remarkable coherency of views of fluoridation partisans, who regularly line up in opposition on every issue, as described in chapter 3. Thus, in order to understand the deployment of arguments, it is necessary to place them in the wider context of polarized confrontation.

In this chapter I have described how the partisans seek not just to destroy the arguments of those on the other side, but also to minimize or destroy their personal credibility by citing endorsements, refusing to debate, making derogatory personal comments, and implying guilt by association with unsavory individuals and stigmatized groups. This form of attack has been most successfully used by the proponents against the opponents, mainly because the proponents have had a near-monopoly over authoritative backing and the professional resources to undertake this style of struggle. The opponents, by contrast, have had insufficient professional authority or control over professional resources to launch a similarly effective attack on the proponents.

In this aspect of the struggle, scientific and nonscientific aspects of credibility and authority are intertwined. It was precisely because Waldbott both had a reputation as a scientist and was heavily involved in campaigning against fluoridation that he was a prime target for attacks on his credibility.

An evaluation of the scientific aspects of the fluoridation issue is impossible without an assessment of the impact of the various techniques used to highlight or downplay certain scientific findings and to bolster or denigrate the reputations of the scientists presenting them. The struggle over credibility is a key to understanding both the acceptance or rejection of claims of scientific knowledge and the use of science as a tool in the power struggle over fluoridation.

5

PROFESSIONAL ATTACK

What I have called in the previous chapter the "struggle over credibility" has mainly been carried out using rhetoric, namely written and spoken language. In spite of the viciousness of some of the verbal attacks, language has its limits. By itself, rhetoric does not have the capacity to prevent a scientist from doing research nor does it bar a dentist from dental practice.

Rhetoric is a way of exercising power, but there are other ways. In the fluoridation controversy, methods of struggle have not been limited to rhetoric. In this chapter, I present a number of cases in which attempts have been made to stop antifluoridationists from expressing their views, doing research, and practicing dentistry.[1]

The implication of these examples is that the fluoridation debate has used more than rhetorical tools. Various other forms of power have been deployed. It is necessary to realize the extent of this activity in order to understand the dynamics of the fluoridation issue. In particular, assessing the technical disputes over fluoridation requires a simultaneous assessment of the wider exercise of power.

Most of the cases of the sort presented here have been documented by antifluoridationists. Some may be incorrect or overstated. But the number of cases is very large, and they fall into comprehensible patterns. In my study of this phenomenon in other areas, there are always many more cases occurring than end up being documented.[2] So I am convinced that these cases point to an important dynamic in the fluoridation controversy. What the cases actually *mean* is something to which I will return to later in this chapter.

SOME CASES

Dr. John Neilands, professor of biochemistry at the University of California at Berkeley, signed a ballot argument against fluoridation. A local proponent of fluoridation wrote to the chancellor of the university requesting that Neilands be reprimanded, and called for him to be expelled from his professional society.[3]

Ivan H. Northfield, a dentist living in Duluth, Minn., made a speech against fluoridation during a campaign in 1965. As a result, his local dental society suspended his membership for one year, without allowing him to speak in his own defense.[4]

In 1964, a sociology student at a U.S. university carried out a survey of a medical society and found that only half of the respondents favored fluoridation while a third opposed it. George Waldbott reports that "The assistant dean, prompted by the fluoridation chairman, wrote a letter berating the student for allegedly abusing the good name of her school." Although threat of a legal action by the student forced a retraction of the letter's allegations, the attack discouraged the student from publishing her data.[5]

While Edward Groth III was a graduate student in biology at Stanford University in the late 1960s, he became interested in the fluoridation issue and, after studying the arguments, wrote a letter to the president of the university suggesting that a ballot argument for the proponents had falsely claimed that there was no evidence of harm. Groth sent copies of his letter to two proponents whom he had interviewed. One of them approached the head of the biology department and vehemently attacked Groth at length, suggesting that he should be expelled from graduate school. But the department head defended Groth.[6]

Dr. Chong W. Chang had done work showing that fluoride interfered with the biochemistry of living tissues. Chang said in a 1972 letter to Waldbott "I have been associated with six years of basic research on fluoride since my study at the University of California and the USDA [U.S. Department of Agriculture] here. However, in recent years, USDA keep demanding me to do the research area which is not related to fluoride. After careful consideration, I have strongly determined to find some other position where I could continue my research on fluoride."[7]

Virginia Crawford, a registered nurse living in Detroit, found that she was severely affected by fluoridated water, and became a vocal opponent. In 1964, she stated that many people had threatened that her nursing license would be taken away because of her activities.[8]

According to George Waldbott, in the 1950s "one internist, still practicing in Detroit, received a warning from a member of his hospital staff. Should he continue to publicly oppose fluoridation he would jeopardize his consultant practice, even his hospital staff appointment. He was profoundly distressed. Reluctantly he withdrew. He had no other choice."[9]

A doctor in Windsor, Ontario who recommended in 1962 to a patient to stop drinking fluoridated water in order to overcome a stomach ailment asked the patient to refrain from revealing his diagnosis to anyone so that his position in the eyes of colleagues, especially Windsor's medical officer for health, would not be jeopardized.[10]

Waldbott also described a case of misrepresentation in 1965, in which prominent profluoridationists presented themselves as antifluoridationists to a woman whose doctor had advised her to avoid fluoridated water in order to overcome health problems. After she revealed the name of her physician, five profluoridationists visited him. "After their visit he had no choice but to remain silent."[11]

A letter from an independent fluoridation promotion group, the Committee for the Betterment of Oral Health, based in Allentown, Pa., stated in 1961 that "We now have spies in most of the established national organizations opposed to fluoridation and can now anticipate the moves they are making and we can really hit hard now, of course, this is not for publication."[12]

Waldbott said that, whereas many presidents or secretaries of dental or medical societies would privately express concern about fluoridation, to do so openly would mean the end of their careers in these societies.[13]

Carol Farkas, a Canadian researcher who has studied the levels of fluoride in foods and warned that some people may be ingesting too much fluoride,[14] gave a talk on this subject to the Canadian Dental Association's annual meeting in the 1970s. After the talk, several dentists came forward, asked for her phone number and said they would call. Five of them did so, "saying they agreed with what I had said but couldn't say so in public because they would get black-balled from the CDA."[15]

In 1963, Dr. R. J. Berry of Oxford published results of research showing a reduction in the rate of growth of cancer cells in the presence of 0.1 parts per million of fluoride.[16] This sounded good in terms of cancer, but actually pointed to the dangers of fluoride for normal cells. At any rate, Berry decided to abandon further work on fluoride after being criticized and subjected to "veiled threats."[17]

Hans Moolenburgh, a doctor and leader of the campaign against fluoridation in the Netherlands, reports that he was instructed by a medical official not to write articles against fluoridation.[18] A friend of Moolenburgh's, named Mien Bulthuis, did research for her dissertation on the role of fluoride in inhibiting the activity of the enzyme cholinesterase. A special committee of the Netherlands' Health Board discussed the dissertation in May 1973. According to the minutes of the meeting, "Mr de Wael remarks [that] he has had a telephone call from Mr Drion (Chief Inspector of Health), who requested that he exert his influence in order to prevent remarks relating to the possible effect of fluoride on humanity from being published in the Bulthuis dissertation, as the subject was already receiving so much publicity that it could cause unrest among the population."[19]

John Polya, associate professor of chemistry at the University of Tasmania, claimed in 1973 that his staff and equipment had been taken away because of his public opposition to fluoridation.[20]

Geoffrey Smith in 1979 worked as a dentist at Proserpine Hospital in Queensland and supervised a dental therapist at a local primary school. He drew attention to the high level of dental fluorosis in children there, and began collecting data on this and on dietary sources of fluoride. He claims he was officially warned by the Queensland Health Department to cease the research and, after media coverage elsewhere in the country, was fired.[21]

Mark Diesendorf worked until 1985 as a principal research scientist at the Commonwealth Scientific and Industrial Research Organization (CSIRO). Officials of the Australian Dental Association wrote letters to the chairman of CSIRO and to the federal

Minister for Science and Technology, who was responsible for CSIRO, complaining, for example, that Diesendorf had "mis-used his CSIRO connections to lend weight to his views on subjects outside his expertise," and requesting the taking of "all necessary steps to ensure [that] this deceptive practice does not continue." CSIRO defended Diesendorf in correspondence on the grounds that he had made clear that he spoke about fluoridation in his "private capacity."[22]

In 1986, Mark Donohoe, a doctor, wrote a letter to the editor of a regional Australian newspaper, attacking fluoridation. He received a letter from the state medical board informing him that the board had received a complaint about his letter to the editor, that the board had concern that his comments were not in agreement with standard medical views, and that a newspaper was not the most appropriate place to present his views on fluoridation.[23] This is an example of what Waldbott would call a "veiled threat."

John Colquhoun describes the difficulty of assessing the role of pressure against antifluoridationists in the following manner.

> In New Zealand the late R E T Hewat resigned from his position with the Medical Research Council in the same year that he revealed to his colleagues his doubts about the paradigm. The author knows that he was fulfilling a long-held wish to go farming, but to what extent he was influenced by pressures to make his decision at that particular time, with the Hastings experiment just started, is not known. The minutes of the Dental Association show that some within the profession believed he resigned under pressure. The late Owen Hooton was a respected Auckland dentist, in private practice, who felt bound by conscience to write to the newspaper dissociating himself from support for fluoridation and agreeing with Sir Arthur Amies' assessment. He was visited by Evan Williams, an officer of the Dental Association, and told that he (Hooton) should desist from such public differences with his colleagues. Hooton promised to reconsider, but after doing so wrote explaining why, in the light of the evidence available to him, he could not change his stance. He added, "The majority of people are against fluoridation. I make that statement on the evidence of the ten referendums held in New Zealand. The methods being used by both the Health Department and the NZDA to force the issue are just repugnant to me." Hooton resigned from the

Association in 1968, and died soon after, saddened by the ostracism he had suffered from most of his colleagues.[24]

Colquhoun himself experienced direct pressure. After being quoted, in a newspaper article, as warning parents about the danger of their preschool children swallowing fluoride toothpaste, he received a letter from his employer, the Director-General of the New Zealand Health Department. The letter stated that "a staff member who is required to carry out instructions which are abhorrent to him should seek a transfer to another position where this conflict will not exist, or he should resign."[25]

A colleague of Colquhoun's who made a similar warning in a newspaper, but anonymously, "was visited by a superior officer who had learned her identity and warned that she had committed 'a dismissable offence'" since she, like Colquhoun, had contradicted the official policy that recommended fluoride toothpaste for all children with teeth, namely two-years six-months and older.[26] In New Zealand in the 1950s, the profluoridationists even arranged for the police to secretly investigate the political affiliations of opponents.[27]

The combination of direct attacks on some public opponents of fluoridation, their fears about loss of grants, and the general labeling of opponents as ignorant and misguided combine to discourage many scientists from doing research or speaking out on the issues. The relative lack of open opposition, in turn, encourages a perception of the "fringe" position of critics.

The direct attacks that occur, plus fears of jeopardizing careers, help to ensure that research projects which may lead to criticism of fluoridation are less often undertaken, and create an atmosphere in which those studies that *are* carried out are affected by a profluoridation bias.[28] Hence, relatively few articles critical of fluoridation are ever submitted to scholarly journals. Of those that are, there is evidence that it is more than usually difficult to obtain publication.

Mark Diesendorf submitted an article critical of fluoridation to the Australian journal *New Doctor*. It was rejected because "it might encourage the antifluoridationists." The editor did not supply the referee's comments, and would not even write in a letter that the article was rejected. He offered this information only over the telephone.[29]

Sohan L. Manocha, Harold Warner, and Zbigniew L. Olkowski submitted a paper about enzyme changes in monkeys who drank fluoridated water to the *Journal of Environmental Health*. One reviewer wrote that the paper "appears to be written with the intent to discredit the use of fluoridated water for the maintenance of dental health" and wondered, since the safety of fluoridated water had been demonstrated "exhaustively and repeatedly," whether there was any point in "reviving an issue that has already been resolved." Another reviewer gave, as a reason for recommending against publication, this statement: "this is a sensitive subject and any publication in this area is subject to interpretation by anti-fluoridation groups. Therefore, any detrimental fluoride effect has to be conclusively proven." The paper was rejected. The authors were warned by their head of department not to seek publication in any other U.S. journal, since the head had been cautioned by the National Institute of Dental Research that the results would hurt the fluoridation cause.[30]

British scientist R. S. Scorer wrote, "I know of one paper rejected by a prestigious British journal on the grounds that it would cause public alarm if published—it raised the issue of a possible relationship between fluoride and cancer mortality."[31]

Waldbott, in a court hearing, was asked, "How did it happen that the *Journal of the American Medical Association*, the *Annals of Internal Medicine*, the *Journal of Gerontology*, and *Annals of Allergy* turned down your articles on fluoride poisoning?" Since the question enumerated "every single journal that had ever rejected an article of mine," Waldbott inferred that Public Health Service officials, as editorial consultants, must have advised the editors of these journals to turn down the articles, and that the editors had provided the information that they had done so.[32]

Albert Schatz, often noted as the codiscoverer of streptomycin, sent three separate letters to the editor of the *Journal of the American Dental Association* in the 1960s. Apparently because Schatz was a known critic of fluoridation, all three certified letters were refused and returned to Schatz unopened.[33]

On 15 to 17 October 1962, a conference on the toxicology of fluorine was held in Bern, Switzerland. The conference was originally planned for the Netherlands but, due to "opposition from dental interests" there, it was transferred to Bern. The conference proceedings were to be published as a book. One publisher of medical and dental literature set the text in type, investing some 10,000 Swiss francs, before pulling out. The publisher was allegedly threatened by a boycott from the dental profession, and was offered compensation for dropping the book.[34]

Philip Sutton reports that after the first edition of his monograph *Fluoridation: Errors and Omissions in Experimental Trials* was published by Melbourne University Press in 1959, copies were dispatched to the press's United States agent, Cambridge University Press. The executive director of the Nutrition Foundation, a body funded by the American food industry, wrote to Cambridge University Press, saying "The professional standing of the Cambridge University Press among scientists and educators would seem to preclude publication of such a book by Cambridge University Press."[35]

Sutton also says that the type of his monograph was, without authorization, melted down soon after publication and had to be reset for the second edition only a year later. At that time, Melbourne University Press normally kept type for at least six months.[36]

The *Index to Dental Literature*, published by the American Dental Association, did not include either the first or the second edition of Sutton's book. It included negative reviews of the book, but not positive ones.[37]

Not surprisingly, journal editors usually deny any improper behavior on their parts. In 1957, dental editors responded to charges of bias by issuing a resolution which stated that "no dental journal is restrained or has been restrained from being free to publish both sides of all controversial matters."[38] Of course, it is quite possible for editors to believe that they are unbiased, while bias, as inferred by others, is at the same time, present.

The above cases are examples of attacks on antifluoridationists.[39] I have heard of only one exception to this pattern. The Australian journal *Simply Living* has published several articles critical of fluoridation. After one of them appeared, Gordon Medcalf, a dentist, submitted a brief reply. The editor rejected it, saying that the views on fluoridation expressed in Medcalf's article were contrary to the facts as *Simply Living* understood them.[40]

The attacks against antifluoridationists predictably are documented almost entirely by antifluoridationists themselves.[41] It is not normally considered proper to reject a scientific paper or deny a research grant simply because of a person's views on fluoridation. Therefore, such cases are not normally publicized by profluoridationists, but are, sometimes, referred to by opponents in order to condemn the methods of the proponents.

Most of the cases have been documented by leading opponents of fluoridation who are scientists rather than, for example, members of citizens' groups. There are several reasons for this.

First, leading opponents who are scientists attract a disproportionate share of the attacks because it is especially important to proponents to reduce the effectiveness which derives from their greater credibility. If an accountant, bricklayer, or homemaker makes claims about fluoridation, it is easy for dentists, doctors, and scientists to dismiss the claims as coming from uninformed sources. In the public debate, and in many scientific forums, the credibility of a statement relates more to the formal status of the *person* who makes it rather than to the *content* of the statement itself. For the purposes of the fluoridation debate, the claims of relevant professionals—epecially those who have written and done research in the field—take on an exceptional significance.

Then, too, because most professionals have favored fluoridation, the few public opponents play a special role. If their credibility can be damaged or their activities which hurt fluoridation can be reduced, this can help change the situation from debate—however unbalanced it may be—to unanimous professional support. Therefore, the leading opponents are much more likely to be targeted for attack.

Also, leading opponents are likely to document attacks because they are prominent nodes for communication. People hear them give talks, read their articles, and, as a result, send them further information. These key figures thereby obtain masses of information, some of which they may publish as accounts of attacks on opponents.

Finally, leading opponents are more able to publish accounts of attacks—especially attacks on themselves—because they have little to lose and something to gain by doing this. They are already prominent in their opposition. Others may not want to spend their lives as antifluoridation partisans, but may simply want to continue work as dentists or medical researchers. For such people, to publicize attacks on themselves would be to bring further attention to their activities and perhaps induce further problems. A safer path is often to simply say nothing and avoid arousing the antipathy of fluoridation proponents.

Attacks on opponents probably have the greatest impact on those who are less prominent in the debate. They provide moral lessons in what may happen to those who take up the "wrong stand."

The normal idea of professional practice holds that measures such as dismissal are taken only against those who are incompetent, unethical, or simply "not good enough." A decision to reject an article submitted to a professional journal is supposed to take place on the basis of peer review, itself based on scientific or scholarly criteria. Membership in professional societies is normally withdrawn only from those who have severely breached professional ethics. How, then, are the sorts of attacks on antifluoridationists described here to be interpreted?

Some profluoridationists perhaps see continued open opposition to fluoridation as evidence of poor judgment, scientific incompetence, unethical behavior, or worse. The imposition of measures against certain opponents is quite justifiable in this context.

Furthermore, no doubt, some of the cases can be explained (or "explained away") as exaggerated accounts or paranoid interpretations by people who have "an ax to grind." But this does not explain the full pattern of attacks.

Most antifluoridationists see the use of professional power against opponents as a violation of professional principles, and as evidence of the unscrupulous behavior of promoters of fluoridation. Opponents of fluoridation frequently raise these cases of "suppression" as showing the political rather than the scientific basis for the promotion of fluoridation. By highlighting discrepancies between the stated norms of scientific behavior and the actual behavior of certain scientists, the opponents use the category of "unjustifiable behavior" as a resource in their struggle.

A middle-of-the-road approach might categorize these examples as unfortunate excesses, not representing proper behavior and possibly being counterproductive for the proponents. But, since the opponents are believed to be wrong and have so little professional credibility, it is not worth making a big fuss about particular cases.

This apparently moderate and balanced view ignores one thing: the organized efforts within the dental profession to denigrate the reputations of antifluoridationists.[42] The dossiers published and distributed by the American Dental Association create a climate of contempt, in which attacks on antifluoridationists become more acceptable. The opponents are, the dossiers suggest, "only cranks anyway."

In summary, the profluoridationists, through their influence in dental and medical associations, their positions and influence with health authorities—especially the U.S. Public Health Service—and their influence over the editorial policies of journals and publishers, have created a climate in which some zealous proponents use a variety of aggressive techniques to stop the expression of antifluoridation views by professionals.[43]

This point again illustrates the impossibility of assessing the fluoridation issue without a full consideration of the dimension of power. An assessment of the scientific evidence is incomplete without knowledge of what research may have been inhibited from being done in the first place, prevented from being published, or relegated to marginal status by attacks on the credibility of the researchers. To assess the impact of these processes, it is necessary to understand the exercise of power both in the fluoridation controversy itself and in the society in which it takes place. To proceed in the analysis, I now turn to the issue of professional power.

PROFESSIONAL POWER

It might seem that activities such as character assassination, maintenance and distribution of dossiers, blocking of grants, removal from professional societies, and denial of publication are incompatible with proper behavior for professionals. The usual idea of a "profession" is of a group of skilled practitioners who act collectively to ensure high standards, ethical behavior, and service to the public. Indeed, a common explanation for the dental profession's support for fluoridation is the altruistic commitment of the occupation to community dental health, even at the expense of reduced earnings. Surely, the unsavory practices involved in "suppression of dissent" on an issue such as fluoridation would not be considered as proper professional conduct.

The explanation for this apparent contradiction lies in a reexamination of the nature of professions. The traditional view of professions as bodies designed to serve community welfare has been challenged since the 1970s by a different analysis. In this alternative view, a profession is essentially a way of organizing an occupation in order to gain and protect wealth and status.[44] Using this perspective, it can be argued that the interests of the profession are not necessarily hurt by the promotion of fluoridation.

The first point here is that the supporters of fluoridation are not all the same. To say that dentists stand only to lose business because of fluoridation, and that, therefore, they are entirely altruistic in supporting it, is to hide differing interests within the dental profession.

Dental researchers who have built a reputation on research into and support for fluoridation constitute one small group with a clear career and personal interest in promoting fluoridation. For example, Noel Martin did some of the early research in Australia into the effect of fluorides on tooth decay. His research in this area provided one basis for his academic advancement at the University of Sydney, where he became a professor and Dean of the Dental School. If history had been different and fluoridation in Australia had never gained acceptance, someone like Noel Martin might never have gained his status and influence.

There is no doubt that Noel Martin, like most other researchers and promoters of fluoridation, is completely sincere in his support for the measure. An analysis of the promotion of fluoridation in terms of interests does not depend on any assessment of the motivations of individuals. What it *does* depend on is the existence of some benefit, material or symbolic, accruing to individuals or groups. A person such as Noel Martin may gain some career benefit from promotion of fluoridation while being, personally, completely disinterested in considerations of prestige or career.

The same process can be explained in terms of the structure of the dental profession. The hierarchies of government health departments, university dental schools, and professional dental associations provide opportunities for individuals to gain in terms of income, status, and power. Promotion of fluoridation is one path to this income, status, and power—assuming that fluoridation is or becomes widely accepted as a "good thing" and, therefore, that those who lead the profession toward it can claim to be worthy of plum positions.

There is also a psychological factor involved here—namely, the commitment that develops when one campaigns for a cause. Most people who take a conspicuous public stand on a subject become more reluctant to admit they were wrong. They are more likely to search out supporting evidence and sympathetic people. As described in chapter 3, the polarization of viewpoints on fluoridation owes much to the ongoing public debate, in which a backdown by any prominent individual would be highly distressing to those with the same view.

Psychological commitment explains some of the passion and rigidity of viewpoint in the fluoridation debate, but it does not explain why so many dentists support fluoridation. One important factor here is dental education.[45] Dental students are more often taught the "correct view" rather than taught to make a critical and independent assessment of the evidence and arguments. When profluoridationists are influential in the teaching of preventive dentistry, most students are taught the fluoridation paradigm. For example, the Sydney University Dental School has turned out a whole generation of profluoridation dentists, thanks to the efforts of leading proponents Noel Martin and Graham Craig.[46] When teachers are not solidly profluoridation, students are also less so.[47]

Another factor is the image of the profession as a whole. A comparison to the medical profession provides a useful starting point. It can be said that the history of medicine is something that the medical profession needs to forget. The era of "scientific medicine" really began only during this century. It is not so long ago that many methods used by physicians did more harm than good—such as applying leeches or delivering babies in contaminated conditions. The status and power of the medical occupation was immensely improved by the discoveries of antibiotics and other "wonder drugs."

A number of critics of medicine argue that most of the reduction in mortality from common diseases such as tuberculosis and typhoid occurred *before* the medical "breakthroughs" which are normally claimed to have been responsible.[48] This decline in incidence and mortality happened because of social improvements, such as public hygiene, better working conditions, and better nutrition. According to this critique, medical science, although responsible for some valuable developments, has unjustifiably been credited for health improvements in which it was not primarily responsible.

For the purposes of the argument here, however, it doesn't matter so much whether medical "breakthroughs" are *really* responsible for dramatic reductions in mortality from particular diseases. The point is that most people think they are, and the profession has fostered this belief and used it to its advantage. Massive government funding of clinical treatment and medical research is provided, even in countries where medicine is ostensibly "private." This sort of funding would be harder to justify if it were not for the reputation of medicine as a worker of miracles.

While more than public image is involved in explaining the power of the medical profession, that image is important. And it is at the level of image that the dental profession usually comes off second best.

Dentistry has taken advantage of scientific and technological developments. Dentists routinely use X-rays, anesthetics, molding techniques, new bonding materials, and the like. These techniques, associated with modern science and technology, help raise the status of dentistry.[49] But none of these techniques is uniquely associated with dentistry as a "great advance." Furthermore, none of these technques can claim to have caused a miraculous reduction in dental problems, similar to the claims for some of the "wonder" drugs used in medicine.

Fluoride is the best candidate for dentistry's claim to a "scientific breakthrough." The early and later research was done by dental researchers. The measure claims a massive and dramatic improvement in dental health and the method is via a "magic bullet," an added substance that causes the improvement. In all these ways, fluoride against tooth decay mimics the established pattern of medical "breakthroughs." In the words of a major Canadian report on preventive dental services, "The 30 to 40 years of epidemiological studies which established the relationship of natural fluoride in the drinking water to the prevention of tooth decay is dentistry's most distinguished contribution to improving the public's oral health."[50] A document published by the Australian Department of Health states more baldly that "Fluoridation of water is perhaps the greatest single development in the history of dentistry."[51]

Fluoride thus provides the basis for an elevation of the public image of the entire dental profession. Fluoridation becomes one way for dentistry to distinguish itself from "technical" occupations, such as physiotherapy or auto repair. The implementation of fluoridation requires sophisticated scientific understanding—such as epidemiology required to measure its effectiveness—and this provides a knowledge base from which dentistry can claim a higher status. So, it can be argued that fluoridation provides the basis for an elevation of the status of the dental profession as a whole.

As in the case of medical "breakthroughs," it doesn't matter whether fluoridation is *really* responsible for a massive reduction in tooth decay. What counts is that most dentists think it is, and that they have been able to convince enough people in the community of the accomplishment.

John Colquhoun has carried out a study arguing that, in New Zealand, the rate of tooth decay was constantly declining for decades before fluoridation and fluoride toothpastes were introduced, and that their introduction had no dramatic effect on the rate of decline.[52] Colquhoun's results are very similar to those observed for diseases such as tuberculosis.

Earlier in the century, British dentists were receptive to the unfounded theory of oral sepsis, which posited that infections in the mouth led to disease in other parts of the body. To stop this alleged problem, teeth were extracted. According to Gilles Dussault and Aubrey Sheiham, the theory's lack of scientific foundation was of little relevance, so long as it seemed sound to dentists and doctors. They argue that the acceptance of the theory of oral sepsis was "determined as much by its capacity to fit the social and economic needs of practitioners as by its apparent validity or its therapeutic virtues."[53]

But what about the objection that dentists will be worse off if tooth decay is reduced by a large fraction? Once again a comparison with medicine is valuable.

Doctors were not put out of business after the introduction of vaccines and antibiotics because of two main reasons: there are plenty of other medical problems for doctors to treat, and entry to medicine is influenced by the medical profession itself. Both these factors apply to dentistry as well.

The traditional idea of a profession—of which the prototypes are the clergy, law, and medicine—is of a "calling" in which work is done to serve community welfare according to special ethical standards and with control over entry and performance by colleagues. The revisionist view is that a "profession" is really just another occupation, except that, by claiming to have special standards and requirements, the members of the occupation attempt to gain money, power, and prestige. Trade unions and industrial struggle for better wages and conditions constitute one strategy for members of an occupation. Claiming professional status is a somewhat different strategy.

A key characteristic of professions is that they regulate entrance to an occupation. For the most lucrative professions—medicine and law—entry to the occupation is regulated by the state. This is done through government-supported and restricted training in higher educational institutions and through licensing by government-authorized bodies. Not just anyone can set up practice as a dentist. Unlicensed "quacks" will be prosecuted.

In some other areas—such as becoming a potter, a singer, or an athlete—no formal qualifications are required. Success is dependent mainly on public perceptions of performance. By contrast, in licensed occupations, the supply of qualified practitioners is usually limited so that wages are kept up. Once granted a license to practice in the occupation, there is little or no market test of the quality of one's performance. Only a tiny minority of doctors or dentists are struck from the register for poor-quality work. In short, a profession is a protected monopoly.

Why should the state grant such a license to an occupation? The process involved is complex, but it can be boiled down to a power struggle. A profession is basically an occupation in which some members have successfully mobilized around a claim to a monopoly over certain knowledge and skills, and won over key parts of the state to provide it with legitimacy through licensing. The more effective the mobilization of practitioners, the more effective the exclusion of competing practitioners and the more likely the winning of concessions from the state.[54]

In countries where doctors and lawyers have been most successful, they are strongly protected by state licensing but weakly regulated by the state itself. This is the case in the United States, where doctors and lawyers are powerful and their average incomes are high.

In Britain, by contrast, the medical profession is similarly protected, but there is strong intervention in provision of professional services through the national health service. In the Soviet Union, the state is even more interventionist, controlling most of the conditions of work. Relative salaries of doctors are much lower, and there is no immediate analog for the legal profession as known in the West.

Those in other occupations are well aware of the advantages of holding a monopoly over the exercise of skills as licensed by the state, and many of them have sought state regulation as a way to improve their conditions. In various parts of the United States, for example, it is illegal to do plumbing, electrical wiring, or tile laying without a license. In this way, full-time plumbers, electricians, and tile-layers seek to improve their status and income.[55]

This perspective on professions does not exclude service to the public, but neither does it guarantee it. The key to a profession's success lies in convincing its clients that its services are both necessary and unobtainable elsewhere. Even if the profession does little or nothing helpful—such as the medical profession until perhaps half a century ago, before which there were few cures for diagnosed diseases—both the professionals and the clients may sincerely believe that the services are essential, beneficial, and provided out of altruistic motives. The practitioners may believe they are altruistic, while, at the same time, the practice of the profession provides them with both material and symbolic benefits.

DENTISTRY AND TOOTH DECAY

This perspective on professions has been systematically applied to dentistry by Peter Davis in his book *The Social Context of Dentistry*.[56] Davis describes the rapid professionalization of dentistry and the way in which dental practice has developed to combine clinical science and personal delivery of services.

The main emphasis in dentistry has been on treatment of individuals rather than changing institutions; this provides traditional dental practitioners with a continuing professional role. Most dental interventions are either at the treatment stage, such as restorative measures, or aimed at the individual, such as attempts to change individual dietary practices rather than policies of the food industry.

In this context, the promotion of fluoridation is an apparent anomaly. Unlike most of dentistry, fluoridation is a preventive measure directed at the collective level, namely community water supplies.

Davis does not systematically discuss the fluoridation issue. However, some preliminary observations can be made on how the perspective on professions as occupational power systems can also explain why reductions in tooth decay are not threatening to dentists.

Even in earlier decades when tooth decay was much more widespread in the community, fillings and extractions accounted for only part of any dental practice. As tooth decay has declined in most industrialized countries, this has not meant unemployment or drastically lowered incomes for dentists.

First, in most countries there are simply not enough dentists to treat all the dental problems in the community.[57] There is a large untapped demand, and at least some of the many people needing treatment are able to pay for it in countries where there is

no public dental scheme. There have been plenty of additional patients to counteract loss of income due to declining tooth decay
rates. Some effort, however, may be required to get more people
to go to dentists. School dental programs and public-education
campaigns serve this function.

Second, restorative dentistry has gradually replaced extrac-
tive dentistry. In earlier years, a bad set of teeth would simply be
removed. Today, the preference is to retain as many teeth as possible and to use crowns, bridges, and other devices to keep them.
In addition, regular check-ups and cleaning have become standard. All this requires a lot more treatment and costs more. Increased standards of living mean that more people can afford to
have this done and, thereby, keep dentists in business.

For example, orthodontics, the branch of dentistry concerned
with the straightening of irregular teeth, has expanded enormously
in the past several decades. Early in the century, crooked and
misplaced teeth were simply "lived with." Today, it is commonplace for children to have braces and other treatments to bring
teeth into a more pleasing alignment. Orthodontic treatment for
adults is also becoming popular.

There has been plenty of time for changes to occur in dental
practice to match altered conditions. This is because changes in
dental health have not occurred overnight. Even when dramatic
reductions in tooth decay have been claimed—as due to fluoridation—this applies only to particular cohorts of children. The
overall rate of dental problems, including nondecay problems, has
changed more gradually.

A third reason why reduced tooth decay rates have not put
dentists out of business is that the supply of dentists is regulated in
part by the profession itself. It is impossible for people "off the
street" to set themselves up as dentists. They must be licensed by a
professional body. Usually, this means years of training in a certified dental school. Entry into dental schools, then, is a crucial
point for controlling the supply of dentists. It is in the interest of
practicing dentists as a whole not to allow excessive numbers of
entrants into the field—assuming that current numbers can ade-
quately cope with those who are able to pay for dental
treatment—since this would reduce average incomes.

In Australia, for example, dentistry is taught at universities.
There is a limited number of positions for students, and, because
dentistry is a lucrative career, entry into the dental course is highly
competitive. A very high score on the relevant entrance examina-

tion is required. It is also very difficult to get into medicine and law, two other professional areas with attractive career prospects. By comparison, university-entry requirements for science and humanities are relatively low, since career prospects in these areas are not nearly so lucrative.

Entry requirements into dentistry are not high because special aptitudes are required of dentists. Indeed, the entrance examination has no special relevance to dentistry. They are high because there are many more students who want to become dentists than are allowed to do so. The reason dentistry is so popular is precisely because the number of dentists is limited, and, therefore, their average incomes are higher than those in most other occupations.

There are, then, at least three reasons why reductions in tooth decay are not particularly threatening to the financial interests of dentists. First, there were never enough dentists to start with. Second, dental practices are changing towards more labor-intensive cleaning and restoration. And third, the dental profession regulates entry, preventing a severe over-supply of dentists.

Undoubtedly, many dentists are personally altruistic in supporting fluoridation in the hopes of massive reductions in tooth decay, even though they realize that their practices may suffer to some degree. But this altruism must be understood within the occupational situation of dentists, a situation which buffers them from any dramatic loss of income.

This, then, is an alternative perspective on why so many dentists have supported, or not resisted, fluoridation.[58] There are a small number of promoters—especially those in research positions—who have built careers on fluoridation and who have reputations as well as many years of personal commitment at stake.

Most dentists are not active promoters, but they do support or accept fluoridation. As a "miracle" treatment provided by the profession, fluoridation promises to raise the status of the occupation of dentistry in a way similar to medical "miracles." In any case, most dentists do, indeed, care about the suffering of their patients, and fluoridation promises to reduce this without suddenly eliminating the need for regular dental treatment. In this perspective, altruism is quite compatible with maintenance of professional status and income.

There is some evidence which can be interpreted as supporting this perspective. A study in 1967 found that, when later-year dental students were asked the question, "if a cure of dental caries is found in the next 5 years, do you feel that this benefit to mankind will affect your income as a dentist?," twice as many answered "No" as answered "Yes."[59]

A detailed comparison by supporters of fluoridation of dental practices in matched pairs of fluoridated and unfluoridated American communities concluded that "fluoridation did not affect dentists' incomes, fees, and nature of treatment to any significant degree."[60] This study found that there were slightly fewer dentists in fluoridated communities and that they had higher salaries.

Antifluoridationists also point to statistics which show that the number of dentists in particular communities has not decreased after fluoridation, but has often increased.[61] But a detailed test of the competing perspectives on why dentists support fluoridation has not been made.

It is possible to spell out a number of hypotheses on the basis of the just-mentioned perspective. For example, it predicts that support for fluoridation would be stronger, other things being equal, in countries where the profession itself has greater control over entry into the profession. It predicts that support for fluoridation would be greater where there is an undersupply of dentists. It predicts that support for fluoridation would be greater among dental researchers and prominent figures in the profession. These and other predictions remain to be tested. The amount of cross-national data on the fluoridation controversy is so limited as to allow widely divergent interpretations of available evidence.

One other point is worth noting. Once the dental profession made a strong commitment to fluoridation, it staked its reputation on the measure. It became very difficult to reverse or even modify the policy, because this would be tantamount to admitting that the dental experts were wrong—both scientifically and ethically—in promoting an insufficiently tested procedure.[62]

This commitment applies even when there are good reasons to change policy. One supporter of fluoridation, Dennis H. Leverett, noted in a 1982 article in the prestigious journal *Science* that the prevalence of fluoridation has meant that fluoride is increasingly found throughout a variety of foods, such as reconstituted fruit juices. Therefore, people are getting much more fluoride in their diet than they would have in earlier years.

Leverett commented, "the definition of the optimum concentration of fluoride in community water supplies needs to be

reassessed. It is important to remember that efficacy of fluoridation and standards for its implementation were established when
water fluoridation was the exception, rather than the rule."[63]

This point has not been taken up openly by proponents of
fluoridation.[64] In the context of the ongoing debate, it would be
taken by opponents as a sign of weakness and retreat. Instead,
Leverett was privately criticized, especially by proponents within
the USPHS, for expressing this view.[65]

In 1987, A. S. Gray, director of the Division of Dental Health
Services in the British Columbia Ministry of Health, made comments about reconsidering advice about fluoridation in an article
in the *Journal of the Canadian Dental Association.* Noting that
decay rates in British Columbia, which is mostly unfluoridated,
are less than in other Canadian provinces with more fluoridation—and are continuing to decline—he states that "we may not
need fluoridation as much as we once did."[66] But, rather than
becoming a "talking point" for the proponents, Gray's article was
quickly picked up by antifluoridationists who have widely
circulated its quotes. This shows the difficulty in trying to modify
a policy which has been long defended in a highly polarized situation.[67]

CONCLUSION

This analysis of the dental profession as a system for organizing the power of an occupation is valuable for understanding the
attack on opponents of fluoridation. Fluoridation was vital to the
careers of some researchers and to the image of the profession as a
whole. In the struggle over the issue, any means available were
liable to be used. It just so happened that the proponents of
fluoridation were able to capture control of professional resources
in the United States and many other countries. These
resources—including access to professional journals, membership
of dental associations, and availability of research funds—were
then used in the struggle against opponents.

The actual details of attacks on opponents cannot be
predicted in this manner, since decisions to threaten a critic depend
on individuals and particular circumstances. What can be said is
that the pattern of attacks reflects the distribution of power in the
controversy. Because it is the proponents who have access to
resources associated with the dental profession, it is the proponents who are capable of making these sorts of attacks—and
they sometimes do!

The limits to attacks on opponents are the limits of professional power. There has been little violence in the fluoridation debate, because neither side has any special hold over the legitimate use of violence. However, if fluoridation had been promoted or opposed by, for example, the military, then it is likely that violence, or the threat of violence, would have been used to promote or oppose it.

There are also tactical considerations which limit the use of professional power. The abuse of power can be counterproductive. Striking dentists off professional rolls is a very serious step, and many profluoridation dentists are likely to be reluctant to see this happen simply on the basis of a dentist's public expression of views against fluoridation. There is always the danger of generating a countermovement of dentists opposed to such serious measures.

Antifluoridationists may seem to be more pure-minded, since they have not been responsible for a similar number and range of attacks on proponents. But, arguably, this is simply because they have not had access to the same professional resources as had the proponents. In many of their writings, antifluoridationists project themselves as highly intolerant of proponents. It is safe to predict that should antifluoridationists capture control of the dental profession in particular countries, the stage would be set for similar sorts of attacks, this time on dissident proponents.[68]

This analysis of the role of professional power can readily be extended to the use of other sorts of power in the struggle. Both proponents and opponents have attempted to influence politicians, trade unions, the mass media, and community groups. Each side uses whatever resources it can acquire in its struggle, whether from support by a political party, popular expression of support through rallies, letters to newspapers, or the commitment of supporters who are willing to distribute leaflets and arrange speaking engagements for civic organizations. The antifluoridationists have been more conspicuous in doing this, especially in relation to referendums, partly because they have *not* had the authoritative support of dental bodies. But especially in countries with decentralized decision making, such as the United States, both sides have done enormous amounts of day-to-day work which is typical of communities organizing on all sorts of issues.

Because the resources associated with the dental profession are so powerful, it has been vital for the success of fluoridation to capture control of the profession in the sense of having support from the leading figures. From this perspective, the early efforts by the "Wisconsin dentists" and other proponents to obtain endorsement by the USPHS, the ADA, and the AMA were crucial. Without professional support for fluoridation, it would have been very difficult to implement the measure.

Following the vital early step of capturing professional support for fluoridation, it has continued to be vital to maintain the appearance of professional unanimity. As long as the opponents have no scientific or professional credibility, they can be more easily typecast as "unknowledgeable cranks," and thus rejected.

This strategy has depended on discouraging professionals from taking vocal open stands against fluoridation. In this context, the attacks on opponents are a logical outgrowth of the initial way in which fluoridation was promoted. In the highly polarized and vehement controversy, it was only to be expected that professional power would be used for professional attack.

6

A CORPORATE CONNECTION?

Proponents typically portray support for fluoridation as coming from responsible professionals, community organizations, and citizens. For example, one writer says that "Proponents of fluoridation have included dentists and their professional organizations, public health officials, and a wide variety of civic groups, from parent-teacher associations to veterans groups."[1]

The proponents often describe the opposition, by contrast, as associated with groups with special belief systems. The same writer states that "The opposition has consisted of a coalition of groups with varied interests, including the politically ultraconservative John Birch Society, health-food enthusiasts, chiropractors, and some members of religious groups such as Christian Scientists."[2] In other words, proponents are responsible members of the community, while opponents are likely to be from groups with "axes to grind."

Opponents offer a different picture. They portray opposition as coming from a wide cross section of the community, including a substantial fraction of dental and medical professionals who are deterred from taking an open stand. Some opponents see support for fluoridation as driven by vested interests, including aluminum and fertilizer companies that want to get rid of fluoride wastes, and government bureaucracies and dental elites seeking to impose their wills on the population. In short, opponents are ordinary concerned members of the community, whereas support for fluoridation derives from financial and bureaucratic vested interests.

In this chapter, I pursue the role of interest groups in supporting and opposing fluoridation, a task begun in the previous chapter with the analysis of the role of the dental profession.

THE OPPOSITION

The standard ways in which opposition to fluoridation has been explained are in terms of irrationality, alienation, or confusion. All of these have been explanations in terms of problems suffered by individuals. Instead, I seek explanations in terms of "interests" which typically involve money, power, or prestige. Are there any groups with an interest in opposing fluoridation?

The only group with an obvious interest in this regard is dentists. Dentists might be thought to have a professional (financial) interest in opposing fluoridation, since they believe it will drastically reduce tooth decay and therefore reduce the demand for their services. But dentists, by and large, do not oppose fluoridation. It is hard to find any similarly obvious reasons, in terms of material interests, that exist for the opposition.[3]

There is very little money to be gained by opposing fluoridation. Some antifluoridation groups benefit financially from sales of water purifiers, but this is far from providing a material interest in stopping fluoridation. After all, their sales would decline if fluoridation were ended. At most, they would have an interest in a continuing controversy in fluoridated areas.

Many members of the health-food movement, especially stores selling so-called health foods, have been involved in the opposition. Part of the promotion of health foods consists in establishing their purity and naturalness in terms of being unrefined, free from added colorings and flavorings, and grown in the absence of pesticides and artificial fertilizers. Those who want to eat so-called natural foods are also likely to want to drink what they consider to be pure water, adding that fluoride can be claimed as making water impure.

There is not much of a link here which involves money or political power. Indeed, health-food shops stand to make money by selling unfluoridated water in fluoridated areas. The health-food industry is much more threatened by measures such as laws to limit sales of vitamins, against which they have strongly mobilized. Opposition to fluoridation is not something which has been backed by the organized power of the health-food industry in the same way that fluoridation has been promoted by dental associations. Many people who consider themselves to be supporters of health foods oppose fluoridation, but only a minority of these people take an active role in the debate.

The connection is more at the level of beliefs than of material interests. If "interests" can be said to be involved, it would be an interest in publicly maintaining a coherent stand against various threats to so-called natural food and drink.

Similar sorts of comments apply to the participation of chiropractors and Christian Scientists in the opposition. In both cases, fluoridation is opposed as a threat to the sort of society these groups prefer. While some individual opponents have come from the ranks of chiropractors and Christian Scientists, neither professional associations nor churches have taken a leading role.

Especially in the 1950s and in the United States, extremist right-wing and racist groups were opposed to fluoridation, including the John Birch Society and the Ku Klux Klan in the United States and the League of Rights in Australia. Opposition to fluoridation provided a vehicle for such groups to vent their opposition to "big government." But the antifluoridation rhetoric of such groups apparently has not persisted much past the cold-war period of the 1950s,[4] and so does not provide a satisfactory explanation for opposition to fluoridation. The significance of the extreme right's involvement against fluoridation—even in the early years—remains to be properly investigated.

On the other hand, the wide-circulation weekly right-wing newspaper, *The Spotlight*, has published antifluoridation articles in recent years,[5] as well as many other articles advocating pure foods and numerous advertisements for vitamins and health foods. But Liberty Lobby, publisher of *The Spotlight*, is inconspicuous in antifluoridation campaigning. Certainly profluoridation groups have not articulated such a connection. This limited evidence suggests that certain right-wing groups may adopt antifluoridationism if it has widespread social support, but they are not the driving forces behind it.

Another set of people involved in the opposition, more amenable to being "explained," is those who are employed by national organizations. Their opposition can be attributed to their personal gain from wages. This approach does not carry one very far.

The closest thing to a national organization in the United States in the 1950s and 1960s was the publication, *National Fluoridation News*. This was originally edited and published by Edith Waldbott, George Waldbott's wife. But it was hardly a vehicle for personal gain. Waldbott himself said he made a point of never accepting payment from patients for complaints thought to be related to fluoride in order to avoid any taint of self-interest.[6]

More recently, the National Health Federation has been involved in campaigning against fluoridation, especially when it employed John Yiamouyiannis. It is possible to explain the opposition of Yiamouyiannis by the fact that he was paid to do work compatible with the antifluoridation stand of the NHF. But another explanation is that Yiamouyiannis was willing to work for such a group because he was already convinced of the case against fluoridation. After all, Yiamouyiannis had opposed fluoridation before joining the NHF, and, since leaving it, he has continued antifluoridation campaigning with the Center for Health Action, in spite of no longer receiving a salary for his work. Furthermore, there is no obvious financial or political interest behind the involvement of the NHF in opposition to fluoridation.

In summary, the opposition to fluoridation is not easily explained in terms of money, power, or prestige to be gained by identifiable groups. This is compatible with the simple observation that the antifluoridation movement is an opposition movement. It has no obvious positive program of its own, but, instead, is basically a reaction against initiatives by the proponents. This suggests that it might be more fruitful to look further at the role of interests in the promotion of fluoridation.

THE PROPONENTS

In attacking fluoridation, opponents have made various claims about who is really behind it. Some right-wing groups have said that fluoridation is a Communist plot to sap the health of Americans. A more common theme is that fluoridation is being forced on people by government, meaning a type of bureaucratic "big brother." But these claims have been mainly rhetorical, and not backed up with much argument or evidence.

Just because these claims are made unrigorously does not mean that they are necessarily wrong. But it makes sense to pursue the more carefully crafted arguments first. The two most developed arguments that are available focus on the role of the dental profession and of particular types of corporations in promoting fluoridation. The role of the dental profession, discussed in the previous chapter, is quite conspicuous. The role of corporations is less obvious, but some opponents have pursued this argument.[7]

There are three types of corporations with a potential financial interest in fluoridation: first, aluminum and fertilizer companies, and other producers of fluoride waste; second, producers of sugary foods; and third, producers of fluoride toothpastes, mouthwashes, and similar products.

THE ALUMINUM AND FERTILIZER INDUSTRIES

One of the major wastes produced during the production of aluminum is fluoride. Fluoride is produced by aluminum companies in massive amounts, enough to seriously pollute whole areas of the countryside. Fluoride can appear in the form of a sludge which must be disposed of somewhere—typically in landfills—or may be airborne. Recycling the waste is possible, but can be very expensive.

In the United States, at least since the 1940s, farmers, local communities, and others have protested against companies whose fluoride emissions have caused economic loss and environmental harm. Damages were awarded in a number of court cases against the polluting companies. Thus, fluoride wastes were, and continue to be, not only a serious public relations problem but also a potentially serious financial problem. The companies must either install expensive antipollution equipment or risk costly legal suits.

In the simplest explanation, aluminum companies supported and promoted fluoridation since they were able to profit by selling, to be put into public water supplies, what would otherwise be waste material. A number of bits of evidence are frequently cited in support of this claim.

The trend in the 1930s was to remove fluoride from water. Waterworks engineers recommended that the maximum level of fluoride in water be set at 0.1 parts per million. This would allow a factor of 10 as the margin of safety. A level of 1.0 ppm was considered to be the maximum allowable by the United States Public Health Service (USPHS).

Contradicting this trend for lower fluoride levels was the recommendation to add fluoride, first made in 1939 by Gerald J. Cox who was then working at the Mellon Institute, which had been founded by Andrew and Richard Mellon, former owners of the Aluminum Company of America. The Mellon Institute provided facilities for research in a range of areas, and useful findings were turned over to the relevant manufacturer.

Cox later went on to become a major promoter of fluoridation. He was, for example, on the Food and Nutrition Board of the National Research Council, where he presented arguments for fluoridation. This body provided close links between government and industry.

Another early link between aluminum companies and fluoride research was the Kettering Laboratory. George Waldbott, Albert Burgstahler, and Lewis McKinney wrote that "Kettering Institute scientist E. J. Largent, who subsequently became consultant for Reynolds Metals Company, has written a book entitled *Fluorosis: The Health Aspects of Fluorine Compounds*, which was expressly designed, as indicated on its jacket, to 'aid industry in law suits arising from fluoride damage.' This book has been used as a reference source by many physicians and health organizations and strongly supports the use of fluoride in drinking water and discounts or minimizes its toxicological effects."[8] Antifluoridationists often reproduce an advertisement from a 1950 issue of the *Journal of the American Water Works Association*, which says "Fluoridate your water with confidence. Use high purity Alcoa sodium fluoride."[9] This advertisement symbolizes the connection between aluminum companies and fluoridation.

The argument that aluminum companies are implicated in the promotion of fluoridation rests on two claims. First, fluoridation serves the interests of the companies. Second, there were some links between the companies and the early promotion of fluoridation.

Does fluoridation serve the interests of aluminum companies? The usual connection spelled out is that the companies have a direct financial interest in selling fluoride, as in Alcoa's advertisement for sodium fluoride. In contrast is the argument that fluoride wastes from aluminum smelters cannot be used directly for water fluoridation.

According to fluoridation proponent John Small, Alcoa has not sold sodium fluoride since 1952. Some smaller companies market sodium fluoride for various purposes, but, among chemicals, it is the third choice for fluoridation in the United States. Furthermore, the U.S. aluminum industry is a major *consumer* of fluosilicic acid, the chemical most often used in water fluoridation. Thus, the aluminum industry might actually benefit financially if water-supply authorities were not competing for supplies. Finally, sodium fluoride was never a waste product from aluminum manufacturing, but had to be produced separately.[10] According to this evidence, the view that aluminum companies gain financially from sales of fluoride wastes has never had much basis.

Today, most fluoride for community water fluoridation in the United States comes from fertilizer companies. For them, fluoride *is* a waste product. Antifluoridationists can claim that fertilizer companies have a vested financial interest in fluoridation. A letter from an official of the federal Environmental Protection Agency spells out the connection quite clearly.

> In regard to the use of fluosilicic acid as a source of fluoride for fluoridation, this Agency regards such use as an ideal environmental solution to a long-standing problem. By recovering by-product fluosilicic acid from fertilizer manufacturing, water and air pollution are minimized, and water utilities have a low-cost source of fluoride available to them.[11]

But this argument is limited by the fact that fertilizer companies make only a small proportion of their profit from selling fluoride wastes.

Wendy Varney has elaborated on the more sophisticated argument that aluminum and fertilizer companies mainly benefit from fluoridation not through sales of fluoride but through an altered public perception of its toxicity. Before fluoridation, fluoride was something to avoid if at all possible. But with the push for fluoridation, fluoride became touted as beneficial and as something that people need to have.

In other words, the existence of fluoridation does not change the toxicity of fluoride wastes from aluminum smelters and fertilizer factories, but it may well change the public perception of those wastes. It might be more difficult to win law suits against companies for fluoride pollution if fluoride is constantly proclaimed as a great boon to humanity. Likewise, it might become easier to argue for dumping of fluoride waste or the construction of new plants if fluoride has a good public image. Fluoridation, according to this argument, provides significant symbolic benefits for the aluminum and fertilizer industries, and these symbolic benefits can translate into financial benefits.

This argument is harder to dismiss outright, but it also needs more evidence to be convincing. It made more sense in the early years of the promotion of fluoridation and before the rise of the environmental movement. Since the 1960s, the public has been increasingly attuned to the hazards of environmental chemicals. In this context, it may be more accurate to say that industrial fluoride pollution hurts the cause of water fluoridation than to say that fluoridation does much good for industrial fluoride polluters.[12]

The second strand of the argument that aluminum companies are implicated in the promotion of fluoridation is that there are direct links between the companies and promotion of fluoridation. This evidence dates mostly from the 1940s, in the period before the major endorsements of fluoridation. As noted earlier in this chapter, Gerald Cox is one link between aluminum companies and fluoridation, via the Mellon Institute. Another link is Oscar Ewing, an attorney, who was employed by the Aluminum Company of America in 1944 at a salary stated to be $750,000.[13] Ewing then stepped down to become the Federal Security Administrator, a position which put him in charge of the USPHS. During his time in this position, the USPHS endorsed fluoridation in 1950. Another connection is that Andrew Mellon, founder of Alcoa, had earlier been Treasurer of the United States, at a time when the USPHS was part of the Department of the Treasury.

Do such connections show that aluminum interests were behind fluoridation? By themselves, the roles of these individuals suggest the possibility that fluoridation was seen as compatible with the interests of aluminum companies. But whether this evidence is convincing or not is likely to depend on a person's view about fluoridation. The evidence would hardly seem to be enough to show to everyone—as it does to Waldbott, Burgstahler, and McKinney—that "Industry's vital role in promoting fluoridation cannot be doubted nor can the leadership of ALCOA be denied in this affair."[14]

It is recognized, even by antifluoridationists, that aluminum companies have not played any substantial visible role in the promotion of fluoridation since the 1940s. Furthermore, there is little evidence that fertilizer companies have ever played an overt role. The claim is that they were implicated in the early stages of promotion—which got it going in the first place—and that, since then, the companies have left the running to others. This is a weak formulation of corporate influence in fluoridation, and hardly different from saying that they have never been active promoters but, perhaps, have been passive beneficiaries of fluoridation campaigns.

THE SUGARY FOOD INDUSTRY

Sugar and sugary foods are widely recognized by dietary specialists—and the public alike—as responsible for tooth decay. It is in the interests of corporations which manufacture and sell sugary foods to minimize the impact of this problem on their sales and profits. There are various ways to do this. Blaming people for not brushing after every meal or snack is one example. But there are limits to this approach, especially since people do not like to blame themselves when they or their children suffer excruciating toothaches.

Another approach is to find some other way to reduce tooth decay, with "other" referring to any way that doesn't involve less consumption of sugary foods. Sugary-food interests have funded research in a variety of areas, including the search for a vaccine against caries and the search for "protective factors" in foods which might naturally prevent decay.

Fluoride is, in many ways, the ideal solution from the point of view of sugary-food interests. It is something to be added to the diet; therefore, attention is drawn away from the decay-producing characteristics of sugar. It is paid for by the consumer or the community, either in the form of individual purchases of fluoride tablets or fluoride toothpastes or in the form of community-wide provision of fluoridated water. Finally, the impact of fluoride on decay is considered to be large.

The point is that decay, instead of being perceived as caused by sugar in the diet, is seen as being due to a deficiency of fluoride. Indeed, promoters of fluoridation frequently talk about "fluoride-deficient waters."

The manufacturers of sugary foods have no *direct* financial interest in fluoride products, but there is an obvious indirect benefit. If campaigns against sugar by dentists, parents, and health groups are diverted, if only in part, by the refocusing of their concerns toward the need for fluoridation, then a potentially serious threat to profits is thereby defused.

There are also some suggestive intermediate links between sugary-food manufacturers and the promotion of fluoridation. In Australia, the Dental Health Education and Research Foundation (DHERF) provides a link between industry and the dental profession. DHERF devotes a significant part of its efforts and funds to the promotion of fluoridation. For example, it spent $40,000 to support fluoridation in a referendum campaign in 1979. Wendy Varney reports that "Donors to, and members of, the Foundation include an array of manufacturers of sweets [candy], biscuits [cookies], soft drinks and cereals: Colonial Sugar Refining Co. Ltd; Australian Council of Soft Drink Manufacturers; Arnott's Biscuits Pty Ltd; Cadbury Schweppes Pty Ltd; Kellogg (Aust.) Pty Ltd; Scanlens Sweets Pty Ltd."[15]

Although its stated general objective is to improve dental health education and improve dental research, Varney reports that DHERF has not taken any steps to help restrict the amount of sugary foods in school cafeterias or to put tighter controls on advertising of food on children's television programs, two areas where there has been considerable activity by groups of concerned parents and citizens. DHERF thus appears to embody the interest of sugary-food manufacturers in promoting fluoridation as a preferred option for combating tooth decay.

Similar to but less focused than DHERF is the American Council on Science and Health (ACSH), which describes itself as "a national consumer education association directed and advised by a panel of scientists from a variety of disciplines. ACSH is committed to providing consumers with scientifically balanced evaluations of issues relating to food, chemicals, the environment and health." ACSH is heavily supported by corporate donors, including many manufacturers of sugary foods. It prepares reports on a wide variety of topics—such as cancer, fast foods, cigarette smoking, alcohol, pesticides, and saccharin—almost always taking a position congenial to corporate interests. Its report on fluoridation is strongly supportive.[16] Also, some of the members of ACSH's Board of Scientific Advisors—such as Stephen Barrett and Sheldon Rovin—are ardent fluoridation proponents.

There are also a number of individual researchers who seem to serve the interests of sugary-food manufacturers in a similar manner to DHERF and ACSH. Some leading proponents of fluoridation—including Frederick J. Stare at Harvard University, and

Elsdon Storey at the University of Melbourne—have received large research grants from sugar interests. In addition, Stare has been one of the seven members of the Board of Directors of ACSH. This is compatible with the idea that sugar interests consider that they benefit from the promotion of fluoridation.

For sugary-food manufacturers, fluoridation provides little or no direct benefit. But there are very large indirect benefits, which arise by diverting potentially damaging attacks from consumer interests into the promotion of fluoridation or, indeed, into the debate over fluoridation. In addition to this general argument, there is some evidence of corporate research contributions to researchers and organizations which promote fluoridation.

TOOTHPASTE MANUFACTURERS

Most toothpastes today contain fluoride. Superficially, it would seem that water fluoridation would not be in the interest of toothpaste manufacturers, since, if tooth decay is prevented by fluoridation, people would have no need for toothpaste. Indeed, some promoters of fluoridation argue that brushing the teeth has no demonstrated benefit so far as tooth decay is concerned—aside from fluoride in the toothpaste—although it is important to prevent the serious problem of gum disease.

As in the case of aluminum and sugary-food manufacturers, the benefits of fluoridation for toothpaste manufacturers are indirect and symbolic. If fluoride is widely perceived as beneficial, and if people are aware that toothpastes contain fluoride, then they are more likely to buy fluoride toothpastes. This has been a successful marketing strategy, especially since the endorsement by the American Dental Association in 1960 of Crest, a toothpaste produced by Proctor and Gamble. The sales of Crest in the United States dramatically rose after the announcement of this endorsement and its use in advertising. Other toothpaste manufacturers have seen the necessity to include fluoride in their product. The only exceptions are some manufacturers of fluoride-free toothpastes catering to the minority of people actively trying to avoid fluorides.

Toothpaste manufacturers have supported a favorable image for fluorides. For example, a representative of Colgate-Palmolive is one of the six governors of DHERF. Although there has been some friction between promoters of water fluoridation and fluoride toothpastes, they seem to support each other today, or at least do little that is hostile.

There are also some other industrial interests which have some stake in a favorable image for fluoride, notably pharmaceutical manufacturers that produce fluoride tablets and other industries that produce fluoride waste. But it is the aluminum, fertilizer, sugary-food, and toothpaste manufacturers that are most affected by the image of fluoride, while the sugary-food and toothpaste industries have been the most prominent in providing funds to investigate fluoride and to promote fluoridation. This provides the basis for the claim that industrial interests are "behind" fluoridation.

CAPITALISM AND THE DENTAL PROFESSION'S PROMOTION OF FLUORIDATION

Although manufacturers of aluminum, fertilizer, sugary foods, and fluoridated toothpaste have an interest in a favorable image for fluoride, there is still only relatively limited evidence that these companies have been directly involved in promoting fluoridation. As described in previous chapters, it has been the dental profession and research scientists—or more precisely a minority of activists within these groups—who have been the driving force behind fluoridation. How can the alleged influence of profits be accommodated to the central role of the dental profession?

One way to look at the problem is in terms of "alternative paths" for the dental profession. In the 1940s, there were several directions which the dental profession might have taken to deal with the problem of tooth decay. These included:

1. Promoting fluoridation of public water supplies;
2. Promoting voluntary uses of fluoride such as tablets, toothpastes, and topical treatements;
3. Emphasizing oral hygiene;
4. Mounting a continuing campaign to limit easy access to sugary foods; and
5. Promoting voluntary restrictions on eating sugary foods.

In practice, some dentists have been involved in each of these areas. Nevertheless, there have been differences in emphasis. Fluoridation has been tackled much more vigorously than has limiting access to sugary foods. The question is: Why have some directions been pursued more strongly than others?

My hypothesis is that dentists collectively have moved along a path bounded by at least three sometimes conflicting aims: improving the dental health of the population, protecting the interests of the dental profession, and avoiding major conflict with powerful groups in society.

I have already described how fluoridation can be interpreted as a measure which adds status to the dental profession while not substantially threatening the jobs of dentists. The added point, in this instance, is the aim of avoiding conflict with powerful groups in society.[17]

Promotion of fluorides does not put the dental profession in conflict with any powerful interest group. The aluminum and fertilizer industries, even if they are not much involved in promoting fluoridation, certainly have nothing to lose by the measure. The manufacturers of foods which promote tooth decay are more crucial, however. They are a powerful interest group which would be greatly threatened by a major and continuing campaign to provide controls over eating habits. By not confronting these industries in a major way, but, instead, promoting fluoridation or just promoting individualistic steps to better oral health, the dental profession has taken a path of less resistance.

In the light of the massive resistance to fluoridation in numerous countries, it may seem that the profession has not really taken an easy path. But the opposition to fluoridation has provided relatively little threat to the status of dentists, especially as the profession has been able to paint opponents as "cranks." The opponents have included only a few individuals of great standing, and are backed by little money or influence. This contrasts greatly with what the food industry might organize against dentists should it be inclined to do so.

Imagine a different scenario, in which the dental profession led a campaign to outlaw the sales of foods with added sugar, or to penalize the sales of refined carbohydrates by crippling taxes. By analogy to fluoridation, the policy of "nonsugarization" could be justified by demonstrated benefits of improved dental health, and also improved physical health as well. Under such a policy, it would still be possible to obtain sugary foods, just highly inconvenient, much in the same manner as it is highly inconvenient to obtain fluoride-free water where water supplies are fluoridated. One could develop a close analogy between fluoridation and nonsugarization. For example, nonsugarization could be portrayed as ensuring that members of all social groups receive an optimally nutritious diet, the same way in which fluoridation is portrayed as providing an optimal level of fluoride for dental health.

The arguments about freedom of choice are potent ones against a policy of nonsugarization. People should have the right to choose the food they eat, even if it is not always the best for them. This argument is not fundamentally different from the freedom-of-choice argument against fluoridation. But there is a basic difference in the circumstances. That difference is the food industry, a massive industrial interest promoting selling refined carbohydrates and opposing nonsugarization. Meanwhile, there is no substantial industrial or other powerful interest opposing fluoridation.

The very idea of enforced nonsugarization probably sounds ludicrous to most people, precisely because the concept of "consumer choice" is promoted so heavily—although mostly implicitly—through the market system and through advertising. Most people believe they have every right to buy sugary foods, and any suggestion to the contrary is dismissed as "heavy-handed interference." My argument is that the logic of this is similar to the logic of the case against fluoridation. The difference in people's responses is due to the vastly different array of interest groups involved, and the way in which perceptions of acceptability have been shaped over the years.

Arguably, the dental profession unconsciously took a path of least resistance in promoting fluoridation rather than nonsugarization, precisely because of the difference in powerful interests which would oppose these policies. This is not to say that the profession took a "wrong" path. It is possible that a path of least resistance is one which also achieves more in the circumstances which shape the paths. But it cannot be said, if we accept this analysis, that the profession's path was one shaped entirely by scientific evidence and concern for dental health. An unconscious accommodation to vested interests seems also to have been important.[18]

So there are, according to this perspective, two factors which explain the continuing commitment to fluoridation by dental elites and most dentists. One is the profession's investment of its own credibility in the measure. Rejecting fluoridation would mean losing a lot of face and admitting culpability for imposing a risk on the public. The second factor is the continuing power of the manufacturers of refined carbohydrates, which make a major challenge to commercial interests in current dietary patterns into a risky and difficult venture for dentists.

Although this explanation may seem plausible for capitalist countries, it has difficulties in explaining the introduction of fluoridation in communist countries where the selling of refined foods is not linked to profit. Whether bureaucratic imperatives shape the decision-making context in a fashion similar to capitalist societies in this area is, to my knowledge, completely unexplored.

INTERESTS AND SCIENTIFIC KNOWLEDGE

Corporate interests have influenced the role of scientific knowledge in the fluoridation debate in several ways. Most directly, corporate funding of research in particular areas—such as fluoride toothpastes—has led to results which are taken up in the debate. Just as importantly, the failure of corporations to fund more research in particular areas than they actually do—such as on diet and tooth decay—means that certain kinds of results are *not* available to be taken up in the fluoridation debate. Some corporations have directly or indirectly supported partisan activity in the fluoridation struggle. Finally, corporations, by their presence and potential for action, have provided part of the political environment which has encouraged the dental profession's emphasis on fluoridation as a method for combating tooth decay.

In this chapter, I have focused on the role of corporate interests in the fluoridation controversy. There are other areas that also deserve attention.

The state (government and related institutions), which has played a key role in decision making about fluoridation, has received some consideration from analysts.[19] The legal system is a key part of the state, which deserves further analysis.[20] Very little comparative analysis of the dynamics of the fluoridation controversy has been done in different countries as a function of different social and political structures.[21]

The role of patriarchy has also been unexplored and unmentioned. Whereas most leaders of the dental profession—and most leading promoters and opponents of fluoridation—have been men, women have usually taken the greatest responsibility for the oral hygiene and diet of their children.

The significance of this and other gender-related differences remains to be studied. The ways in which the state, the legal system, the national political structure, and patriarchy have shaped the struggles over scientific knowledge in the fluoridation debate remain to be studied.

7

MAKING A DECISION

How should—or could—a decision be made about fluoridation? If science is not a solution, neither is politics. There is no political system which is free from the inherent difficulties of decision making when claims of scientific knowledge are disputed and issues involve both scientific and political dimensions.

The foregoing chapters have shown several ways in which to examine the debate. At the level of ideas and arguments, there are ongoing disagreements and disputes over the evidence about the benefits and risks of fluoridation, and the relation of fluoridation to human rights. In the minds of the leading partisans on the issue, the arguments are tied together into unified assemblages, which serve either to support or oppose fluoridation. What we have is not a disparate set of arguments, but rather two different pictures of the world. Each side tries to win adherents to its own coherent picture.

Evidence, logical arguments, and emotional appeals are involved in the case presented by each side. But the struggle goes beyond this into attacks on the credibility of those on the other side who claim to be experts. To establish authority, both in the relevant professional communities and the wider political scene, soundness of evidence and argument apparently is not seen as sufficient. Credentials and authoritative bodies are trotted out whenever possible, and the credibility of those on the other side is belittled, both subtly and blatantly. Of importance here is the circulation of dossiers of derogatory comments.

There is also the more direct use of power, notably the mobilization of the resources of the dental profession on occasion to attack opponents by expelling members from dental associations, denying publication, and blocking research funds. When the dental profession has been captured by profluoridationists, then all available professional power may be brought to bear against vocal dissidents.

Finally, there is the overall political and economic context of the debate, especially with relevant corporations and the state. These can influence the direction of initiatives within the dental profession by making some strategies for tackling dental decay more feasible and attractive. Rather than directly confronting corporate interests, it may seem more natural or sensible to deal with the problem by another route.

Do these perspectives provide any insight into what should be done about fluoridation or, without committing oneself to a particular stance, how a decision should be made?

FLUORIDATION AND DEMOCRACY

Some social scientists, examining the bitter struggle, have concluded that democracy is an inappropriate decision-making procedure for dealing with public health issues such as fluoridation. Harvey Sapolsky, a political scientist at the Massachusetts Institute of Technology, wrote in 1968 that "The experience with fluoridation seems to confirm the inappropriateness of direct citizen involvement in policy-making."[1] Sapolsky assumes that a rational, scientific evaluation shows the safety and benefits of fluoridation, and contrasts this to citizen opposition. He concludes that democracy, in the sense of citizens being involved in social decision making, is incompatible with scientific advancement in society. His solution is the familiar one of representative democracy in which the citizens choose political leaders, who then evaluate the measure by using expert advice.

Donald McNeil, historian and long-time supporter of fluoridation, takes a similar stance. He states, "It would be reassuring if elected officials could dispassionately weigh the factual information on fluoridation, then calmly make the decision, with the public abiding by the overwhelming body of scientific evidence that fluoridation is effective, efficient, inexpensive and safe."[2] He considers that the continuation of the fluoridation controversy, rather than the complete implementation of fluoridation, is a price that Americans pay for their open political system.[3]

The trouble with these formulations is that they draw conclusions about citizen participation on the basis of a presumption that the scientific case for fluoridation is conclusive. Profluoridationist Russell Scobie, who is opposed to referendums on fluoridation, encapsulates this assumption in his statement that "A referendum cannot establish or destroy a scientific fact."[4] This view is flawed in two ways. First, it ignores or dismisses the scientific criticisms of fluoridation. Second, it assumes that fluoridation is strictly a scientific issue, whereas actually it has crucial ethical and political dimensions.

A preference for decision making by elected representatives is convenient for supporters of fluoridation in the United States because, on the basis of experience there, public officials are easier to convert to fluoridation than is the general public at a referendum. Yet, a look at decision-making procedures elsewhere in the world casts doubt on this view. It is actually in the countries which are more open to citizen involvement, with more frequent referendums and decision making by local government units, where there is usually a higher implementation of fluoridation. This includes Australia, Canada, New Zealand, and the United States. In liberal democratic societies where administrators and politicians at the national level have more sway—notably in a number of European countries—there is little or no fluoridation. As mentioned in chapter 3, there are a number of possible explanations for the lack of fluoridation in Europe, and research to test these explanations remains to be done.

Most debates about decision-making procedures over fluoridation are really part of the debate over fluoridation itself. It is no coincidence that proponents support, at least in principle, decision-making methods that they think will lead to fluoridation, and, similarly, that opponents support methods that they think will allow it to be stopped.

DECISION-MAKING STRUCTURES

There is a considerable literature concerning decision making on science policy,[5] and, indeed, quite a lot on the ways in which fluoridation decisions are made.[6] Almost none of this, though, confronts the implications of a struggle for credibility and using all available resources at the level of scientific knowledge. Rather than deal with the full range of issues concerning decision making—including everything from campaigning techniques to the politics of science policy—I have a limited objective here. I intend to examine a number of contrasting political systems to determine whether any of them provides any way of handling the fluoridation controversy by addressing the problems raised by struggles over the production, assessment, and credibility of scientific knowledge claims.

DICTATORSHIP is a political system based on rule by a single person or, by extension, a small group. Once a dictator has made a decision, it is supposed to be implemented throughout the society. A dictator can be benevolent, malevolent or, more likely, a combination. For the sake of argument, let us assume that the dictator considering fluoridation is benevolent, and desires the greatest good for the greatest number of the people, aside from political participation. On the surface, the dictator can simply examine the evidence and arguments and make a decision.

But this does not solve the problem, for, unless the dictator is also the world's foremost scholar on all aspects of fluoridation, the dictator has to rely on advice. This could be from dentists, epidemiologists, political advisors, ethicists, economists, or secret police. The point is that the system of dictatorship does not resolve the issue because the struggle over fluoridation will take place at the level of advisors. The people who make the presentation and the particular evidence and arguments presented to the dictator will shape the decision.

In the modern world, however, classical dictatorships are rare.

BUREAUCRATIC STATES, in which a system of government bureaucracies makes key administrative decisions with little outside input, are more common. The bureaucratic state characterizes much about communist societies and, as well, quite a lot about capitalist societies. Once again, let us assume for the sake of argument that the relevant health bureaucracy is benevolent, seeking to maximize community welfare in a way that is compatible with continued maintenance of the bureaucracy itself. In the bureaucratic system, outside pressure groups such as dentists, environmentalists, or defenders of individual rights have little access to the corridors of power.

It might seem that the bureaucrats could simply listen to all relevant experts and representatives of interest groups, make a decision, and implement it—subject, of course, to convincing their nominal political masters. But bureaucracies are not exempt from power struggles. Indeed, a bureaucracy can be considered to be a type of political system, in which various groups struggle within the organization's hierarchy, division of labor, and regular routines to implement measures which will cement their own positions within it.[7] Bureaucracies commonly have an "old guard" committed to long-established policies. Young rebels challenge the status quo, not only because they believe in different ways of doing things, but also because this is a way to advance their careers.

If the issue of fluoridation had been left entirely to bureaucratic states, it is quite likely that it would never have gotten underway in the first place. Remember that, in the 1940s, the USPHS was resistant to premature promotion of fluoridation, and succumbed only to an impassioned and effective lobbying process coming partly from the outside. In a more bureaucratized state, the energy of the dentists from Wisconsin might never have succeeded against entrenched conservatism. Communist bureaucracies have investigated and implemented fluoridation only *after* it was widely promoted in many other countries, especially those with more pluralist political systems.

TECHNOCRACY or direct rule by experts is another option. In practical terms, this might mean that a decision on fluoridation would be reached by a panel of experts or an expert inquiry with executive powers. Technocracy sounds attractive to some scientists and other experts, but, in practice, it degenerates into a type of dictatorship or bureaucratic state. Those experts who take on the role of decision making must inevitably deal with issues outside their immediate range of expertise, and this process leads quickly to a more bureaucratic role. Furthermore, the structure of a technocracy demands an answer to the question of who are the real experts. The answer, in practice, will depend on a struggle for power.

REPRESENTATIVE DEMOCRACY is based on election of representatives who have formal decision-making power. In pluralist systems with elections and political parties, representatives are subject to pressure from a range of interest groups, including constituents, lobbyists, government bureaucrats, political party officials, and the media. The wide range of pressures means that there can be no preordained conclusion on fluoridation. The intense activity by both profluoridationists and antifluoridationists in systems with elected representatives testifies to their belief that political mobilization is crucial, and the political system does not automatically lead to any one decision.

This applies even when legislators set up a committee to hear testimony from experts and citizens, and then make a judgment. In practice, such committees have served as one more forum for the continuation of the fluoridation debate, rather than as a method for resolving it.

REFERENDUM is another system. Suppose, for the sake of argument, that all fluoridation decisions are implemented without question on the basis of a majority vote by people in a given public water supply area. Whatever conditions are imagined, this would still allow the losing sides to dispute the result as unfair.

There can be disputes about the wording of the referendum and disputes about resources available for informing the public. For example, one side or the other might claim that only those with certain types of education can fully understand some of the evidence; therefore, the education system may influence the result. Factors of gender, ethnicity, class, and geography could also play a role. Almost always, there will be a disgruntled minority, some of whom may decide that pressure group tactics are warranted in the case of defeat at the referendum. Thus there is no guaranteed conclusion to the controversy.

UNANIMITY is another decision-making procedure. Everyone must agree before a decision is made and implemented. This is feasible only in small communities. As a decision-making procedure, unanimity gives incredible power to the status quo.

CONSENSUS is a modified system in which all that is required is that no one strongly objects. Some may disagree but not feel sufficiently strong about it to seek to block the group's action. Consensus, in this sense, has been used considerably in collectives of various sorts, and is the implicit method in settings, such as the New England town meeting, where voting is the formal system.[8]

Under consensus, a single strenuous objector to fluoridation could stop its implementation or, if fluoridation were already introduced, a single objector could keep it from being removed. Consensus systems usually lead to an intense effort to find a solution which satisfies everyone. For example, a possible resolution would be to fluoridate the public water supply but provide free unfluoridated bottled drinking water to anyone who wished to have it.[9]

Consensus systems have their own power struggles. Because the decision-making process is open—rather than the secret ballot common in elections—the pressure on dissenters to conform in order to reach a decision can be intense.

In any of these systems—from dictatorship to consensus—the role of economic structures and interests, as well as other groups such as professions, should not be forgotten. Corporate and professional interests may be crucial in putting fluoridation on the political agenda rather than some other issue relating to dental health.

Even without this caveat about wider structures, it appears from this brief survey of political systems that there is no neat resolution available of the fluoridation issue. The debate over fluoridation includes a political struggle, and no political system is exempt from such struggle. Only the form of struggle—and the likely outcome in different historical circumstances—is different.

Some of the participants in the debate may pine for a system in which the issues are dealt with logically and clearly, and a decision is made and then implemented in a clear, sensible, and effective manner. Any system which alleges to do this would be "papering over" a multitude of problems, conflicts, and commitments.

Looking through the literature on political philosophies—whether they be liberalism, Marxism, or anarchism—it is remarkable how little help is provided in dealing with controversies such as fluoridation. The problem is that disputes over scientific knowledge are intertwined with disputes over values. They also become involved with wider power struggles, and traditional political philosophy assumes that claims of scientific knowledge can be unambiguously adjudicated in a realm of science which is separate from ethics and politics.

Arguably, science is always inherently bound up with systems of power.[10] But, even short of this claim, it is certainly the case that science related to fluoridation is carried out in a situation where knowledge is entwined with power struggles. The traditional assumption that adjudication of claims based on scientific knowledge is separate from social decision making does not hold true. A minimum response is the open recognition of this situation, so that social claims are less able to disguise themselves as claims about scientific knowledge.

In order to have credibility throughout the community, a decision-making method should be able to deal simultaneously with both the technical and value aspects of any issue in a way that reflects both the interests and values of the entire affected community. The trouble with systems that put elites and experts in crucial decision-making roles is that the interests of the elites and experts themselves are likely to intrude.

Elections provide far too indirect a connection with community concerns, and politicians are notoriously susceptible to pressure groups. The more populist alternative of referendums also has a crucial shortcoming: that is, most people do not have the time to study all the arguments of fluoridation—not to mention all sorts of other controversial issues—and, hence, referendums often become political carnivals. Therefore, it is worthwhile to focus more closely on methods that involve a group of people making a careful assessment of the issues. This includes formal inquiries, the science court, and the citizens court, among others.[11]

The fluoridation issue has two features which make most of the decision-making methods of this type inadequate or inappropriate. First, the facts are inseparable from values. This is apparent, for example, in the coherency of viewpoints across technical, ethical, and political issues. Any method that assumes or requires a separation of facts and values will be unable to deal satisfactorily with the issue. The proposed science court—which relies on a panel of neutral experts hearing testimony and adjudicating factual matters only—falls into this category.

Second, there are almost no experts who are not identified with one side or the other. The tremendous polarization of viewpoints means that there is hardly anyone having credibility with both proponents and opponents. Any decision-making methods that include experts—such as a science hearings panel composed of both scientists and lay people—can readily be accused of bias on two counts. First, the scientists may have commitments, professional affiliations, or friendships which jeopardize their appearance of objectivity. Second, the members of a science hearings panel are appointed, and those making the appointments can be accused of bias.

These same objections also apply to many prominent laypeople, and this limits the value of a citizen court which relies on appointed lay individuals. Similarly, formal inquiries, whether conducted by judges or others, require appointments to be made in the polarized situation.

One approach that has the potential to overcome both these difficulties is the "policy jury." A group of individuals is selected randomly from the relevant community, making sure to obtain a statistically representative sample by sex, age, and other criteria. This group acts as either a decision-making body or an advisory body. The group listens to, examines, and discusses evidence, arguments, and submissions on all aspects of the issue, both technical and ethical. It is backed up by research and secretarial assistance.

The advantages of the policy jury are that those chosen are unlikely to have any vested interest in the outcome. They are representative of the community, yet have the time to examine the nominated issue in depth. Finally, there is no pretense that scientific issues can be separated from value aspects.

Policy juries have been run in Minnesota on several controversial topics, including the effect of agriculture on water quality and a proposal to introduce school-based clinics to deal with teenage pregnancies and sexually transmitted diseases. The randomly selected jurors have taken their roles extremely seriously, shown a good grasp of the issues, and evaluated the jury process very positively. The results of these jury deliberations have been received favorably by both the media and politicians.[12]

Similar exercises have been carried out in West Germany. "Planning cells," which are groups of randomly selected citizens, have dealt with issues such as energy policy, town planning, and information technology.[13]

I believe that the policy jury or planning cell is one of the few decision-making methods that has the potential to deal with the fluoridation issue in a widely credible way. But it will not satisfy those who believe that nonspecialists can not nor should be making judgements about issues with a significant technical component.

CLOSING THE DEBATE

Let us turn now from how the debate in principle should be resolved to possible reasons why the debate might actually be closed in the future.[14] If the key to the debate is struggle using a range of resources from rhetoric to professional power, then changes in the available resources can readily change the state of the debate.

One way in which long-standing debates fade away is through gradual withdrawal or death of leading advocates on one side. For example, some physicists did not accept the innovation of relativity in the early 1900s. But this "old guard," never very strong, became less vocal and its leading figures eventually died.

The fluoridation debate has gone on for well over a generation. Many of the original partisans have died or withdrawn. Professor J. D. Jackson, a leading advocate in Britain, died in 1987. George Waldbott, the leading opponent in the United States for many years, died in 1982, and Dean Burk died in 1988. But new partisans have stepped into the breach on both sides, such as proponent Brian Burt and opponent John Lee. There is little evidence that either proponents or opponents are failing to attract new adherents. In other words, the debate is not fading away as an "old guard" withers on the vine.

Since only a minority of dentists, doctors, and scientists openly oppose fluoridation, the antifluoridationists are more vulnerable to the loss of a few key individuals. On the other hand, they continue to attract considerable popular support, and there is a sufficient body of scientific literature to maintain activism even without many active experts.

Another way in which the debate could be transformed is through switches of allegiance. On an issue as highly polarized as fluoridation, the defection of a few prominent figures can be extremely influential. The best example here is John Colquhoun's change of opinion.

Colquhoun supported fluoridation throughout most of his career, in which he rose to become Principal Dental Officer of Auckland, New Zealand. He went on a world tour shortly before retirement to examine the case for fluoridation, and ended up deciding against it. Since 1984, he has been one of the world's leading opponents.[15] Changes of position of this sort are especially effective because the individual has an intimate knowledge of the "other side" in a way in which no active partisan would be offered.

Colquhoun's switch of allegiance, while very damaging to proponents, was not as significant as it would have been if he had earlier been a more highly prominent proponent. Indeed, it is hard to find a single example of a leading partisan who has switched sides. They are much more likely to drop out of the debate entirely.

Another way in which the balance of power in the debate might change is through new issues and new supporters. This possibility arose in 1987 with a brief report in the prestigious scientific journal, *Nature*, that, when water boiled in aluminum pots was fluoridated, a much greater concentration of aluminum entered the water than when the water was unfluoridated.[16] In other words, it was suggested that fluoridated water was leading to much higher intakes of aluminum. This was seen as significant because some scientists have linked aluminum intake to Alzheimer's disease, which involves degeneration of brain connections and is said to be widespread especially among the elderly.[17]

If this report had been replicated and vindicated and the aluminum-Alzheimer's connection shown more conclusively, it might have brought a new constituency into the fluoridation debate, that of doctors and citizens concerned about Alzheimer's. The solution would not necessarily have meant ending fluoridation, since it is also possible to replace aluminum pans, but this example shows, nevertheless, the potential for mobilizing new supporters. As it turned out, the reported results were refuted and retracted,[18] a result readily accepted by antifluoridation scientists such as Albert Burgstahler and Mark Diesendorf. Burgstahler carried out the experiment himself and found no unusual aluminum leaching. But this was not before many antifluridationists had proclaimed that the initial findings vindicated their opposition.

Fluoridation proponents have tried to expand their constituency through a connection between fluoride and the disease osteoporosis. In osteoporosis, the bones become porous and prone to breakage, a problem especially likely to affect postmenopausal women. The usually recommended antidotes are estrogen replacement therapy, calcium supplements, and regular exercise.

Another approach is heavy doses of fluoride. Not surprisingly, this method is touted by profluoridationists. There have been a few studies which show that fractures in the elderly are less common in regions with fluoridated water,[19] and other studies which contest this correlation.[20] If profluoridationists can convince people that fluoridation helps to reduce the incidence of osteoporosis, this would attract a new constituency to the cause of fluoridation. So far this has failed to occur.

Convincing new constituencies of a striking new risk or benefit of fluoridation has the potential to change the balance of the debate dramatically. The best example of this effect is the claims about fluoridation and cancer presented by Yiamouyiannis and Burk, which greatly helped the opponents in the 1970s. Note that claims do not have to be scientifically correct in order to be persuasive. The claims about fluoridation and cancer were effective politically even though many scientific refutations were published. Similarly, profluoridationists have made claims for decades about the beneficial effects of fluoridation for bones without much scientific backing, although, in this case, the benefit for the fluoridation cause has not been great.

The most important potentially new constituency in the debate is the environmental movement, which could put fluoridation on its agenda as a form of pollution and a health hazard. So far, this has happened only to a limited extent, with some individuals, such as Ralph Nader, and organizations openly opposing fluoridation. Mainstream environmental groups have not adopted the antifluoridation cause. If this were to occur, it would shift the balance in the debate.

Edward Groth III has been watching the debate for decades, and he does not expect any sudden change in the balance of power. He believes "the balance is like a limestone formation in a cave; each new study or recruit is like a drop of water that leaves a tiny residue, and the mass of evidence and informed people gradually grows on the anti side. On the pro side, political victories and recruits are also piling up slowly. If the balance eventually is shifted, it will probably not be catastrophic, but gradual, and not necessarily centered on any one event or new research report."[21]

SIDESTEPPING THE DEBATE

There are several other scenarios in which the fluoridation debate is not resolved but, instead, becomes irrelevant. A decline in tooth decay so that it becomes a rare problem is one way in which this could happen. The declines recorded in industrialized countries—both fluoridated and unfluoridated—over the past few decades already hold the possibility for ending the debate, except that the cause for the decline is disputed.[22] As long as the decline can be attributed in substantial part to fluoridation, the debate can continue.

On the other hand, if decay were virtually eliminated by some other means, the fluoridation issue would become irrelevant. One unlikely possibility is that the diet for young people would become very wholesome, without the refined carbohydrates that lead to decay.

Another possibility is that an alternative "technical fix" for tooth decay could be developed. One area of study is the use of casein and other compounds found in natural foods, such as milk and cheese, and which reduce decay, as additives to other foods such as candy.[23]

Another area being studied is vaccines against decay.[24] If either of these came up with a solution recognized as effective, then fluoridation might be rendered unnecessary.

The reduction in tooth decay provides a way to sidestep the debate, because neither side needs to admit it was wrong. Proponents can continue to insist that fluoridation was needed in earlier years, and that it is only with the widespread use of fluoride toothpastes, better oral hygiene, and perhaps other unknown factors, that water fluoridation has become less urgent. Opponents can continue to make their claims about the hazards and lack of benefits of fluoridation.

GOOD STRATEGY FOR THE PROPONENTS?

Using the benefit of hindsight, let me offer a few comments on the strategy used by proponents of fluoridation. The proponents had enormous early success in winning over to their side the key government and professional bodies. This was gradually translated into actual implementation of fluoridation in the United States and some other countries. The credibility of scientists who were opponents was demolished, but continuing opposition came from local communities with little or no open support from dentists and doctors.

The strategy of the proponents can be seen, from an outsider's point of view, as one of, first, capturing the key public health and professional organizations, and then using the power of these organizations to marginalize opponents and persuade communities.[25] This strategy might have had more difficulties if the push had started later since, with the rise of the environmental movement in the 1960s, new chemicals have been given exceptional scrutiny. But, by this time, the antifluoridationists had been typecast as "right-wing cranks." In the succeeding years, the environmental movement, while showing some interest in the issue, has not put fluoridation fully on its agenda.

In spite of the apparent effectiveness of this profluoridation strategy, there has been continued and bitter citizen resistance, backed by a small minority of professionals. This opposition, while lacking the powerful professional standing of the proponents, has been effective politically. The antifluoridation forces have not faded into obscurity as expected by proponents.

Arguably, the massive early push for fluoridation, which brushed skeptics aside, laid the seeds for its own lack of complete victory. The aggressive promotion in the early years, which drew public attention to the issue, ironically also helped stimulate opposition.[26] The resulting polarization has persisted and acted as a "dogged brake" on greater expansion of fluoridation. Perhaps a quieter and less urgent early promotion would have led to greater success in the long run.

It is possible that a different approach to the testing of benefits and risks could have reduced later criticism. The early trials of fluoridated and unfluoridated cities were criticized by Philip Sutton on a number of methodological grounds. One response would have been to invite Sutton and other critics to be consultants in experimental design, thus co-opting their dissent. Instead, Sutton was attacked. His criticisms have returned to plague the profluoridationists in the 1980s through the studies by Colquhoun and Diesendorf.

Similarly, a greater willingness to respond to and work with early critics, such as Frederick Exner and George Waldbott, who claimed there are health hazards from fluoridation, might have moderated the passion of the opposition. One risk in this is that some of the claims of the critics might have been verified. This could have weakened the passion of the promoters.

Bending over backward to respond to scientific criticisms would not necessarily have eliminated the critics, since any experiment, no matter what its protocol and results, can be challenged and explained away.[27] The fluoridation trials comparing the cities of Tiel and Culemborg in the Netherlands and Anglesey and Mon in Britain are much more sophisticated than those criticized by Sutton, but have, nevertheless, come under attack.[28] But responding to scientific criticisms sometimes can serve to restrict areas of disagreement. More willingness to deal with the critics on their own ground might well have mollified some of them and weakened their alignment with citizen antifluoridation groups.

Fluoridation of public water supplies is only one way to get fluoride to people's teeth. The promotion of water fluoridation has been a mixed success, with nearly complete failure in Western Europe. But fluoride toothpastes have quietly had almost total victory, in the sense of being widely adopted without significant controversy. The antifluoride campaigners have largely targeted water fluoridation, to a considerable extent, because of its compulsory aspects. If water fluoridation has been the front line of the struggle, the supporters of fluoride against tooth decay have, in effect, been well inside their opponents' territory, having won over most of the population to fluoride via toothpaste.[29] In fact, the struggle over water fluoridation can be interpreted as a side issue, which has attracted the bulk of the attention, while the major changes were happening through fluoride toothpastes and oral hygiene.

This can be interpreted either as a highly successful though unintentional strategy for bringing fluoride to teeth, or as a wasteful expenditure of professional effort which could have been better spent in less contentious efforts at education and routine professional care.

Good strategy for the opponents?

The opponents have been able to muster an extraordinary degree of popular support through the years, especially when local decisions are involved. This has been in spite of having the open support of only a tiny minority of experts and in the face of the endorsement of fluoridation by most authoritative bodies. As a populist movement, antifluoridationism has been an amazing success, holding back the tide of fluoridation in English-speaking countries and preventing its widespread adoption in Europe.

It is easy to make criticisms of the antifluoridationists. Their campaigning is frequently riddled with numerous gross exaggerations and misleading claims. Certainly sodium fluoride is used as a rat poison, but there are many substances which are harmful in large doses and beneficial in small amounts. The frequent wild statements about the hazards of fluoride can make serious critics wince. Whether or not the exorbitant claims help or hurt the cause of the opponents more than a sober assessment of shortcomings in the evidence for fluoridation is difficult to say.

Hans Moolenburgh, a leader in the campaign against fluoridation in the Netherlands, argues that aggressive techniques—including calling the proponents liars—are effective and necessary.[30] Arguably though, many thoughtful critics and potential opponents may have been inhibited from voicing or developing their concerns due to a reluctance to appear associated with the extremes of antifluoridation rhetoric.

The cause of the antifluoridationists would have been helped by documentation of hazards by ever more researchers. Waldbott, no doubt, had good reason to be reluctant to expose his patients and files to critics, especially given his experience in being misleadingly "exposed" by Hornung.[31] But, if the phenomenon of fluoride intolerance is to be accepted, investigations by many researchers and clinicians, including skeptical ones, is essential. This is the obverse of the shortcoming of the proponents' campaign in failing to respond to criticisms by the opponents. A careful documentation of intolerance, reproducible by others, would add greatly to the credibility of claims of that particular hazard.

Another problem of the antifluoridation campaign is that it has been almost entirely negative and reactive. The agenda was set by the supporters of fluoridation in the 1940s, and, ever since then, the opponents have been on the defensive. The opponents are *against* the measure, whether because of concern about hazards or individual rights. It is not so clear what they are *for*.

Some of them do take the problem of tooth decay seriously, especially those who push for a better diet. Others are concerned about wider issues of fluoride pollution, including that done by industry. But these other issues can be lost in the passion of the fluoridation debate. Furthermore, by being continually negative and without a prominent positive program, the image of the opponents is also more negative.

The negative side of the opposition is most apparent in the dynamics of fluoridation decision making. When a national or local government moves to make a decision, the opponents mobilize, often impressively. But while the issue is stabilized, either with or without fluoridation and with little chance of a change, the antifluoridationists are inactive. With some exceptions, they are not conspicuous in ongoing campaigns for better oral hygiene, better diet, protection of civil liberties, or environmentally sound policies for industry.

If more of the opponents were prominent in other campaigns—especially those with a positive angle—their credibility on the fluoridation issue would be greater. The involvement of environmentalists such as Mark Diesendorf, Robert Mann, and Wendy Varney may indicate a change in this direction. If the antifluoridationists can win over mainstream environmental groups to their cause, their campaigning effectiveness will be immensely strengthened. This strategy may be analogous to the winning over of the USPHS, the American Dental Association, and the American Medical Association by the profluoridationists in the late 1940s and early 1950s.

CONCLUSION

Many people like to believe that there is a correct or rational answer to social and political dilemmas. Most of them want to know simply whether fluoridation is right or wrong, rather than spend lots of time studying the issue. Part of the attraction of the belief in scientific objectivity is that science may provide an avenue for determining an answer.

Unfortunately for the "black-and-white" picture of the world, there is no final arbiter for many issues involving science. Fluoridation is not purely a scientific issue, since it involves considerations of community welfare, economics, individual rights, ethics, and decision making. But even the "science" of fluoridation is problematical. Judging the scientific evidence on the issue brings in considerations involving the exercise of power, since such considerations have affected the type of research conducted, the opportunities for publication, and the credibility of scientists.

Few decision-making methods acknowledge the power struggles going on over scientific knowledge. Yet, there seems to be no political system which can avoid these struggles. In this sense, politics is not a solution to the fluoridation debate, and it is unlikely that any formal method can be used to satisfactorily adjudicate it. The actual closure of the debate is more likely to come through accumulating small successes on one side or the other, or a shifting of the debate to other issues.

A further complication is that the choice of a decision-making method is just as much as part of the struggle over fluoridation as disputes over benefits, risks, and individual rights. Formal assessments by dental authorities usually favor fluoridation. Referendum results, more often than not, oppose it. Those who discuss the pros and cons of different decision-making methods may appear to be just looking for a way to resolve the fluoridation debate. Whether they realize it or not, they have joined the debate itself.

8

STUDYING THE CONTROVERSY

The fluoridation issue has aroused not only the passions of many people, but also the interest of numerous social scientists. The controversy is an interesting one to study. It has been heated, and it has persisted for decades. It has involved both science and politics, and it has involved an exceptional degree of public participation, especially in the form of referendums. There is much rich material in the controversy for sociologists and political scientists to explore. In this chapter, I will briefly review the main types of social analysis of the fluoridation controversy,[1] with a goal of placing my own analysis in perspective.

PREVIOUS STUDIES

Most social research on fluoridation has assumed that fluoridation is scientifically proven. This assumption is often not even mentioned and certainly never justified by a careful review of the scientific evidence. In many cases, the making of the assumption must be inferred from the type of analysis made of the fluoridation controversy. The main aim of this type of research is to explain why people oppose fluoridation.

Demographic Studies

One popular approach has been to look for correlations between people's views on fluoridation and demographic characteristics such as age, education, income, political position, and number of young children. For example, Mausner and Mausner,[2] in one of the earliest prominent studies, found that a smaller fraction of opponents than of proponents had completed high school.

Another demographic finding was that people older than 60 years of age were more likely to oppose fluoridation. This could be due to lower levels of education, to conservatism, or to lack of any personal benefit. People with young children were more likely to favor fluoridation.[3] Antifluoridationist views have also been linked to conservatism through opinion surveys and studies of correlations between votes on different issues.[4]

Although some intriguing demographic correlations with views on fluoridation have been found by some researchers, most have not stood the test of further investigation. For example, Gamson[5] found a more complex relationship between education and attitudes to fluoridation than did the Mausners. Both those respondents with high levels of education and those with very limited education favored fluoridation, whereas those with medium levels of education were more opposed. Likewise, the correlations between political views and views on fluoridation have not stood up.[6]

A basic problem with these sorts of studies is that correlations between education, age, or other variables and attitudes to fluoridation do not, by themselves, explain opposition. In particular, they do not explain the widely noted change in views during debates on fluoridation. Often, opinion polls conducted before fluoridation became an issue show large majorities favoring the measure, but referendum results often show impressive majorities against fluoridation.[7]

The Alienation Hypothesis

Another widely used approach in earlier studies was to look for correlations between opposition to fluoridation and "alienation."[8] Individuals who were alienated from the dominant culture were thought to use opposition to fluoridation to express their frustrations. Antifluoridationism, according to this hypothesis, is essentially a revolt of the powerless who have latched onto fluoridation as a symbol of the impositions put upon them.

Support for this hypothesis was obtained by examinations of antifluoridation literature, by interviews with antifluoridation leaders, and by attitude surveys. There are several difficulties with the alienation hypothesis.[9]

Attitudes portrayed by antifluoridation leaders in their literature are unlikely to be typical of all those who vote against fluoridation. The surveys of alienation have been limited in size, and even the concept of alienation leaves much to be desired. Finally, the alienation hypothesis, like the demographic approach, cannot explain changes in opinion during referendum campaigns.

The Confusion Hypothesis

A third approach is based upon the concept of "confusion."[10] The switch in viewpoints during referendum campaigns is attributed to confusion generated by the debate itself. Voters, having been confronted by conflicting claims presented by those who present themselves as experts, take the "safe" route in opposing fluoridation and any possible health risks.

The confusion hypothesis seems to explain the dynamics of the development of antifluoridation concerns, but does not explain why antifluoridationists have been able to mount campaigns in so many cities over so many years. Nor does it explain why antifluoridation campaigns have continued to succeed, whereas similar efforts against pasteurization faded away.

The demographic, alienation, and confusion approaches each assume that supporting fluoridation is rational, namely, in agreement with scientific evidence and a progressive social outlook. Therefore, support for fluoridation does not have to be explained by using social analysis. Since support for fluoridation is rational, opposition, then, must be, in some sense, irrational. Therefore, the task of social analysis is to explain the opposition.

Note that these explanations use categories which present opponents of fluoridation in an unflattering light. They are uneducated, alienated, confused, or even just plain irrational. The use of such categories would be unlikely without the assumption that fluoridation is correct.

In addition to the specific shortcomings already mentioned, there are several problems with this general approach, which can be empirical or theoretical. Empirically, it is very hard to explain the lack of fluoridation in Europe and many other countries. In most of these countries, there has been less citizen participation in decision making, and certainly less reliance on referendums than in the United States. The decisions not to fluoridate have, in many cases, been made by government bureaucracies advised by various experts—precisely the groups that, in the United States, have more often supported fluoridation.

No doubt, it would be possible to develop a social explanation of the relative lack of fluoridation in Europe. But such an explanation would have to go beyond the use of demographic correlations and the concepts of alienation and confusion, which are inadequate to the task. It is not surprising that those using these approaches have almost always ignored struggles over fluoridation outside the United States.

On the theoretical side, one difficulty with the assumption that fluoridation is scientifically based is that considerations of ethics and public policy are involved, too. There is the issue of compulsion; the issue that the benefits go to only some sections of the population (none to the toothless, for example); the issue that any risks affect only some sections of the population; the issue that alternatives to water fluoridation will lead to a different distribution of costs and benefits; and the issue of who should make the decision. Those who assume that fluoridation is rational have assumed, in addition to its scientific validity, that fluoridation is socially progressive. In other words, fluoridation is assumed to be socially rational, namely the best use of society's resources to achieve a desirable end.

The trouble is that science by itself is quite inadequate to prove that fluoridation is socially rational. Additional assumptions are required, for example, that ensuring benefits of reduced tooth decay to the entire population takes priority over any violations of individual rights to avoid fluoridated water. But, in the social studies of fluoridation, such assumptions are never spelled out nor are they argued for. This would undermine the rationale for trying to explain only the opposition to fluoridation.

These explanations of opposition to fluoridation implicitly ground their social analysis in a particular and inevitably limited view of the social world. This is not necessarily a shortcoming. The problem is that their assumptions about the social world are never made explicitly, and that, furthermore, these social assumptions are usually hidden behind the premise of a purely scientific foundation for fluoridation.

It is appropriate to note that many of the social scientists who have studied the controversy have seen it as their task to help promote fluoridation.

Mausner and Mausner sought to understand the "disease" of anti-intellectualism and develop methods for combating it.[11] Kegeles, in surveying social research on fluoridation, had some hope that "help for the [profluoridation] practitioner will be one of the eventual by-products."[12] Gamson, on the basis of his social psychological studies, offered recommendations for fluoridation proponents on what not to do in referendum campaigns.[13] It is not surprising, then, that there has been a one-sided focus on opponents and a neglect of the social analysis of the promotion of fluoridation. In a review of social studies of fluoridation, Motz[14] pointed out that there is an implicit profluoridation bias, and, hence, some possible research projects have never been undertaken, such as surveys of communities which have never been embroiled in fluoridation controversies.

A second theoretical problem with the usual explanations which focus on the reasons for opposition to fluoridation is that they make social analysis dependent on the current state of scientific knowledge. What if, in the future, scientists were to decide that fluoridation was wrong after all? Then, all the social analyses would have to be redone to explain the newly irrational support for fluoridation.

This is not just a hypothetical objection. There are many cases in the history of science in which the dominant viewpoint has been rejected and sometimes reinstated. Any method of social analysis which looks only to explain the irrationality of opponents of the dominant view would look foolish.

The theory of continental drift, for example, was once the dominant view. Then, it lost favor, and has since become the established view of today.[15] Using social analysis to explain only opposition to continental drift, then to explain only support for it, and finally again to explain only opposition to it, would be a frustrating exercise.

In the case of fluoridation, where the dominant view differs in different countries, this would mean a social explanation for opposition to fluoridation in the United States and a social explanation for support of fluoridation in, for example, India. Indian sociologists have not written much on fluoridation—and certainly not in American social-science journals—so this theoretical dilemma has not been highlighted. One reason is that, in India, fluoride in water has long been seen as a health hazard and fluoridation has not been on the agenda. So, as a social problem, fluoridation has not been of special interest to social scientists there.

The limitations of the standard social science research on fluoridation can be traced to a general assumption that science is done in its own special realm, independent of the exercise of power, and that objective scientific knowledge enters into the social arena in some way or other. This means that power struggles over what counts as valid scientific knowledge are not includ- ed in the analysis. Certainly, that applies to the studies of demographics, alienation, and confusion. The idea of confusion, for example, implicitly assumes that there is a scientific realm in which clearheaded truth, rather than confusion, holds sway. This same assumption of a separation between scientific knowledge and social dynamics is also made in other types of studies of fluorida- tion.

The Group Politics Approach

This type of analysis essentially looks at the dynamics of interest groups in the social struggle over fluoridation. Typically, this means looking at dentists and other groups promoting fluorida- tion, groups organizing opposition, government agencies, and the like.[16] Studies in the "group politics" mold fall into the category of pluralist political science. They focus on tactics, alliances, policies, and outcomes. These studies often avoid the one-sided emphasis on demographic or psychological reasons for opposition, since both proponent and opponent groups are studied.

This type of analysis is useful at its own level,[17] but it usually leaves out any consideration of social struggles over the status of claims about scientific knowledge. In other words, it makes the same assumption that science is carried out in its own separate realm, and becomes subject to social processes only when in- troduced into the public debate.[18]

Combining the group politics approach with one or more of the other approaches would appear to offer greater explanatory power.[19] But the result is still limited by the common assumptions made, such as the neglect of struggles over scientific knowledge and the neglect of struggles outside the United States.

Structural Analysis

Another method of analysis is to use concepts of social structure such as profession, class, capitalism, patriarchy, and the state. The idea of a social structure is a way in which to capture conceptually sets of human interactions which are regular and, in some way, patterned. For example, capitalism can be defined as a set of in- teractions associated with the ownership of the means of produc- tion and with the production and sale of labor power and goods in a market.

Focusing on structures does not mean that the role of in- dividuals must be overlooked. Structures, after all, only come about when individuals behave in regular ways, as when entrepreneurs buy and sell goods in a market situation. In other words, structures are socially constructed. Structures are simply a convenient way in which to talk about certain recurring patterns of interaction.

Indeed, it can be misleading to think of the behavior of individuals as independent of these regularities. Individuals are caught in the structured expectations and behaviors of many others.

For example, a person might think it quite reasonable to move into an empty building. But capitalism is built on the ownership of property, which means that most people do not expect to be able to make use of vacant land or buildings and police can be induced to take action against those who do. Capitalism, thus, depends on people's support for—or acquiescence to—property ownership, with the use of state coercion as an ultimate sanction. But these patterns of behavior are not forced on people. It is possible to challenge behavior associated with property ownership, for example, to undermine the loyalty of police and courts to certain owners. This is precisely what many squatters try to do.

Just as it is misleading to think of individuals as "free agents"—since they are constrained by other people's regular patterns of action—so it is misleading to think of structures as independent of people's activities, since it is always possible for regular patterns of activities to be challenged and changed.

Concepts of social structure can be used to examine scientific controversies, for example, by looking at the influence of professions, corporations, and the state in shaping agendas and pursuing certain goals. This approach has been almost entirely absent from analyses of fluoridation.[20]

As I indicated in chapter 6, it is much easier to apply this sort of analysis to the promotion of fluoridation, whereas, most analysts have looked only at the opposition. Furthermore, structural approaches are more commonly used by Marxian analysts, most of whom seem to have accepted the stereotype of antifluoridationists as "right-wing individualists," and, hence, not found the fluoridation issue as one worthy of study.[21] Structural analysis also has the same limitation as pluralist political analysis in that it does not delve into the struggles over scientific knowledge.

Although most social analyses of fluoridation focus on the opponents—assuming that scientific knowledge backs the proponents—there is a minority position that reverses the assumption. A few critics of fluoridation have analyzed the dynamics of the controversy, focusing especially on methods of promotion, interest groups, and the like. This analysis is more likely to use the group politics approach. But it is in agreement with the rest of the research in the basic assumption that science is essentially separate from the social conflict. The difference is that the critics assume that the science supports the antifluoridation position, or at least does not support *only* the profluoridation stance.[22]

From this brief survey of the main types of social analysis of the fluoridation controversy,[23] it is easier to see where my own analysis differs. I have looked at both the promotion of and opposition to fluoridation, rather than just the opposition. The demographic, alienation, and confusion approaches are not sufficient for understanding the controversy. My main attention is on the struggles over the status of scientific claims about fluoridation. Rather than assume that scientific knowledge is in a separate category and exempt from social analysis, I have begun from the assumption that struggles over scientific knowledge should be analyzed in the same general way as other types of struggles.

SOCIOLOGY OF SCIENTIFIC KNOWLEDGE

My approach grows out of a different tradition—the sociology of scientific knowledge. In this extension of the classical sociology of knowledge, all of science is opened for social examination. The processes by which scientists decide that certain claims deserve to be treated as facts are examined, just as the beliefs about religion, gender, or politics are examined.[24]

The "strong program in the sociology of scientific knowledge"[25] is based on four postulates.

1. All knowledge should be explained as resulting from social causes, called causality;
2. The investigation should be impartial with respect to the truth or falsity of the beliefs analyzed, called impartiality;
3. The same conceptual tools should be used to explain both true and false beliefs, called symmetry; and
4. The analysis should be able to be applied to itself, called reflexivity.

The strong program certainly provides a different entry point to the fluoridation controversy. First, social analysis is applied to claims about scientific knowledge as well as reasons for public opposition, emergence of interest groups, and so forth. Second, the scientific claims, both for and against fluoridation, are analyzed using the same conceptual tools.

One of the most useful concepts is that of "resource" or "tool."[26] A resource is anything that is used by an "actor," meaning, in this instance, someone or some group involved in the controversy. Resources include scientific knowledge, scientific publications, scientific status, and so on. Scientists can try to persuade each other of their views by using data, argumentation, personal prestige, charisma, publications, and many other resources.

One way to interpret this book is to say that, in each successive chapter, I have looked at the use of resources from a slightly different and ever widening point of view.

Chapter 2 deals with the scientific arguments. Scientific data and arguments are resources by which partisans try to convince each other and the public.

Chapter 3 deals with the coherency of viewpoints of partisans. In a sense, the different arguments in the debate are made coherent by the debate itself, and are, thus, made into a congealed, less vulnerable resource for waging further debate.

Chapter 4 deals with the credibility of partisans who are scientists, as credibility is both a resource and a target for attack.

Chapter 5 deals with professional attack. Professional power is a resource.

Chapter 6 deals with corporate power, which is certainly a resource and may have had some impact on the debate.

Finally, chapter 7 deals with methods of decision making, which themselves can be interpreted as resources.

Another valuable concept in analyzing the fluoridation controversy is "interest."[27] In chapter 2, the interests at stake are those of scientists in having a scientifically solid argument. Chapter 3 deals with coherency of viewpoints and could be said to treat the interests of partisans having viewpoints that stand up in public debate. Interests in scientific and public credibility are the core of chapter 4. Chapter 5 deals with the interests of the dental profession, and chapter 6 with the interests of certain corporations.

Long before chapter 7, however, I have gone beyond the usual ambit of the strong program, if not parted company with it.

This is most obvious in the use of professional power and capitalism as tools of analysis. These are categories of social structure, as described earlier. They arise from different theoretical traditions which have seldom been meshed with the sociology of scientific knowledge. This is because the strong program has usually been applied to disputes carried out almost entirely inside the scientific community, such as over the existence of gravity waves or continental drift.

In such disputes, one can look at the shaping of claims of knowledge by general beliefs about society, by the career interests of groups of scientists, and so forth. But, whereas in such disputes there is some, usually tenuous, influence by wider social interests on the course of the scientific controversy, there is usually relatively little converse impact of the scientific controversy on society.

The fluoridation controversy is quite different. Not only are scientific, ethical, and political arguments mixed together in a vociferous debate, but the credibility of scientists has been a subject of intense interest, with strong attacks mounted.

RELATIVISM

The usual theory of knowledge underlying the study of science is that scientific knowledge is an expression of truths rooted in nature, or at least as good an approximation as currently possible to such truths. This positivist approach is the basis of the assumption that controversies can be studied by examining the truth of scientific statements separately from the social dynamics. The strong program, by contrast, is built on a relativist picture of knowledge, which denies that there is any inherently superior way to determine truth rooted in nature. Science is, then, analyzed just as is any other belief system.

Note that in applying the strong program to controversies, only a "methodological relativism" is required. The analyst proceeds as if there were no privileged access to the truth. This is a procedure for social analysis, not a statement about reality or personal beliefs.

A common criticism of relativism is that it means that all beliefs are treated as equally true and that the social researcher—in this case, me—has abdicated responsibility for evaluating the scientific evidence. Both of these accusations are grounded in positivist assumptions. In other words, relativism is attacked on the grounds that it is not positivist. The arguments between positivists and relativists have been traversed at length elsewhere.[28] Instead, let me simply outline how my analysis of the politics of knowledge about fluoridation does carry out a non-positivist evaluation of scientific knowledge.

In looking at the struggles between profluoridation and antifluoridation scientists, I have not sought to determine the "scientific truth," but I have, instead, looked at the strategies used by different partisans. These strategies include presentation of data, theoretical argument, arguments including both technical and social dimensions in a coherent package, assertion of authority, attacks on the credibility of others, and so forth. The elements of these strategies include both what is traditionally called scientific (data and theoretical arguments) and what is traditionally called social (authority and attacks), as well as mixtures (coherent arguments).

In my analysis, I have selected arguments, individuals, and cases which I consider to have been important in the controversy. This means that I have made an evaluation of their scientific and social importance.

For example, I have given considerable attention to arguments about the benefits of fluoridation. My assessment is that these arguments are important because the science in the area has been persuasive. The proponents have used arguments about benefits—and evidence to back these arguments—as the foundation of the promotion of fluoridation. The opponents have used arguments and evidence critical of claims about benefits as effective tools to challenge fluoridation.

On the other hand, I have given little attention to attacks on fluoridation on the grounds that sodium fluoride is used as rat poison. While this argument is regularly brought up by lay opponents—and sometimes, in a rhetorical fashion by opponents who are scientists—it has played a subsidiary role in the controversy, so far as the use of scientific claims is concerned.

Note that my selection of arguments does not require an assessment of scientific truth rooted in nature, as assessed by authoritative experiments and the like. Rather, I examine the scientific claims in the social context of the debate. But I have not treated all claims as equal. Not all are worthy of the same attention.

Rather, I concentrate on claims which are the most potent or persuasive in practice. This can be because they are, in positivist terms, either scientifically convincing or politically convenient. In practice, from the relativist's perspective, these two categories of science and politics are not separated.

In my analysis, I have certainly made judgements about the quality of evidence, argument, and intervention. I have concentrated on opponents of fluoridation who are scientists, such as John Colquhoun, Mark Diesendorf, Philip Sutton, George Waldbott, and John Yiamouyiannis, because their contributions have been perceived as sufficiently influential to mobilize supporters and disconcert proponents. I have given less attention to scientists on the fringes of the debate, either because their scientific merit has less credibility even with knowledgeable opponents or because, whereas their science is respectable, their work has not been brought center-stage in the controversy.

A similar selection and evaluation process applies to my discussion of proponent arguments. I have cited works of individuals such as Brian A. Burt, Frank J. McClure, John J. Murray, and Andrew J. Rugg-Gunn because their contributions to the debate, both scientific and social, have been treated with great seriousness.

What I have *not* done is attempt an assessment of the scientific evidence for and against fluoridation as if that evidence is separate from the social evaluation of the controversy. Indeed, my analysis is designed to show why such an assessment, if presented as separate from social considerations, can be misleading.

Knowledge about fluoride is not separate from society, but has been generated in a context in which therapeutic use and, since the early 1940s, policy decisions have been key considerations. The context of much fluoride research as been highly charged and often polarized into profluoridation and antifluoridation molds. "Nonscientific" ethical and political considerations are crucial, and have been tightly linked to scientific claims throughout the debate.

Even more dramatically, the attacks on the credibility and activities of scientists among the leading opponents have been important in the assessment of the scientific status of both profluoridation and antifluoridation claims. The attacks have also undoubtedly been important—although in ways which can only be guessed at—in shaping both research into fluoride's effects and research into alternatives to fluoridation.

Relativism liberates the social scientist from the constraints of acquiescing to the current scientific orthodoxy. The social analysis can range more deeply into scientific areas. That, of course, may offend powerful scientists and their allies, and perhaps this is one reason why relativism is applied to current controversies less often than it might be.

From the point of view of the strong program, there is no such thing as a neutral, unbiased assessment of scientific evidence. Rather, those assessments that are more persuasive, and that seem to others to be more objective, are the assessments which are sensitive to the diverse facets of the social context in which the science is embedded. It is a compliment rather than a criticism to say that Edward Groth III, in his writings on fluoridation and including his commentary in this book, accomplishes such a persuasive assessment precisely because of his awareness of the social influences on fluoride research. He is willing to consider scientific evidence damaging to fluoridation in spite of its rejection by proponents because he is aware of the processes used to destroy the credibility of critics.

But he is also willing to be critical of evidence often raised by antifluoridationists. He is aware of the polarized nature of the dispute and uses this awareness to assist him in avoiding the assumption, encouraged by partisans on both sides, that, if evidence doesn't support one side, it must support the other. A positivist might say that Groth is surveying the scientific evidence. A relativist might say that he is presenting a persuasive account of the scientific evidence, informed by his assessment of the social context.

THE ROLE OF THE RESEARCHER

For all their differences, the positivist and relativist approaches have a surprising convergence when it comes to studying contemporary controversies.[29] Each of them assumes that the researcher is a separate, neutral observer. This is obvious enough when it is assumed that objective knowledge is to be sought about science and society. Being a partisan on the issues would certainly seem to make objectivity difficult if not impossible. As a result, it is usually assumed without discusion that analysts are not and should not be involved in the controversy themselves. If they are, then bias is assumed.

More intriguingly, relativist approaches lead to the same result. The strong program in the sociology of scientific knowledge is actually based on the traditional scientific method. Causal explanations are sought, and the same explanatory mechanisms are used to analyze all social beliefs, including scientific knowledge. Ironically, in this respect, relativism is more like the traditional positivist model of science than is positivism in the social sciences. There is no suggestion that the researcher can or should be involved in the controversy.

The strong program's requirement of reflexivity—that the theory should apply to itself—would seem to allow for researcher participation. But in practice reflexivity is taken to mean that methods of explaining beliefs should also be able to be applied to the beliefs of the analyst. The social explanation of the rise of social theory is one thing; involvement in the controversy being studied is another. In practice, relativist analysts of controversies have almost exclusively studied either historical cases, which allow a nice separation of the researcher and the researched, or contemporary cases that are restricted to fairly narrow disciplinary communities. In the latter case, the analyst's involvement does little to disturb the controversy itself, especially when the products of social research are esoteric articles in specialist social science journals.

Separation of the researcher and the researched may work in some cases, but practical experiences show that it often cannot be sustained in dealing with contemporary controversies with a strong public involvement. To some extent, the social researcher is inevitably involved in the controversy being studied.

I have already described the commitment to fluoridation by many social scientists who have studied the controversy. In some cases, the social scientists were "recruited" by profluoridationists to study the issue. For example, the initial incentive and funding for the major study by Robert Crain, Elihu Katz, and Donald Rosenthal was provided by the United States Public Health Service (USPHS).[30] These researchers were obviously sympathetic to fluoridation.

It is not surprising that such studies are quite useful to proponents and have often been cited by them. For example, J. M. Dunning, in a textbook on dental health, states that social scientists are the allies of profluoridationists.[31] The social scientists sometimes become involved in overt partisan activity. Historian Donald R. McNeil, author of the classic history *The Fight for Fluoridation*, has repeatedly taken a strong profluoridation stand.[32]

This sort of involvement by earlier social scientists in the fluoridation issue was not seen as a problem, nor as a violation of objectivity. This is because they accepted a positivist picture of science, accepted the claims of dental authorities about fluoridation, and believed that fluoridation was socially progressive. Therefore, partisan involvement meant being a partisan on behalf of truth, which was treated as unproblematic.

Just as there is a strong connection between assuming that fluoridation is scientifically proven and undertaking a social analysis of reasons for opposition, so there is a strong connection between opposing fluoridation and undertaking a social analysis of the promotion of fluoridation.

Opponents can use structural analysis to explain the promotion of fluoridation in terms of other than rationality. Explaining also becomes "explaining away." Strictly in terms of logic, explaining the promotion of fluoridation by its compatibility with the interests of powerful groups does not mean that fluoridation is any less desirable. But, in practical political terms, structural explanations are threatening to those policies which are "explained." Structural analysis is a challenge to any claim of pure rationality.

Aside from the crude statements by opponents that fluoridation is a plot by big business and big government, there have actually been few studies which have developed even a moderately careful analysis of the promotion of fluoridation. In each case, the analysis has been linked to opposition to fluoridation.

An early important study was by Michael Wollan, who wrote an article entitled "Controlling the Potential Hazards of Government-sponsored Technology" which was published in 1968 in the *George Washington Law Review*.[33] The article examined how technology assessment was being performed in the United States, and analyzed three case studies: weather modification, engine noise from supersonic transport aircraft, and fluoridation. In discussing fluoridation, Wollan focused on the vested interest of the USPHS in a measure which it had endorsed, making impossible a proper continuing assessment of the measure.

Opponents have frequently cited Wollan's article and distributed copies of it. Wollan was not involved in the opposition to fluoridation before this article, but, after it appeared, he opposed fluoridation on a few occasions before his early death in an automobile accident.

Another important study was done by George L. Waldbott, Albert W. Burgstahler, and H. Lewis McKinney, and included as part of their 1978 book, *Fluoridation: The Great Dilemma*.[34] The primary author of this book was Waldbott, and, indeed, it is written in the first person singular. Waldbott was the leading opponent of fluoridation in the United States for some twenty years, beginning in the mid 1950s. Burgstahler, professor of chemistry at the University of Kansas, has also been an active scientist opposing fluoridation. McKinney is a professor of history of science at the University of Kansas. The structural analysis in *Fluoridation: The Great Dilemma*, thus, forms a part of their overall case against fluoridation.

Wendy Varney's book, *Fluoride in Australia: A Case to Answer*, published in 1986, is the most important recent structural analysis of fluoridation.[35] Varney's treatment is the most careful and comprehensive yet available, drawing on theoretical accounts of capitalism and the professions as well as a large amount of data about fluoridation in Australia and elsewhere. Varney's book is based on a thesis done in the Department of Government at the University of Sydney. Before doing this study, Varney had been an environmental activist but had played no role in the fluoridation issue. But after writing the book, she took a public stand against fluoridation on a number of occasions, both in talks and interviews.

Mark Diesendorf, a leading opponent in Australia, collaborated with Varney in writing an article on "Fluoridation: Politics and Strategies," published in 1986 in the Australian journal, *Social Alternatives*.[36] This article develops an analysis along the lines of Varney's analysis and draws conclusions about how to oppose fluoridation. John Colquhoun, a former dental public health officer who switched sides to become a leading opponent of fluoridation in the 1980s, later wrote his doctoral thesis at the University of Auckland on the topic of education and fluoridation, including a structural analysis of the promotion of fluoridation.[37]

These examples show the strong link between making a structural analysis of the promotion of fluoridation and opposing the measure. Waldbott, Burgstahler, Diesendorf, and Colquhoun were active opponents of fluoridation who were scientists and who later wrote about the role of corporations and the dental profession in promoting it. Wollan and Varney, as social scientists, apparently did their analyses along these lines first, and then were drawn into the debate on the opposition side.

What these examples show is that the type of analysis which a person makes of the polarized fluoridation controversy is influenced both by his or her stand on the issue and, in turn, influences his or her further participation in the argument. Any hope of a value-free analysis, or a value-free mode of analysis, appears to be misplaced. Those who want to maintain the misleading appearance of value-free social-science research are best advised to avoid studying contemporary controversies, or, as an alternative, to publish only abstruse articles in obscure specialist journals so that partisans are not tempted to use the research for their own ends.

This is not my aim in writing this book. Rather than attempting to keep myself separate from the debate, my involvement may actually lead to deeper insights than are otherwise possible. My own experiences serve to illustrate this.

My initial study of fluoridation was made possible without much personal interaction with the controversy, simply by obtaining and studying various documents that are readily available to the public. But this changed when I undertook interviews with leading Australian partisans who are scientists, as described in chapter 3. Only a few of the opponents and proponents knew me, or had even heard of me, before I interviewed them. But a viewpoint was formed in some cases.

Halfway through my long interview with fluoridation proponent Elsdon Storey at the University of Melbourne, he told me that he knew what I was going to say in my research, because he had seen a copy of a paper I had presented describing cases of suppression of dissent in several fields, including fluoridation.[38] Storey informed me that he did not wish to be quoted in my paper unless he was given a complete draft to okay before anyone else saw it.

After returning from my interviews in Melbourne, I received a letter from Jack Martin, another Melbourne proponent whom I had interviewed before meeting with Storey. Martin also requested inspection of the full manuscript before it was seen by anyone else. He added that he was surprised that my university was funding such an "unscientific" study.

What I did in response to these requests was to remove from my draft paper any direct reference by name to views expressed in the interviews with these two individuals.[39] I then sent the draft paper (the essence of which is chapter 3 in this book) to all 17 proponents and opponents whom I had interviewed. I invited their comments. Five of the six opponents furnished comments, some of which were quite critical. By contrast, not a single proponent provided comments. The only replies were from Storey, who criticized my standard of work and said he did not want to be associated with my article in any way; and Martin, who said the article was trivial and biased and requested that his name be omitted.

The obvious explanation of the different responses to my paper lies in the symmetrical approach that I had adopted. I described the coherency of viewpoints of both proponents and opponents, and I presented the arguments on both sides. Since proponents generally maintain that there is no credible scientific opposition to fluoridation, my analysis appeared to give the opponents far too much credibility.

A similar one-sidedness prevailed when I tried to obtain comments on the first draft of this book from scientifically knowledgeable proponents and opponents of fluoridaton. I had no difficulty in obtaining significant comments from the only three opponents whom I approached—Albert Burgstahler, John Colquhoun, and Mark Diesendorf—which was not surprising since each had readily corresponded with me earlier. Obtaining comments from proponents was more difficult. In the end, I wrote to twelve leading proponents in several countries before obtaining comments from Brian Burt, Michael Lennon, John Small, and Donald Taves. Had I not received their comments, it would have been more difficult to obtain a good picture of the proponents' case, and easier to have been drawn into the opposition camp.

My point is that, as soon as one begins interacting with partisans in a polarized controversy, there is no neutral position. If I had adopted a strong profluoridation position, dismissing critics as "not to be taken seriously," then it would have been difficult, to say the least, to maintain communication with the critics. On the other hand, taking a symmetrical position meant alienating many of the proponents. Even my symmetrical position—which apparently led the Australian proponents to cease communications—has led to criticisms from some antifluoridationists who believe I have given too much ground to the proponents.[40] The pressures for becoming an overt partisan—or avoiding the controversy altogether—are considerable.[41]

One possible way around this problem would be to delay publication and the revelation of one's perspective until all research is completed. Unfortunately, this strategy does not allow for a crucial part of social research: that is, the development of the researcher's credibility with particular audiences. By publishing, one's authority can be boosted in the eyes of some participants in the controversy, and this can lead to acquisition of materials and insights not otherwise obtainable.

This was apparent in my correspondence with numerous individuals involved with fluoride around the world. Before I had written anything about fluoridation, I received helpful replies from some to whom I wrote. But, after writing drafts of papers and, even better, having had papers published, my status as a person to be reckoned with was increased. From several individuals, I received valuable personal information and documents that I am sure would not be sent to the casual inquirer. This sort of response was more likely to come from opponents of fluoridation or from those not necessarily against fluoridation, but who had run afoul of the proponents. But I also received some very valuable materials from proponents. On the other hand, many proponents—and some opponents—did not supply material which they might have shared.

There is nothing exceptional about this sort of response. Most people are more likely to spend time and effort and to reveal information to those whom they believe are likely to treat it responsibly and to have an impact. Sending prior publications is an excellent way of showing the sort of results one is likely to produce in the future.

Another consequence of writing about fluoridation was that my articles were taken up by partisans for their own purposes. Several opponents have told me that they have circulated copies of my papers to others, and the papers have also been cited on occasion by opponents. I am less sure of how proponents have treated the papers. In any case, the point is that a researcher, intentionally or otherwise, can be incorporated into the controversy by partisans. In my case, the involvement has been mainly via my publications. Ironically, my status as a social scientist who is entirely separate from the controversy allows my work to be used more effectively by partisans.

Partisan involvement is a more difficult issue for relativists than positivists, although it is not necessarily more compromising. As already indicated, a relativist analysis of claims to knowledge normally must be supplemented by an analysis of power relations. Part of this latter analysis can involve an examination of the ways in which partisans are able to mobilize or neutralize others, including social scientists. In other words, the analysis can be applied to itself.

The researcher who is studying scientific controversies makes value judgments in a number of ways, including many detailed points such as which bits of evidence to emphasize, which partisans to give credence to, which arguments or power plays to discuss, and so forth. But, prior to these detailed judgments, come some wider choices.

What issue should be studied? Dealing with a historical case usually allows the analyst to escape scrutiny by partisans. Dealing with a bitterly contested issue with public dimensions makes it more difficult to appear to be neutral.

What is the audience of the research? Writing recondite social-science jargon for specialist journals means that partisans will take less notice. It also means that social scientists have abjured making a contribution to the debate.

What conceptual tools are used in the analysis? Positivism is generally useful for supporting the side with strongest claims to scientific backing. Relativism is generally more useful for supporting the side with less scientific credibility. But it remains possible to try to adapt any particular analysis to counter these tendencies.

Finally, to what degree is the analyst involved in the controversy? Research built on assessment of documents without interaction with partisans, and publication in esoteric specialized journals, allows low involvement at the expense of the understanding to be gained through direct contacts, inside channels of information, and participant observation.

My position is that there is no "best way" to study the fluoridation controversy. A "best way" assumes agreement on the aims of the social analysis, and that agreement does not exist.

Many analysts have supported fluoridation and, consciously or unconsciously, used their analysis to support the cause of fluoridation. For this purpose, a positivist framework and relatively accessible publications are most suitable. The same applies to the very few analysts who have opposed fluoridation.

Many analysts, it is safe to say, use studies of the fluoridation controversy primarily as a means to "contribute to social science," as well as enhance their own reputations and promote their careers. For this purpose, a more independent stance toward partisans and an orientation toward specialist publications is dictated. A low-key, tacit support for fluoridation may also help, since most editors and referees for relevant journals have also automatically supported fluoridation.

But the intellectual marketplace is a competitive one, and so, some researchers may find it to their advantage to stake out new conceptual territory, tying their prestige and careers to unconventional ways of doing things. They will, naturally, justify their approaches in terms of contributing to a deeper understanding of the social world—just as did those following the prior orthodoxy. This is one way to put in perspective the development of the strong program in the sociology of scientific knowledge. This approach provides new insights, presents new dilemmas and, most importantly for social researchers, opens up new areas for analysis.

That is what I have tried to do in this book. I wanted to show how the science in the fluoridation controversy can be studied in its social context. Personally, I am not particularly concerned about supporting or opposing fluoridation. My interest lies in the exercise of power within science and the implications of this for democratic decision making. I believe that the method of analysis which I have chosen helps in dealing with these issues.

But my own intentions are only part of the story. Having analyzed the fluoridation controversy, my own work becomes a part of it. Others will now make their own decisions about how to use it.

THE FLUORIDATION CONTROVERSY: WHICH SIDE IS SCIENCE ON?

A Commentary by Edward Groth III

(EDITOR'S NOTE: Edward Groth III is a biologist who has specialized in the study of policy decision-making processes on environmental and public health issues. He holds an A.B. degree in biology from Princeton University, and a Ph.D. in biological sciences from Stanford University. His doctoral dissertation concerned a study of two issues of science and public policy—air pollution control and the fluoridation controversy. He worked for five years on the staff of the Environmental Studies Board of the National Research Council in Washington, D.C., preparing reports on environmental problems for the federal Environmental Protection Agency and other government agencies. Since 1979, he has been on the staff of Consumers Union, the publisher of *Consumer Reports* magazine, where he is currently associate technical director for Policy and Public Service. The views expressed here are his own, and do not represent positions of Consumers Union or any other organization.)

INTRODUCTION

In this book, Brian Martin has produced the most penetrating and authoritative analysis of the fluoridation controversy yet to emerge from the multidisciplinary social studies of science. (And, from my perspective, it's high time someone did!)

Nevertheless, Martin's assessment leaves me unsatisfied. I want it to say more about two key questions.

First, he takes the existence of the controversy as a given. Then, he examines the arguments and behavior of the advocates on each side. But *why* does controversy persist over fluoridation, after fifty years of debate? Is this, as the proponents often insist, a "fake" controversy, without real merit, and spurred by unscientific "antis"? Or is the idea of fluoridation intrinsically controversial?

Second, the fluoridation debate is dominated by disputes over scientific issues. While Martin recounts what both sides say on many of these questions, he makes no attempt to assess the quantity or quality of evidence for the arguments of each side. Who is right? Are they both wrong? We need to know.

Evaluating such a massive, complex body of data is a daunting task, even for an author steeped in the environmental health sciences. But to omit doing so is like leaving yeast out of bread dough; the end product is flat and unsatisfying without that vital ingredient.

In this essay, I will attempt to fill those two voids. I will demonstrate—rather decisively I believe—that the controversy over fluoridation is, indeed, inherent in the proposal and absolutely unavoidable. On the second task, I will venture into somewhat riskier territory. A detailed review of the literature is neither appropriate for the expected audience of this book, nor is it feasible in the available space. I plan, instead, to present my own admittedly subjective impressions of the evidence, based on several thousand papers which I have read over twenty years. My statements will necessarily be very general. For readers who prefer not to accept my characterization of the evidence, I will supply references to more detailed scientific reviews as reasonable starting points for independent examination of the literature.

A GENUINE CONTROVERSY

Proponents of fluoridation often assert that there really is no legitimate debate. Political controversy persists, the argument goes, only because misinformed, antiscientific opponents refuse to accept the overwhelming scientific evidence of fluoridation's effectiveness and safety. As one often-cited American propagandist has stated, "The survival of this fake controversy . . . represents one of the major triumphs of quackery over science in our generation" (*Consumer Reports* 1978).

When "pros" take that posture, an analysis like Martin's or my own (Groth 1973, 1980) that treats the controversy symmetrically—that is, looks critically at arguments and behavior of *both* the proponents and the opponents—legitimizes the opposition by implicitly treating the controversy as genuine. It is, thus, incumbent on us, I feel, to state explicitly why we believe that the controversy over fluoridation is legitimate.

A Clash of Values

The first key to the answer lies in looking closely at what the dispute is really *about*. A casual observer might think that the debate over fluoridation is a scientific dispute, but that's not so. The controversy is really over a question of social policy: Shall the public water supply be used as a vehicle to treat the population with fluoride to help prevent tooth decay?

Assessments of risks, benefits, and economic effects of the measure are, to be sure, scientific tasks. But science cannot say what degree of risk is acceptable in exchange for expected benefits. Neither can science say whether it is morally acceptable to treat the public with a prophylactic agent through the water supply, or whether universal effortless treatment to prevent tooth decay should take precedence over a citizen's right to decide what treatments—and what risks—he or she will accept.

These issues are pure value judgments. They require social choices among competing priorities. And people clearly disagree, often vehemently, over such value judgments. There is no single "right" answer to such policy questions. They demand political solutions, and, significantly, the political choice posed by fluoridation has no compromise outcome. A water supply is either fluoridated, or it isn't. It is, therefore, not surprising that the debate over the measure is polarized into committed "pro" and "anti" camps.

A Clash of Risk/Benefit Perceptions

Social psychologists have recently documented how average citizens perceive risk/benefit issues quite differently than many experts do (Slovic 1987), which helps explain why experts often have trouble communicating with the public about risks.

Although a minority dissents, most experts on fluoridation see the benefits of the measure as solidly proven and large, and they view the risks as unproven, remote, and minuscule—if, indeed, any risks exist at all. From that viewpoint, fluoridation seems sensible and sound.

But the public sees things somewhat differently. To most average people, the benefits of fluoridation are invisible. Nobody "sees" cavities their children don't get. Most people also do not regard tooth decay as an especially serious health problem.

When it comes to risks, experts tend to demand some concrete evidence of hazard. But consumers expect products and health treatments to be proven safe. They are more inclined than experts are to see sketchy evidence as grounds for concern about safety. The public in general is also risk-averse. Given a choice, they would prefer to accept zero additional risk, especially when lower-risk or no-risk alternatives are available.

While experts generally focus on the *magnitude* of a risk as its critical dimension, and judge risks below a certain size to be trivial and socially acceptable, average citizens seem much more attuned to the *quality* of the risk. Certain qualities also greatly magnify public reluctance to accept a risk. Natural hazards are much less frightening to most people than hazards that originate from technology or human actions, even if the latter are identical—as in artifically versus naturally fluoridated water—or objectively much smaller.

Voluntarily assumed risks—those in which the individual feels in control of his or her own fate—are tolerated much more readily than even negligible risks that are imposed on people without their choice or control. If the risk is perceived as morally unacceptable, involuntary risks may provoke outrage far out of proportion to the size of the risk. For instance, people may smoke cigarettes but object strenuously to minute pesticide residues in their foods (Sandman 1987).

The public's point of view on these matters is no less "rational" than is that of the experts. The two views are just *different*. Such differences help explain why experts and average citizens often don't see eye-to-eye on fluoridation.

A Clash of Moral Perceptions

Scientific questions about fluoridation hold out at least a hope of being answerable with objective evidence, but the moral dimensions of the debate are intensely and irremediably subjective. Here, too, the issue is polarized.

To health authorities, fluoridation advances social justice by providing dental caries prophylaxis to all children, including many of the poor who would not otherwise be able to afford proper dental care. In the eyes of profluoridationists, it is morally wrong for a community not to provide that benefit.

To antifluoridationists, fluoridation is, in itself, morally wrong, because it violates individuals' rights to determine what happens to their own bodies. Even those who see the value of fluoride treatment consider the administration of uncontrolled dosages through the water supply to be a violation of medical ethics. "Antis" reject "pro" comparisons with vaccination and chlorination, arguing that dental caries is neither life-threatening nor is it spread through the water supply. Thus, compulsory mass treatment to prevent dental caries is unjustified. Each side sees its own as the morally superior position, and attacks the other side's posture in ethical terms, such as "denying poor children the benefits of fluoridation"or "forcing medication down our throats," respectively.

Decisions by courts—which have ruled both for and against fluoridation in different cases—don't resolve this dispute, as legality and morality are rightly perceived as separate issues.

A Clash of Experts

Disputes over value judgments in fluoridation decisions would persist even if the scientific evidence were complete and unequivocal, and all experts agreed on what it meant. But it is unreasonable to expect such unanimity of either science or scientists. The science on *any* debate over an environmental health issue shares these common features:

Uncertainty. Research simply cannot answer all questions that "matter" on any environmental health topic. Even the best studies raise new questions while offering tentative answers to old ones. Available research tools are rarely potent enough to yield unqualified proof of cause and effect, especially when effects of environmental agents on human health are concerned. Critical knowledge gaps always remain.

Expert Judgments. Because of the irreducible uncertainties inherent in the science itself, policy decisions depend on extensive interpretation of the evidence by experts who must make many subjective judgments in the process.

What is a "good" study? How much evidence does it take to be "convincing" on a particular point? What are the implications of particular evidence for human health? When two different studies on a key issue reach conflicting conclusions, where does the truth lie?

Such questions have no unequivocal answers. Two equally qualified experts can study the same body of research and reach opposing scientific conclusions. Experts are human, and their own values and social views are often intermingled with their "scientific" advice.

For instance, an expert whose chief concern is dental caries prevention might look at inconclusive evidence of harm from fluoridation, and advise that there is no proof of adverse effects. So, fluoridation should proceed. An expert whose chief concern, however, is avoiding unnecessary risks might look at the same body of evidence and conclude that fluoridation should be held in abeyance until more definitive proof of safety is available. The experts might actually disagree less over the evidence than over the philosophical issue of where the burden of proof should lie in disputes over public health procedures.

Disagreement among experts is the norm in public-policy debates with scientific components. It is both commonplace and appropriate for policy makers and the public to hear conflicting scientific opinions. The common profluoridation claim that *all* "qualified" experts support the effectiveness and safety of the measure is simply not credible; science and scientists are never so unambiguous. The apparent unanimity on fluoridation has its origin in political processes as described in Martin's analysis, not in the underlying science, as I will show later.

A Clash of Professional Perspectives

Two distinct professional fields—dental public health and environmental health—might lay claim to research on the possible effects of fluoridation. Each has its own unique perspective, and the two fields differ in basic goals, concepts, methods, and intrinsic biases, enhancing the likelihood of disagreements among experts on questions related to fluoridation.

Dental Public Health. Fluoridation research originated within this field nearly 60 years ago. The basic goal of this subdiscipline is the general promotion of oral health, including the prevention of tooth decay. Dental public health practitioners see fluoridation as a most valuable weapon in the war against dental caries. Their primary scientific goal has been to demonstrate that adding fluoride to unfluoridated water supplies has the same beneficial effects observed in naturally fluoridated communities. Secondarily, they have sought to demonstrate that neither natural nor artificial fluoridation poses unacceptable health hazards for people who drink the water for a lifetime. From the dental public health perspective, fluoride research should be used to support a major public health benefit.

Environmental Health. This second field of knowledge treats fluoride as it would any other toxic natural element. It seeks to assess exposure from all sources; to identify populations with excessive exposures or risk-enhancing personal characteristics; to identify potential biological effects of exposure and their underlying physiological mechanisms; to determine the dose-effect and dose-response relationships that link exposure and effects; to identify risk-enhancing or risk-reducing variables; to estimate the likelihood and magnitude of effects at any given level of exposure; and to assess safety margins between typical dose levels and those that may cause adverse effects. Experts trained in the environmental health perspective are concerned primarily with risks, and with protecting the public from possible harm. They use research primarily to support health and safety standards and pollution control regulations.

These two legitimate and well-established professional perspectives are, inherently, somewhat adversarial toward each other. While dental public health practitioners seek to use scientific data to promote benefits, environmental health practitioners try to use research to protect against potential health hazards. In public policy debates, these two legitimate points of view would normally clash, and policy makers would have to resolve conflicting interpretations and priorities.

But the fluoridation debate is not a normal policy-making context, and the two clashing perspectives generally have not received balanced attention in the dispute. The reasons for this are largely historical and political.

A BRIEF HISTORY OF FLUORIDATION RESEARCH

The scientific and political histories of fluoridation are inextricably intertwined. Once fluoridation became an explosively controversial political issue around 1950, the dispute had profound effects on the subsequent conduct of research and the interpretation of results.

Martin's monograph recounts the familiar history of early fluoride research. Studies beginning in the 1930s correlated fluoride levels in community water supplies with resistance to dental caries. The idea that tooth decay could be largely prevented by adjusting the mineral content of water supplies proved irresistable to public health leaders, and "demonstration" projects with artificial fluoridation were begun in 1945.

While those studies were under way, enthusiastic advocates of fluoridation began an intensive lobbying campaign to attain widespread official approval for and endorsement of the measure. Those early "pros" believed that naturally fluoridated communities provided all the evidence needed that fluoridation was effective and safe. They campaigned tirelessly, and met with much political success. In 1950, the United States Public Health Service (USPHS) yielded to the pressure and, over the objections of its own scientific authorities who felt that an endorsement was premature, officially endorsed fluoridation. Proponents rapidly accumulated endorsements from professional societies and health organizations and felt that their battle had been won. They were wrong.

Early promotional efforts were met by strong opposition to fluoridation, for all the reasons described earlier. Many early opponents were scientists, who criticized the "pros" for failing to complete the demonstration studies before endorsing fluoridation, and who raised questions about possible toxic effects that had been inadequately investigated.

In truth, the USPHS had conducted very few studies to assess potential toxicity of fluoridated water at the one-part-per-million level. In the next fifteen years, numerous safety studies were done. But most were conducted by USPHS scientists who were openly defending a controversial policy from vigorous political attacks. These studies can therefore be criticized for obvious potential bias, as well as subjected to normal scientific criticism.

While this research proceeded the political battle raged, and the controversy rapidly polarized. Proponents of fluoridation learned that the public, aroused by allegations from the "antis" of harm from the measure, would not accept objective statements on questions of safety. Rather than say, "None of the evidence we have seen so far indicates a significant risk, but there are still unanswered questions," the "pros" found that they had to be dogmatic: "Research has proven, beyond question or doubt, that fluoridation is absolutely, unequivocally safe for everyone." To say less was to invite political defeat.

By the mid–1960s, research on potential adverse effects of fluoridation had essentially come to a halt within the USPHS. The emphasis had shifted to political promotion. Proponents felt the earlier studies were adequate to support their case, and that continuing research on questions which had supposedly been answered could prove to be politically awkward. Thus, for the past twenty-five years, there has been little or no official effort to search for possible side-effects of fluoridation, at least in the United States. The USPHS has pursued reactive research, seeking to counter claims or findings used by the antifluoridationists, but has not actively sought evidence of possible harm.

The seeds of the imbalance between the two scientific perspectives on fluoride reserch—noted in the previous section—are evident in this history. Virtually all research supporting fluoridation was done by proponents of the dental public health (DPH) perspective, including USPHS scientists; those associated with the "demonstration" studies; and a few outside experts who were recruited to assist in promoting this novel public health measure. Although research on the potential adverse effects of fluoridated water might obviously fall within the environmental health (EH) perspective, in this case, the work was done almost exclusively by USPHS scientists and others in the DPH camp. The few scientists with EH credentials who participated in research on fluoridation were willing converts, most of whom also played important roles in political advocacy of the measure.

Historical accidents account for the dominance of the DPH perspective in fluoridation research. The same agency (the USPHS) was responsible both for promoting fluoridation and for assessing its safety. Today, such a conflict of interest would likely be recognized and dealt with. For example, in the United States, nuclear power is promoted by one agency, while its safety is regulated by another agency. But political institutions had not come to terms with this problem in the 1950s. Perhaps more significant was the lack, in the early years of fluoride research, of a well-defined discipline of environmental health. That field really came into its own in the 1960s and 1970s. Neither the concepts and methods now used routinely in environmental health research nor institutions that would foster such research (such as the U.S. Environmental Protection Agency or the National Institute of Environmental Health Sciences) existed much before 1970.

While fluoride research has been dominated by DPH scientists in countries where fluoridation has been actively promoted, work done to support fluoridation is a small part of the total international scientific endeavor on biological effects of the ion. Wide-ranging research has explored dental effects of fluoride, and its potential hazards as an air pollutant, a workplace contaminant, and a natural constituent of water supplies. In India and many other countries, fluoride toxicity from naturally fluoridated water is a major public health problem.

Most of that research approaches fluoride from EH perspectives, and could be very useful for appraising the possible health risks of fluoridation. But it has had minimal impact on the fluoridation debate, at least in the United States. Scientific discussion of fluoridation in this country has been dominated by DPH experts, whose objective is promoting fluoridation, not seeking new insights into potential adverse effects. Such research is often cited by "antis" as evidence of potential hazards. Then, political profluoridationists usually try to discredit the work, or to dismiss that research as "irrelevant to fluoridation."

Few American scientists experienced in EH research have ever sought to study possible effects of fluoridation. The USPHS and other DPH authorities have effectively defined research on this topic as their "turf," and they have asserted that all relevant questions were answered long ago, giving the impression that fluoride toxicity is an "old" issue. Relatively little funding is available to support such research. And the intense public controversy over fluoridation deters many objective researchers from studying the topic. Few scientists want to do research that is likely to embroil them in an emotional controversy. It is easier to choose other environmental problems to study.

The result is an odd disparity. In most countries, fluoride research is carried out by EH scientists, seeking to protect the public from adverse effects. But in countries where the fluoridation debate has had major impact, research has been dominated by DPH scientists, and the few EH researchers willing to pursue active studies of potential adverse effects of fluoridation are usually also politically active opponents of the measure. The polarized political dispute in those countries has infected the body scientific, and argument permeated with political advocacy has effectively crowded out objective scientific inquiry on many important questions.

THE QUALITY OF THE EVIDENCE

In the struggle for credibility, described in Chapter 4 of Martin's monograph, the credibility of divergent "pro" and "anti" interpretations of scientific evidence looms large. The scientific quality of the evidence itself is, thus, a central concern that cannot be avoided here.

The world literature on biological effects of fluoride is enormous. It was said twenty years ago to comprise at least fifteen thousand published reports. That number may have doubled by now. It is not really feasible for any reviewer to summarize—let alone critically appraise—such a body of knowledge in a brief essay. Instead, I will offer some concise and admittedly subjective impressions. For readers who may be reluctant to accept the word of any one "expert"on this vital topic, I will provide references to a few solid review documents for those who may wish to pursue their own assessments.

To simplify the task a bit, I will arbitrarily divide the vast and complex body of fluoride research into seven parts.

- Studies of the dental benefits of fluoridated water
- Other studies on the anticaries effects of fluoride
- Studies of dental fluorosis or mottled enamel
- Studies on the safety of fluoridation, conducted by or for agencies promoting the measure
- Studies suggesting adverse effects of fluoridation, often done by antifluoridation scientists
- Other research on toxic effects of fluoride, usually done by independent scientists with no involvement on either side of the fluoridation controversy
- Reviews of the literature, written from any of these three perspectives: "pro," "anti," or noninvolved

Benefits of Fluoridation

Research in this category consists primarily of epidemiological studies of two basic types: surveys of dental health in communities with naturally fluoridated water; and demonstration studies in which changes in rates of dental caries associated with artificial fluoridation were assessed. Prototypes of both kinds were done in the United States, and they have been imitated in many other countries (Newbrun 1986a). According to Newbrun, more than one hundred reports of similar studies have been published.

The vast majority of these studies report substantial reductions in the incidence of dental caries where water supplies had around 1 ppm or more fluoride. The commonly quoted figure of a 50 to 60 percent reduction in tooth decay is a rough average of the results reported in some of the prominent early studies.

Many authorities regard the great number of similar studies and the close agreement of their results as overwhelming proof of fluoridation's large beneficial effects. Nevertheless, these studies are open to many scientific criticisms.

Virtually none of the studies had appropriate controls for factors other than fluoridated water that might affect tooth decay rates. A few had contemporaneous controls in the form of nearby unfluoridated cities; but some such control cities were fluoridated during the course of the studies, and, in other studies, changes in decay rates in the control cities went unexplained. With very few exceptions, the investigators knew where the children examined lived, and their expectations might have influenced subjective assessments of decay status. The random design and statistical rigor commonly expected of, for example, drug-efficacy trials, field studies, and epidemiological research, were either impossible or simply absent from most of the fluoridation studies.

The first substantial scientific critique of the fluoridation studies was published by Sutton (1959), and it has never been effectively shown to be in error. Recently, Diesendorf (1986) cited extensive evidence that tooth decay rates have declined substantially both in countries without widespread fluoridation and in those that have fluoridation. He concluded that factors beyond fluoridation are reducing tooth decay, and that reported improvements may have been improperly credited to fluoridation, rather than to more complex, not fully understood multifactorial causes.

In 1989, an American antifluoridation leader, John Yiamouyiannis, obtained unpublished data from a national survey of the incidence of dental caries which was conducted in the mid-1980s by the National Institute of Dental Research (NIDR). Yiamouyiannis' analysis of comparative tooth decay rates in fluoridated and unfluoridated communities showed no differences, a claim which he publicized before his paper appeared in a scientific journal (Yiamouyiannis 1990).

In response to the publicity, NIDR scientists argued that Yiamouyiannis had improperly focused on the number of decayed, missing or filled teeth—one of the more widely used indices of decay status in past studies—as his measure of dental caries rates. Using another index—the number of children with no tooth decay at all—the NIDR claimed to see 25 percent less decay in fluoridated cities. The NIDR response was also publicized before its scientific publication (Brunelle and Carlos 1990).

Whether dispassionate scientists, working out of the glare of public dispute, may soon reach consensus on this issue or not, a significant shift in the debate seems to have occurred. The "pro" side now seems to be arguing that, in today's health environment, fluoridation may be expected to reduce dental caries by up to just 25 percent. Only a year or two ago, the benefit was still commonly claimed to be a 50 or 60 percent reduction. If, in fact, the "best" estimate of benefits is now lower, we may soon look for revised perceptions of the balance between benefits and risks as well.

These critical perspectives on benefits are well within the realm of legitimate scientific debate, and most are substantive enough to be taken seriously. While they do not discredit the hypothesis that fluoridation reduces tooth decay, they do cast serious doubt on the actual magnitude of the caries-preventive effect. A reassessment of this issue seems to be under way at present among experts, even strong advocates of fluoridation.

Other Research on Fluoride's Anti-Caries Effects

This category includes a great number of animal experiments, clinical trials, and other studies designed to explore the mechanisms of fluoride's caries-preventive effects, and to support a range of applications of fluoride against tooth decay (Newbrun 1986b). Most of this research has been independent of the political fluoridation controversy and, thus, insulated a bit from the distorting impacts of that dispute.

Without going into detail, I believe this large body of research provides almost indisputable evidence that fluoride is an effective anti-caries agent. That leaves open the issue of *how large* the effect of community water fluoridation on the incidence of dental caries may be, but it does make the hypothesis that it has no effect at all quite difficult to entertain.

Studies of Dental Fluorosis

Dental fluorosis, or mottling of the tooth enamel, was the first effect of fluoride on dental health to be extensively studied. Epidemiological surveys in naturally fluoridated areas in the 1930s, conducted primarily by H. Trendley Dean of the USPHS, showed a clear-cut dose-response curve, with both the incidence and the severity of dental fluorosis increasing as fluoride content of a water supply was increased. The relationship was widely confirmed by other investigators and in other countries.

Dean classified cases of dental fluorosis into five degrees of severity, which he named questionable, very mild, mild, moderate, and severe. His studies (and others) show that some dental fluorosis occurs at fluoride levels as low as 0.5 ppm. At 1 ppm—the level typically used for dental caries prevention—Dean found that 10 to 20 percent of children had dental fluorosis of the questionable, very mild or mild stages, which involve white spots or patches on the teeth. At fluoride levels of 2 ppm or more, moderate and severe stages began to appear, and by 5 ppm, the severe stage involving extensive brown stains on the teeth was quite prevalent. Dean's studies and others showed that dental fluorosis occurs at lower fluoride concentrations in areas with higher average temperatures, presumably because water consumption is greater in hot climates.

In the early years of research, dental fluorosis was considered to be a serious public health problem, and the USPHS initially set a maximum fluoride level of 1 ppm in order to prevent this adverse effect. But as promotion of fluoridation gained momentum, explicit trade-offs were made, accepting the occurrence of some dental fluorosis in return for caries prophylaxis. Dean and others felt that 10 to 20 percent incidence of no more than mild fluorosis was "not objectionable." This is clearly a value judgment, and many people do find mottling of their children's teeth quite objectionable.

To support fluoridation, the USPHS adopted revised fluoride standards, setting a range of "optimal" concentrations which varied with annual average temperature in the community, from 0.7 ppm in hot climates to 1.2 ppm in colder ones. The USPHS set twice the optimal level—1.4 to 2.4 ppm—as the maximum permissible fluoride levels. Although this implies a "safety factor" of 2, there is, in fact, essentially complete overlap between the range desired for dental caries prophylaxis and the range that causes dental fluorosis in sensitive people. The "safety margin" represents a social judgment that the dental damage done by these fluoride levels is acceptable, and not a margin with no damage. In 1985, the U.S. Environmental Protection Agency relaxed the upper limit to 4 ppm for naturally fluoridated communities, arguing that even severe dental fluorosis was acceptable when compared to the costs of defluoridating many small towns' water supplies.

Although dental fluorosis has been well documented for more than 50 years, current scientific understanding of the effect is inadequate. Three important areas are still uncertain and subject to controversy. The first is the toxicological meaning of this effect. Is dental fluorosis an external sign of general cellular toxicity, unique only in its visibility, while less detectable effects occur in other tissues? Or are the ameloblasts—the cells that lay down the enamel as the teeth grow inside the jaw—uniquely sensitive to fluoride? More exact knowledge of fluoride's mechanism of action in causing dental fluorosis could shed light on this pivotal point, but the precise mechanism is still not fully understood.

A second debate persists over whether permanently discolored teeth have any adverse psychological effects on a child. Some psychologists assert that they do, at least in severe cases. In the fluoridation debate, "pros" deny health implications of dental fluorosis, calling it "merely a cosmetic effect." Some even say that mildly mottled teeth are more attractive. These are obviously subjective judgments, and not scientific conclusions.

The final unresolved issue about dental fluorosis is whether its incidence is increasing. A general increase in exposure to fluoride in the diet has been documented over recent decades, and is attributable to the use of fluoridated water in food processing. If total fluoride intake has increased, dental fluorosis should be more prevalent now than it was before fluoridation. Several studies suggest that it is. For instance, Leverett (1986) found dental fluorosis to be 3.5 times as prevalent in nonfluoridated communities and twice as prevalent in fluoridated communities as Dean had observed.

Many experts, including some profluoridation leaders, have suggested that definitions of "optimal" fluoride levels in water should be lowered, to compensate for increased dietary fluoride. Other "pros," understandably reluctant to take a step that would suggest that the margin of safety in current fluoridation levels has been inadequate, have highlighted the uncertainties in the comparisons and called for further study of the question (Szpunar and Burt 1987). This debate has gone on with no major effort to resolve it for some twenty years.

Studies of the Safety of Fluoridation

This body of evidence consists of research conducted by or for the USPHS as part of its program to demonstrate the safety of fluoridation. Most of these studies were conducted between 1940 and 1960. Some involved clinical examinations of people in communities with fluoridated water, usually adults with lifelong exposure to naturally fluoridated water. Others were statistical studies of mortality, looking for differences between death rates from major causes in cities with high- and low-fluoride water supplies. In general, the studies reported no evidence of significant adverse effects. Collectively, they are interpreted by both their authors and other proponents of fluoridation as convincing evidence that there are no adverse health effects of any kind associated with fluoridated water (McClure 1962).

Many valid scientific criticisms of these studies have been published. The total number of studies is small—no more than a few dozen. The clinical studies inevitably examined small numbers of subjects, rendering statistically insignificant even those clear-cut differences in health status that were recorded in several studies. Broader statistical surveys looked only at a few major types of toxicity that fluoride might possibly cause. Neither the clinical studies nor the statistical surveys specifically looked for several kinds of adverse effects that other literature clearly attributes to fluoride.

Many of the studies had obvious methodological weaknesses. For instance, a clinical study of children in Newburgh, N.Y., excluded all subjects who had shown any signs of illness. A survey of autopsy data seeking evidence of skeletal fluorosis excluded every individual known to have suffered from any kidney disease. Because renal insufficiency increases retention of fluoride, and, thus, enhances the risk of skeletal fluorosis, the study excluded those people most likely to show the effect it presumably was seeking.

This research was done before modern criteria for assessing the effects of environmental agents were developed. Most studies looked only for obvious clinical symptoms of health damage, not for the subtler biochemical and physiological changes that are now recognized as precursors of frank impairment. No research specifically focused on subpopulations likely to be at higher-than-average risk, such as people with kidney disease or those with extreme water intake. Judged by the standards of modern environmental health research, these studies were poorly conceived, insensitive, and unlikely to find adverse effects even if some were present.

The studies also had an obvious potential for bias because they were sponsored by an agency and carried out by a handful of scientists who were simultaneously engaged in vigorous political promotion of fluoridation. In my judgment, serious actual bias was present. The authors of the studies consistently interpreted incomplete data and ambiguous findings as persuasive evidence of the absence of risk, and they uniformly rejected every result that suggested potential harm as "clinically insignificant" or "not attributable to fluoride."

In short, the USPHS set out to prove a null hypothesis—that fluoridation could never harm anyone—and perhaps it was politically necessary for them to attempt that impossible task. Even a much larger body of high-quality studies could not absolutely prove safety. The existing studies are certainly much less than conclusive evidence on the question.

Studies Showing Adverse Effects of Fluoridation

This category includes a variety of published reports—many in well-respected, peer-reviewed journals—which are often cited by "antis" as evidence that fluoridation has harmed or could harm some people. Among them are:

- Clinical reports by several authors (Waldbott and others) of reversible illness, interpreted as a toxic response by hypersensitive individuals to small doses of fluoride;
- Case reports of skeletal fluorosis, including several from the American literature, attributed to drinking water with relatively low fluoride content of 2 to 5 ppm;
- Clinical reports of illness and mortality in patients who were treated by hemodialysis with fluoridated water;
- Statistical analyses suggesting an association between fluoridated water and an increased risk of cancer, and a few animal bioassays for carcinogenicity;
- Epidemiological surveys suggesting an association between fluoridated water and an increased risk of Down's syndrome;
- Cellular and animal studies on the mutagenicity of fluoride; and
- Animal studies suggesting adverse effects of fluoride on kidney function, enzyme activity, or other processes.

In general, most of these studies are of adequate scientific quality to be taken seriously. Most have no fatal methodological flaws or implausible theoretical underpinnings. (NOTE: Some "studies" cited by the "antis" may indeed be disreputable, but it is important not to tar all such evidence with the same brush.)

This research is certainly subject to scientific criticism on many grounds. Some studies do have methodological weaknesses that raise doubts as to their accuracy, and probably should not be accepted as valid unless confirmed by more, better-designed research. Other studies with contradictory findings exist on most of these issues, feeding debates about the relative merits of each study and where the weight of the evidence lies. Some reports, such as in vitro mutagenicity studies, may be accepted as valid, but their implications in terms of potential effects of fluoridation on human health are subject to wide uncertainty and varied interpretations.

None of these studies prove conclusively that fluoridation is harmful, but some provide strong evidence that some effects in sensitive people may be likely. Others raise questions that have not been aggressively pursued by research. Indeed, several authoritative independent scientific reviews identified lists of important questions about the safety of fluoridation that still require further research (National Research Council 1977; Marier and Rose 1977; Taves 1979; and Johnson et al. 1979.)

Other Research on Toxic Effects of Fluoride

This category includes a large body of occupational health research, veterinary studies assessing effects of fluoride air pollution, and epidemiological research on populations in other countries such as India, where an estimated one million people have skeletal fluorosis (Teotia and Teotia 1984).

Most of this research is of average, acceptable scientific quality, and some of it is much better than that. The Indian studies of skeletal fluorosis, for example, include hundreds of papers published over a fifty-year period. The research has documented dose-response curves showing a clear risk of skeletal fluorosis even at 1 ppm fluoride in water. It also identified several stages of the disease, including the subclinical changes that precede the obvious symptoms of damage; elucidated mechanisms; identified nutrients and other variables that modify risk for individuals; and identified populations at special risk, including children and people with impaired kidney function.

This research—and much other work on related topics—could be enormously valuable for assessing the risk of skeletal fluorosis and other health effects in the United States and other countries with fluoridated water supplies. But it has been largely ignored in the fluoridation debate.

Most scientists who strongly support fluoridation have generally been unwilling to acknowledge the many implications in such research that water fluoridated at 1 ppm poses actual risks to the public. "Pros" often dismiss the Indian studies and similar research as "irrelevant to fluoridation." Some misrepresent the evidence, asserting, for instance, that skeletal fluorosis in India has been observed only where water contains 10 ppm fluoride or more. The few "antis" who are competent to evaluate the world literature critically have not been able to focus scientific discussion on this research.

Scientific Summaries and Reviews

Given the vast amount of primary literature on effects of fluoride, few people can study it all. Reviews and summaries that interpret the literature—and sometimes, reviews of reviews—are, thus, the predominant source of information for people who want to learn more about the scientific evidence.

Unfortunately, reviews of literature relevant to fluoridation reflect the extreme polarization of both the political and scientific debates that has long characterized the controversy. There are many profluoridation reviews (Newbrun 1986b; McClure 1970; and Royal College of Physicians 1976), and a few competent antifluoridation reviews (Waldbott 1965; Waldbott et al. 1978; and Burgstahler 1965). The "pro" reviews appear widely in dental and medical journals, as well as in books, while most "anti" reviews have been published as books, for reasons explored in chapters 4 and 5 of Martin's monograph.

A reader new to the issue who has not studied the original papers could be seriously misled by the normal assumption that reviews are reasonably objective. One is more likely to make such assumptions about "pro" reviews, because of their respectable trappings, than about more openly biased "anti" tracts. In fact, however, the "pro" reviews are every bit as slanted and distorted as the "anti" ones—and some are worse.

Reviewers on each side are extremely selective, and selectively critical. They cite studies that support their point of view un-critically, often implying—and sometimes asserting—that no contrary evidence or alternative interpretations exist. They bring up studies that the other side cites only to criticize them, and they sometimes misrepresent the evidence in such studies in order to discredit it.

There are some exceptions to this general picture. A few comparatively objective and scientifically credible reviews seek a balanced scientific perspective on the data, rather than to give advantage to one side or the other in the political dispute. Examples include Jolly et al. (1973), National Research Council (1977), Marier and Rose (1977), Taves (1979), Johnson et al. (1979), Dementi (1980), Franke (1979), and Teotia and Teotia (1988).

Summary

The overall quality of the evidence on the health effects of fluoridated water is fairly typical of the evidence on many other environmental health issues. There are good studies and bad studies; questions that have been well answered and others that have been barely answered at all; a great deal of evidence of potential risk but little conclusive proof of harm; and nothing like conclusive proof of safety for various populations using water with 1 ppm fluoride over a lifetime. Substantial scientific uncertainty on most questions makes a range of interpretations possible and precludes absolute answers.

While the scientific picture on fluoridation is typical of science on most such issues—except that many key studies were done a long time ago—the extreme political controversy over social policy in this case has pervaded the scientific debate. That makes objective assessment of this evidence extraordinarily difficult, even in relation to scientific assessments inherent in other environmental policy disputes.

WHICH SIDE IS SCIENCE ON?

Actually, my answer is "Neither side." Ideally, in disputes over public policy involving risks and benefits of an innovation like fluoridation, society needs science to be a neutral arbiter of facts, not a dogmatic advocate of a single policy choice. Pragmatically, the current state of scientific knowledge on questions related to fluoridation makes science effectively neutral. The evidence as a whole can't be claimed by either side, try as they will.

In the rhetoric of the political debate, science often *seems* to be on one side or the other, but it isn't. Professional scientific organizations that endorsed fluoridation expressed their social preferences as citizens, but endorsements have no intrinsic scientific merit. Scientists who campaign for each side are, likewise, acting as citizens, not merely as experts.

Can nonpartisan science resolve the debate? It's tempting to think so, but I doubt it. Here's why.

- Scientific consensus (if it were possible) cannot resolve disputes over value judgments and social priorities.
- The enormous world literature actually fuels debate, rather than defuses it. No one interpretation fits all studies, and advocates of any view can find evidence to support the political position which they favor.
- New research will not resolve debates, even on issues where more research is clearly needed. Any new study is certain to include enough ambiguity to allow those who don't like its results—whichever side that is—to dismiss it as inconclusive, and, thus, sustain their existing beliefs.
- There is no organized demand for objective scientific views on fluoridation. Only the active "pros" and "antis" care passionately about the issue. A balanced "on-the-one-hand-but-on-the-other-hand" scientific discussion helps neither side. Each wants slanted scientific-sounding arguments that will help it win the political debate. Objective scientific voices on the issue—such as those cited earlier—have been drowned out by the clamor of the political battle.
- That same emotional battle keeps most objective scientists, especially environmental health scientists with true expertise, from entering the policy debate. It leaves the field to those whose main goal is political victory, not accurate presentation or advancement of scientific knowledge.

I wish I could be more optimistic about the likelihood that objective scientific inquiry would affect public policy debates over fluoridation. But, in twenty years of watching the controversy, I have seen no signs that leaders on either side—those with the power to change the dynamics of the debate—are willing to alter their time-tested approaches.

Ironically, the "antis," who are usually portrayed as unscientific, often *act* more scientifically in the debate, probably because it is politically useful to do so. For instance, they frequently cite the unanswered questions about risks, and call for further research. While most "antis" are not scientists, they may have absorbed the ideas and approaches of the environmental health perspective by observing other debates over toxic substances in recent years. By contrast, the political profluoridation stance has evolved into a dogmatic, authoritarian, essentially antiscientific posture, one that discourages open debate of scientific issues.

As long as the debate remains centered on the political fate of fluoridation proposals, it seems unrealistic to expect it to be more scientific. As Brian Martin's monograph has effectively documented, even those "antis" who are well-credentialled scientists lack the resources needed to force a change in terms of the debate. Because they have the greatest resources, the "pro" leadership has the greatest control over how the debate is conducted, but they seem locked in a corner, where change may well bring defeat.

The wider scientific community—especially those sectors most concerned with environmental health—does have the resources to affect the debate, but it lacks motivation to become involved. As long as the broader scientific community remains aloof from this dispute, I am afraid history will continue to repeat itself.

REFERENCES

Brunelle, J.A. and J.P. Carlos. 1990. Recent Trends in Dental Caries in U.S. Children and the Effect of Water Fluoridation. *Journal of Dental Research* 69: 723–727.

Burgstahler, A.W. 1965. Dental and Medical Aspects of Fluoridated Drinking Water. *Transactions of the Kansas Academy of Sciences* 68:223–242.

Consumer Reports. The Attack on Fluoridation, Part 2—Six Ways to Mislead the Public. (August 1978): 480–482.

Dementi, B.A. 1980. Fluoride in Drinking Water. Toxic Substances Information Division, Virginia State Department of Health, Richmond.

Diesendorf, M. 1986. The Mystery of Declining Tooth Decay. *Nature*, (10 July) 332:125–129.

Franke, J. 1979. A New Concept of the Effect of Fluorides on Bone. *Fluoride* 12(4):195–208.

Groth, E. 1973. Two Issues of Science and Public Policy: Air Pollution Control in the San Francisco Bay Area and Fluoridation of Community Water Supplies. Doctoral dissertation, Department of Biological Sciences, Stanford University, Stanford, Calif.

Groth, E. 1980. The Fluoridation Controversy: Some Implications for Science and Public Policy. Seminar presented to the Dental Public Health Program, School of Public Health, University of Michigan, Ann Arbor. 28 March, 1980.

Johnson, W.J., D.R. Taves, and J. Jowsey. 1979, Fluoridation and Bone Disease in Renal Patients. E. Johansen, D.R. Taves and T.O. Olsen, eds. *Continuing Evaluation of the Use of Fluorides.* 275–294. Selected Symposia Series, American Association for the Advancement of Science. Boulder, Colo.: Westview Press.

Jolly, S.S., S. Prasad, R. Sharma, and R. Chander. 1973. Endemic Fluorosis in Punjab, I. Skeletal Aspect. *Fluoride* 6(1):4–18.

Leverett, D. 1986. Prevalence of Dental Fluorosis in Fluoridated and Nonfluoridated Communities—A Preliminary Investigation. *Journal of Public Health Dentistry* 46(4):184–187.

Marier, J.R., and D. Rose. 1977. *Environmental Fluoride 1977.* Associate Committee on Scientific Criteria for Environmental Quality, National Research Council of Canada. NRCC Publication No. 16081. Ottawa: NRCC.

McClure, F.J., ed. 1962. *Fluoride Drinking Waters.* Publication No. 825, United States Public Health Service, Bethesda, Md. (A collection of USPHS papers on all aspects of fluoridation from research over a thirty-year period, reprinted in one volume.)

McClure, F.J. 1970. *Water Fluoridation: The Search and the Victory.* National Institute of Dental Research, Bethesda, Md.

National Research Council. 1977. *Drinking Water and Health.* Safe Drinking Water Committee of the Advisory Center on Toxicology and the Assembly of Life Sciences. Washington, D.C. National Academy of Sciences, 369–400. (NOTE: The section on fluoride, written by D.R. Taves, is recommended. Summary sections elsewhere in the volume and written by other authors have a distinct profluoridation bias and conflict with the data on 369–400)

Newbrun, E. 1986a. Water Fluoridation and Dietary Fluoride. 3–32 in Newbrun (1986b), next reference.

Newbrun, E., ed. 1986b. *Fluorides and Dental Caries.* Third Edition. Springfield, Ill.: Charles C. Thomas Publisher.

Royal College of Physicians. 1976. *Fluoride, Teeth & Health.* London: Pitman Publishing, Ltd.

Sandman, P.M. 1987. Risk Communication: Facing Public Outrage. *EPA Journal* (November): 21–22. Washington, D.C.: United States Environmental Protection Agency.

Slovic, P. 1987. Perception of Risk. *Science* 236:280–285.

Sutton, P.R.N. 1959. *Fluoridation: Errors and Omissions in Experimental Trials.* Melbourne: Melbourne University Press.

Szpunar, S.M., and B.A. Burt. 1987. Trends in the Prevalence of Dental Fluorosis in the United States: A Review. *Journal of Public Health Dentistry* 47(2):71–79.

Taves, D.R. 1979. Claims of Harm from Fluoridation. E Johansen, D.R. Taves, and T.O. Olsen, eds. *Continuing Evaluation of the Use of Fluorides.* 295–321. Selected Symposia Series, American Association for the Advancement of Science. Boulder, Colo.: Westview Press.

Teotia, S.P.S., and M. Teotia. 1984. Endemic Fluorosis in India: A Challenging National Health Problem. *Journal of the Association of Physicians of India.* 32:347–352.

Teotia, S.P.S., and M. Teotia. 1988. Endemic Skeletal Fluorosis: Clinical and Radiological Variants. A Review of 25 Years of Personal Research. *Fluoride* 21(1):39–44.

Waldbott, G.L. 1965. *A Struggle With Titans.* New York: Carlton Press.

Waldbott, G.L., A.W. Burgstahler, and H.L. McKinney. 1978. *Fluoridation: The Great Dilemma.* Lawrence, Kans.: Coronado Press, Inc.

Yiamouyiannis, J.A. 1990. Water Fluoridation and Tooth Decay: Results from the 1986-1987 National Survey of U.S. Schoolchildren. *Fluoride* 23(2): 55–67.

APPENDIX

FLUORIDATION AROUND THE WORLD

Beginning in 1987, I wrote to health departments in numerous countries in the world enquiring about fluoridation. My standard letter was as follows:

I am carrying out a social scientific study of the issue of fluoridation of public water supplies to reduce tooth decay. Any information you can provide in relation to the following questions would be most appreciated.

1. What fraction, if any, of the population of your country drinks water to which fluoride is added for the purposes of reducing tooth decay?
2. What fraction of the population drinks water which *naturally* contains fluoride at a level equal to or greater than that considered optimal for reducing tooth decay?
3. What is your government's current policy on fluoridation?
4. Does your government promote other uses of fluoride, such as fluoride tablets, fluoride in table salt, fluoride in toothpaste, and topical fluoride treatments by dentists?

I would be grateful to receive any relevant documents or articles you can provide relating to these issues.

I obtained a list of addresses of health departments used by a government body in Australia. This covered 37 countries. For countries not on this list, I wrote to embassies and high commissions in Australia. This covered many further countries. Finally, for some others not covered by either of these procedures, I simply wrote to the Minister of Health in the capital city of the country concerned. In countries from which I received no official reply, I also wrote to a few individuals whose names were given to me as likely sources of information.

I did not try to contact every government in the world, but concentrated on industrialized countries and the larger Third World countries.

In the following tabulation, and in the interests of accuracy, I have often closely paraphrased replies which were received. Some replies did not provide answers to all my questions. This accounts for missing information in what follows. Population figures are for 1986 unless otherwise stated. Additional information has been used when available and useful.

In some cases, a few further English-language references which deal with fluoridation or the fluoridation controversy have been listed.

Sources:

Auermann, E., and H. Lingelbach. "Status and Prospects of Fluoridation in Europe." *American Journal of Public Health and the Nation's Health*, vol. 54, no. 9 (September 1964): 1545–1550.

Bernhardt, Mary E. "Fluoridation International." *Journal of the American Dental Association*, vol. 80, no. 4 (April 1970): 731–734.

Chaneles, Juan. "Fluoridation in South America." *Journal of the American Dental Association*, vol. 61, no. 3 (September 1960): 331–337.

Experience on Water Fluoridation in Europe. Copenhagen: World Health Organization Regional Office for Europe, 1987.

Farkas, E.J. "Water Fluoridation in Eleven Countries." *Social Science and Medicine*, vol. 16 (1982): 1255–1258.

Forrest, Jean R. "The Effectiveness of Fluoridation in Europe: A Review." *British Dental Journal*, vol. 123, no. 6 (19 September 1967): 269–275.

Frank, R.M. and S. O'Hickey, eds. *Strategy for Dental Caries Prevention in European Countries According to Their Laws and Regulations*. Oxford: IRL Press, 1987.

Oliver, Keven Charles. *Fluoridation in Europe, 1945–1980: History and Documents*. Masters thesis, University of Kansas, 1983.

Ross, W. Stewart. "Fluoridation in Europe." *Journal of the American Dental Association*, vol. 61, no. 3 (September 1960): 324–330.

Scobie, Russell B. "Water Fluoridation: A Survey of the International Picture." *Alabama Journal of Medical Sciences*, vol. 12, no. 3 (1975): 225–229.

Australia

Population, 15.6 million in 1984.

1. 10.2 million or 66 percent drank water with added fluoride.
2. About 136,000 or 0.9 percent drank naturally fluoridated water (0.5 ppm fluoride or more).
3. The National Health and Medical Research Council has supported fluoridation in a series of statements since 1952. Decisions about fluoridation are made at the local level.

Sources:

Commonwealth Department of Health. *Fluoridation of Water: A Collection of Reports and Statements.* Canberra: Australian Government Publishing Service, 1985.

See also: Head, Brian W. "The Fluoridation Controversy in Victoria: Public Policy and Group Politics." *Australian Journal of Public Administration,* vol. 37, no. 3 (September 1978): 257–273.

Myers, D.M., V.D. Plueckhahn, and A.L.G. Rees. *Report of the Committee of Inquiry into the Fluoridation of Victorian Water Supplies.* Melbourne: Government Printer, 1980.

Varney, Wendy. *Fluoride in Australia: A Case to Answer.* Sydney: Hale and Iremonger, 1986.

Walker, Glen S.R. *Fluoridation: Poison on Tap* Melbourne: Glen Walker, G.P.O. Box 935G, Melbourne, Victoria 3001, Australia, 1982).

Austria

Population, 7.6 million.

1. No water supplies contain added fluoride.
2. About 15,000 or 0.2 percent drink water naturally containing 1 ppm fluoride or more.
3. Fluoride tablets are provided to the public.

Source: A letter from Erich Klaus, Secretary Administration, Austrian Embassy, P.O. Box 375, Manuka ACT 2603, Australia, dated 6 August 1987.

Belgium

Population, 9.9 million.

1. No water supplies contain added fluoride.
2. About 100,000 or 1 percent drink water naturally containing 1 ppm fluoride or more. Most drinking waters have less than 0.5 ppm fluoride.
3. Local or regional authorities make the ultimate decisions about fluoridation.
4. The government promotes other uses of fluoride mainly through treatment in medical schools and through general recommendations on dental hygiene.

In the 1950s, there was a limited trial of water fluoridation in a community with a population of about 8,000. It was discontinued for a variety of reasons, one of which was probably economics.

Source: A letter from Dr G. Thiers, Director, Institut d'Hygiène et d'Epidémiologie, Ministere de la Sante Publique et de la Famille, 14, Rue Juliette Wytsman, 1050 Bruxelles, Belium, dated 5 June 1987. *See also:*
Vreven, J. "Dental Caries in Belgium: Preventive and Legal Aspects." R.M. Frank and S. O'Hickey eds. *Strategy for Dental Caries Prevention in European Countries According to Their Laws and Regulations.* Oxford: IRL Press, 1987: 119–125.

Brazil

Population, about 124 million in 1982.

1. Approximately 26 million or 21 percent drank water with added fluoride.
2. Naturally fluoridated water is rare.
3. Oral health is a priority area for government assistance, and fluoridation is being promoted.
4. Fluoride toothpastes are used widely. Other fluoride vehicles are used on a limited scale, including topical treatments and mouth rinses in schools.

Source: A letter from Carol C. Sherman, Science and Technology Section, Embassy of Brazil, G.P.O. Box 1540, Canberra ACT 2601, Australia, dated 29 May 1987.

Canada

Population, 23.0 million in 1976.

1. Approximately 8.38 million or 36 percent drank water with added fluoride.
2. 174,000 or 0.76 percent drank water with naturally occurring fluoride.
3. Decisions about water fluoridation are taken at a local or regional level. With a few exceptions, formal guidelines for preventive dental services do not exist in Canada, nationally or regionally.

Source:

Working Group on Preventive Dental Services. *Preventive Dental Services: Practices, Guidelines and Recommendations.* Canada: Minister of Supply and Services, 1979.

Chile

Population, 12.1 million.

1. 1.26 million or 10.46 percent drink water with added fluoride. These people live in the Fifth Region of Chile, an experimental area for fluoridation.
2. 1.30 million or 10.81 percent drink water with naturally occurring fluoride at a level considered to be "fairly acceptable," although not optimal.
3. The government's National Program of Fluoridation of Drinking Water Supplies began with fluoridation of Fifth Region water supplies. This program will be expanded to cover other regions, subject to budgetary considerations.
4. The Ministry of Health encourages the use of fluoride in regions where the water does not contain added or natural fluoride. The Ministry of Health runs programs for schools which include topical fluoride treatments, as do dental practices which are part of the National Health Services system. Most toothpastes contain fluoride.

Source: A letter from Guillermo Anguita, Second Secretary, Embassy of Chile, P.O. Box 69, Red Hill ACT 2603, Australia, dated 18 August 1987.

Czechoslovakia

Population, 15.5 million.

1. In 1987, about 3.3 million or 21 percent drank water with added fluoride. In 1988, fluoridation ceased in Ceske Budejovice and Prague.
2. There is one locality which has a natural fluoride level higher than permissible. (The World Health Organization guidelines for Czechoslovakia's climate specify 0.8 to 1.5 ppm.) The water in this locality is diluted with water from other sources.
3. The Scientific Board of the Ministry of Health established the Fluoride Committee to regulate the use of fluoride in drinking water. This committee brings together experts from all fields considered to be relevant. Fluoridation is recommended wherever it is deemed effective and suitable. It is not compulsory. If it is recommended by the environmental and health services, it still requires the consent of regional or local authorities.
4. In places where fluoridation is not suitable, sodium fluoride tablets are provided if approved by appropriate medical officers. Fluoride toothpastes are available for purchase.

Sources: A letter from Professor B. Rosický, Institute of Hygiene and Epidemiology, 100 42 Praha 10, Czechoslovakia, dated 20 July 1987; also a form letter from R. Ch. Ziegelbecker and R. Ziegelbecker, dated 24 May 1989, and concerning fluoridation in Ceske Budejovice and Prague.

Denmark

Population, 5.1 million.

1. No water supplies contain added fluoride.
2. Some 150,000 to 300,000 or 3 to 6 percent drink water that naturally contains fluoride.
3. The Minister for the Environment, Helge Nielsen, stated on 5 January 1977 that water fluoridation should not be allowed. Factors involved in formulating this opinion included:

- the cost of fluoridation, considering variations in fluoride levels in groundwater (the major source of the water supply);
- possible impacts of fluoride on plants and animals in marine and fresh waters;
- the narrow interval between the levels of fluoride causing beneficial and harmful effects; and
- possible overdosing of critical groups, including people drinking very large amounts of water, people with reduced kidney function, people undergoing prolonged dialysis, and babies fed with foods using dried milk.
4. Several uses of fluoride are promoted, especially fluoride toothpastes, rinses, and topical treatments, and, to a small extent, fluoride tablets and varnish.

Sources: A letter from Eli Schwarz, Chief Dental Officer, National Board of Health, 1 St. Kongensgade, DK-1264 Copenhagen K, Denmark, dated June 1987. "Fluoridation of drinking water," *Nyt fra miljøstyrelsen.* special issue (February 1977). *See also:*

Schwarz, E. "Dental Caries Prevention and Legislation in Denmark," Frank, R. M. and S. O'Hickey, eds. *Strategy for Dental Caries Prevention in European Countries According to Their Laws and Regulations.* Oxford: IRL Press, 1987: 89–102.

Schwarz, Eli, and Erik Randers Hansen. "Public Attitudes Concerning Water Fluoridation in Denmark." *Community Dentistry and Oral Epidemiology.* Vol. 4, 1976: 182–185.

Fiji

Population, 714,000.

1. Only the population of Suva—71,000 or 10 percent—drinks water with added fluoride. Even so, there are often long periods during which the water in Suva is not fluoridated due to mechanical problems.
2. There is no evidence that Fiji waters contain any natural fluoride.
3. Although the government has no formal policy, it encourages the use of fluoride.
4. All methods of using fluoride are promoted except for fluoride in salt.

Source: A letter from Dr. Devi Singh, assistant director of Dental Services for the Permanent Secretary for Health and Social Welfare, Department of Health, Government Buildings, Suva, Fiji, dated 5 June 1987.

Finland

Population, 4.9 million.

1. Only the population of Kuopio—76,000 or 1.6 percent—drink water with added fluoride.
2. About 200,000 or 4.1 percent drink water with natural fluoride.
3. The government supports fluoridation but has not been very active in promoting it.
4. The government promotes fluoride tablets, toothpastes, and topical treatments, all of which are widely used.

Source: A letter from Dr. Heikki Tala, Assistant Chief Dental Officer, National Board of Health, Siltasaarenkatu 18 A, PB 223, SF-00531 Helsinki 53, Finland, dated 27 May 1987. *See also:*

Hausen, H. W. "The Experience of Drinking Water Fluoridation in Finland." *Experience on Water Fluoridation in Europe.* Copenhagen: World Health Organization Regional Office for Europe, 1987: 37–47.

Tala, H. "Strategy of Dental Caries Prevention in Finland According to the Health Legislation and Other Legal Regulations." Frank, R. M., and S. O'Hickey, eds. *Strategy for Dental Caries Prevention in European Countries According to Their Laws and Regulations.* Oxford: IRL Press, 1987: 103–117.

Hannu Vuori, "Attitudes Towards Fluoridation of Drinking Water." *International Journal of Health Education.* Vol. 41, 1973: 109–118.

France

Population, 55.2 million.

1. No water supplies in France contain added fluoride.
2. Probably about 940,000 or 1.7 percent drink water with fluoride naturally at an adequate level between 0.7 and 1.5 ppm, and about 260,000 or 0.5 percent drink water with fluoride naturally at a possibly hazardous level greater than 1.5 ppm.

3. Fluoridation has not been undertaken because French consultative representatives considered that the large number of distribution plants (more than 20,000) and great regional variations in fluoride concentrations present technical difficulties that cannot be overcome.
4. In 1985, the law was changed to allow fluoridation of milk and of table and cooking salt for a period of five years. Fluoride toothpastes and tablets are sold only in pharmacies.

Source:

Rey, J. "Legal Aspects Related to Caries Prevention in France." Frank, R. M. and S. O'Hickey, eds. *Strategy for Dental Caries Prevention in European Countries According to Their Laws and Regulations.* Oxford: IRL Press, 1987: 155–157.

German Democratic Republic (East Germany)

Population, 16.6 million.

1. Roughly 3.4 million or 20 percent drink water with added fluoride.
3. Karl Marx Stadt was fluoridated in 1959. When technically feasible, water fluoridation is the method of choice for preventing tooth decay, and is part of the government's national health program.
4. The national health program also includes provision of fluoride tablets, topical treatments, and recommendations for using fluoride toothpastes.

Source:

Künzel, W. "The Experience of Water Fluoridation in the German Democratic Republic." *Experience on Water Fluoridation in Europe.* Copenhagen: World Health Organization Regional Office for Europe, 1987: 48–65.

Federal Republic of Germany (West Germany)

Population, 60.7 million.

1. No water supplies contain added fluoride.
3. Sources differ as to whether fluoridation is legally permissible. According to the Minister of Youth, Family, Women, and Health, fluoridation is not allowed because

there are people who must or prefer to drink unfluoridated water whereas, according to commentator H. Pohl, water fluoridation is possible. In any case, there is no fluoridation anywhere in the country, partly due to the activities of antifluoridationists. The city of Kassel was fluoridated from 1952 to 1971.

4. Addition of fluoride to foodstuffs, such as salt or milk, is illegal. The federal government encourages the use of fluoride toothpastes and tablets.

Sources: A letter from Dr. Evers, Der Bundesminister für Jugend, Familie, Frauen und Gesundheit, Postfach 200490, 5300 Bonn 2, Federal Republic of Germany, dated 27 May 1987. *See also:*

Naujoks, R. "Dental Caries Prevention in the Federal Republic of Germany." Frank, R. M. and S. O'Hickey, eds. *Strategy for Dental Caries Prevention in European Countries According to Their Laws and Regulations.* Oxford: IRL Press, 1987: 181–188.

Pohl, H. "Legal Aspects of Caries Prevention in the Federal Repblic of Germany. Ibid: 189–195.

Greece

Population, 10.0 million.

1. No water supplies contain added fluoride.
3. On two separate occasions the Ministry of Health, Welfare, and Social Security moved to fluoridate drinking water in urban areas, but, each time, objections from the Ministry of Public Works stopped implementation. According to the Greek Ambassador in Australia, the decision not to fluoridate was based on the following reasons:
   • There is limited implementation of fluoridation around the world, especially in the developed countries.
   • There is proof that pathological disorders result from fluoridation.
   • Various factors, such as climate, affect people's intake of water, so it is very difficult to specify the most suitable level of fluoridation.
4. There are no organized national programs for prevention of tooth decay. Fluoride tablets, toothpastes, and topical treatments are available.

Sources: A letter from Athanase A. Camilos, Ambassador of Greece, Embassy of Greece, Canberra ACT 2600, Australia, dated 2 June 1987. *See also:*

Mitsis, F. J. and T. M. Athanassouli. "Dental Caries in Greece. Epidemiology-prevention-legal Aspects." Frank, R. M., and S. O'Hickey, eds. *Strategy for Dental Caries Prevention in European Countries According to Their Laws and Regulations.* Oxford: IRL Press, 1987: 75–87.

India

Population, 784 million.

1. No water supplies contain added fluoride.
2. About half the rural population drink water naturally containing 1 ppm fluoride or more. Drinking water in urban areas usually has less than 1 ppm.
3. The issue of government policy on fluoridation does not arise because the major relevant health problem is endemic fluorosis. Defluoridation plants and deep bore water supplies have been introduced to provide drinking water with less than 1 ppm fluoride.
4. Apparently there is no government policy permitting the use of fluorides. Flouride toothpastes and topical treatments are used in some areas.

Source: A letter from Professor S. P. S. Teotia, head, Postgraduate Department of Human Metabolism and Endocrinology, LLRM Medical College, Meerut-250 004, India, dated 19 May 1989.

Iran

Population, 49.9 milion.

1. No water supplies contain added fluoride.
2. Sixteen million or 34 percent drink water naturally containing 1 ppm fluoride.
3. The government plans to introduce fluoridation in urban areas, and also to introduce fluoridated table salt.
4. Some physicians prescribe fluoride tablets, some toothpastes contain fluoride, and some dentists give topical fluoride treatments.

Source: A letter from Ahmad Attari, Ambassador, Embassy of the Islamic Republic of Iran, 14 Torres Street, Red Hill ACT 2603, Australia, dated 25 September 1987.

Ireland

Population, 3.5 million.

1. 2.3 million or 66 percent drink water with added fluoride.
3. The Minister of Health can direct health authorities to add fluoride to water supplies under the Health (Fluoridation of Water Supplies) Act of 1960. A legal challenge to this act failed in both the High Court and the Supreme Court in 1964. Fluoridation in Ireland is compulsory and national. All major centers of population were receiving fluoridated water by 1969. The third of the population not receiving fluoridated water live in rural areas and small towns.
4. Almost all toothpastes contain fluoride, most dentists use topical fluorides,and there are some programs for using fluoride mouth rinses and tablets.

Sources:

Clarkson, J. J. and D. O'Mullane. "The Experience of Water Fluoridation in Ireland." *Experience on Water Fluoridation in Europe.* Copenhagen: World Health Organization Regional Office for Europe, 1987: 66–73.

MacEntee, Sean. "Fluoridation in Ireland: The Spadework." *Journal of the Irish Dental Association.* Vol. 18, 1972: 48–52.

MacNeill, S. "The Fluoridation Case in Ireland—Legal and Scientific Evaluations." *Journal of the Irish Dental Association.* Vol. 18, 1972: 59–67.

O'Hickey, S. "Dental Caries Prevention in Ireland: Legal Aspects." Frank, R. M. and S. O'Hickey, eds. *Strategy for Dental Caries Prevention in European Countries According to Their Laws and Regulations.* Oxford: IRL Press, 1987: 207–222.

Israel

Population, 4.3 million.

1. Approximately 870,000 or 20 percent drink water with added fluoride.

2. About 108,000 or 2.5 percent drink water with fluoride naturally at a level considered to be satisfactory.
3. The current policy of the Ministry of Health follows the guidelines of the World Health Organization.
4. The Ministry encourages a range of fluoride vehicles, such as tablets, toothpastes, rinses, and topical treatments.

Source: A letter from Josephine H. Kaufman, Senior Assistant for Dental Health, Department of Dental Health, Ministry of Health, Jerusalem, Israel, dated 24 May 1987.

Japan

Population, 121.7 million.

1. No water supplies contain added fluoride.
2. Of the 1972 population served by community water supplies, 0.4 percent drank water with fluoride at 0.8 ppm or more.
3. The government does not permit water fluoridation. The water quality standard for fluoride was set in 1978 by the government at less than 0.8 ppm.
4. No uses of fluoride are promoted by the government. The use of fluoride toothpastes is widespread, and some dentists use topical fluoride treatments.

Source: A letter from Humio Tsunoda, Professor and Director, Department of Hygiene and Public Health, Iwate Medical University, 19-1, Uchimaru, Morioka, 020 Japan, dated 31 March 1989.

Lebanon

Population, 2.7 million.

1. No water supplies contain added fluoride.
4. Dentists recommend fluoride toothpastes, which are widely used. Pharmacies stock fluoride tablets.

Source: A letter from the Embassy of Lebanon, 73 Endeavour Street, Red Hill ACT 2603, Australia, dated 10 December 1987.

The Netherlands

Population, 14.5 million.

1. No water supplies contain added fluoride.
2. No water supplies contain fluoride naturally at 1 ppm or higher. The maximum natural level of fluoride is far below this.
3. There is no intention by the government to introduce fluoridation. Earlier, there was widespread fluoridation, but following efforts by antifluoridationists, the Supreme Court of Justice ruled in 1973 that the Water Supply Act was not an acceptable legal basis for it. Legislation prepared to legalize fluoridation was withdrawn from Parliament in 1976 to avoid its rejection and there has been no fluoridation since that time.
4. All uses except fluoride in table salt are promoted. Ninety percent of toothpastes sold are fluoridated. Topical fluoride applications and fluoride tablets are paid for by social insurance.

Sources: A letter from K. Kranenburg, Head of the Dental Division, Department of Welfare, Health and Culture, Postbus 5406, 2280 HK Rijswijk, The Netherlands, dated 17 June 1987. *See also:*

König, K. G. "Legal Aspects Related to Caries Prevention in the Netherlands." Frank, R. M., and S. O'Hickey, eds. *Strategy for Dental Caries Prevention in European Countries According to Their Laws and Regulations.* Oxford: IRL Press, 1987: 67–73.

Moolenburgh, Hans. *Fluoride: The Freedom Fight.* Edinburgh: Mainstream, 1987.

New Zealand

Population, 3.3 million.

1. About 1.65 million or 50 percent drink water with added fluoride.
2. Naturally fluoridated water is found in only a few very small water supplies.
3. Fluoridation has been endorsed by the Department of Health as a "proven health measure" and as the single best community-based method for preventing tooth decay.

4. The Department of Health recommends:
   - the use of fluoride tablets for children older than six months of age in areas where the water supply has less than 0.3 ppm fluoride;
   - the use of fluoride toothpastes by all people; and
   - that dentists and school dental nurses should consider topical fluoride treatments for individual patients.

Sources: A letter from Peter B. V. Hunter, Department of Health, P.O. Box 5013, Wellington, New Zealand, dated 8 June 1987; and Clinical Services Letter No. 222, Department of Health, Wellington, dated 14 September 1983. *See also:*

Colquhoun, John. *Education and Fluoridation in New Zealand: An Historical Study.* Ph.D. thesis, University of Auckland, 1987.

Mitchell, Austin. "Fluoridation in Dunedin: A Study of Pressure Groups and Public Opinion." *Political Science.* Vol. 12, 1960: 71–93.

Taylor, Derek. "Fluoridation Comes to Hastings." *New Zealand Medical Journal.* Vol. 54, 1955:23–31.

Norway

Population, 4.2 million.

1. No water supplies contain added fluoride.
2. About 22,000 or 0.53 percent drink water with fluoride naturally between 0.50 and 0.74 ppm; 8,300 or 0.20 percent drink water with fluoride naturally between 0.74 and 1.99 ppm; and about 6,200 or 0.15 percent drink water with fluoride naturally at unfavorably high levels between 2 and 5 ppm.
3. For fluoridation to become possible, a resolution would have to be introduced in the Norwegian parliament. This has not happened. Currently, there is no political interest in fluoridation, primarily because of public resistance. On the other hand, Norwegian health authorities support fluoridation, in agreement with the World Health Organization.
4. The Public Dental Health Service has made widespread use of different fluoride vehicles such as tablets and rinses. In 1985, 70 percent of toothpastes sold contained fluoride. In most parts of the country, children receive fluoride tablets at no cost.

208 AppendixAppendix

Sources: A letter from Ole W. Sandbekk, Assistant Deputy Director General, and Bente Traeen, Executive Officer, Directorate of Health, P.O. Box 8128 DEP, N–Oslo 1, Norway, dated 30 June 1987. *See also:*
Haugejorden, O. "Legal Aspects of Dental Caries Prevention in Norway." Frank, R. M., and S. O'Hickey, eds. *Strategy for Dental Caries Prevention in European Countries According to Their Laws and Regulations.* Oxford: IRL Press, 1987: 231–241.

Helöe, Leif Arne, and Jan Magne Birkeland. "The Public Opinion in Norway on Water Fluoridation." *Community Dentistry and Oral Epidemiology.* Vol. 2, 1974: 95–97.

Papua New Guinea

Population, 3.4 million.

1. Only the people in Port Moresby (population approximately 250,000 or 7.4 percent) drink water with added fluoride.
2. There is very little information available on natural levels of fluoride in the water.
3. In 1965, the government passed legislation requiring fluoridation of public water supplies at the level of 0.8 ppm. Due to a shortage of qualified personnel, only the city of Port Moresby has been fluoridated.
4. Outside Port Moresby, dental workers are encouraged to provide fluoride tablets and topical treatments. Flouride toothpastes are promoted, but not fluoride in table salt.

Source: A letter from Dr. Bais Gwale, Coordinator of Dental Health Services, Department of Health, P.O. Box 3991, Boroko, Papua New Guinea, dated 4 August 1987.

Philippines

Population, 58.25 million.

1. About 8,300 or 0.014 percent of the population drink water with added fluoride. Only the United States military bases have fluoridation.
2. About 4.5 million or 7.72 percent drink water naturally containing fluoride at or above the level considered op-

timal for reducing tooth decay, which, in the Philippines, is 0.4 to 0.6 ppm.

3. The Fluoridation Law of 1963 authorized the fluoridation of public water supplies. In 1980, an installation to fluoridate metropolitan Manila was initiated, but it has not been completed due to political and financial difficulties. Small pilot projects were started in Limay, Bataan, and San Jose City, but were stopped for the same reasons.
4. The government promotes fluoride mouth rinsing every two weeks. Fluoride toothpastes are widely sold. The government has not yet promoted fluoride tablets or fluoridated table salt. Topical fluoride treatments at rural dental clinics were too expensive in terms of staff and so were phased out.

Source: A letter from Guillermo F. Juliano, Chief, Dental Health Service, Ministry of Health, Manila, Republic of the Philippines, dated 14 July 1987.

Poland

Population, 37.5 million.

1. Less than one million or 2.7 percent drink water with added fluoride.
2. About 200,000 to 300,000, or 0.5 to 0.8 percent, drink water which naturally contains fluoride at a level equal to or greater than that considered optimal for reducing tooth decay.
3. The government supports fluoridation, but there are obstacles to it in particular provinces, some due to antifluoridationists.
4. The government promotes fluoride tablets, toothpastes, and topical treatments.

Source: A letter from Prof. Dr. hab. Zbigniew Jańczuk, Pomorska Akademia Medyczna, Stomatologi Zochowawczej, Al. Powstańców W kp. 72, blok 18, 70–111 Szczecin, Poland, dated 31 July 1987.

Portugal

Population, 10.3 million.

1. Only the small town of Montemor-o-Novo (population approximately 20,000 or 0.2 percent) drink water with added fluoride.
3. The extension of fluoridation nationally is being studied.
4. Since November 1985, there has been a program of fluoride tablets for children of kindergarten age and regular periodic fluoride mouth rinses for pupils in elementary schools. In 1987, a national program of oral health education began which includes a recommendation to use fluoride toothpastes.

Source: A letter from Gabriela Salgueiro, Ministério da Saúde, Gabinete de Relações Internacionais, Lisbon, Portugal, dated 22 July 1987.

Romania

Population, 22.7 million.

1. No water supplies contain added fluoride.
2. About 4.5 million or 20 percent drink water naturally containing an optimum fluoride level of more than 0.5 ppm.
3. The city of Tîrgu Mureş was fluoridated for over a decade from 1961, but this was terminated due to economic reasons.
4. Government authorities support the use of a number of fluoride vehicles. Fluoride toothpastes, mouth washes, and gels are for sale.

Source: A letter from Dumitru Tănăsel, Director, Ministerul Sănătăţii, Str. Ilfov No. 6–Sectoral VI, 70621, Section 5, Bucharest, Romania, dated 31 October 1987.

Singapore

Population, 2.6 million.

1. Since 1958, all of the population drink water with added fluoride.
2. None of the population drinks water with natural levels of fluoride.
3. The government supports fluoridation.
4. Other uses of fluoride are not promoted actively by the government. Fluoride toothpastes make up almost all of

the market. Dentists are free to offer topical fluoride treatments.

Source: A letter from Miss Tan Bee Lian, Public Relations Officer, Ministry of Health, 55 Cuppage Road, Cuppage Centre #09–00, Singapore 0922, dated 16 June 1987.

South Africa

Population, 23.2 million.

1. No drinking waters contain added fluoride.
3. The Health Act, 1977, allows the Minister of Health to regulate for the introduction of fluoridation, but this has not yet happened. The Department of Health is currently investigating fluoridation due to increased interest in South Africa. Principles to be considered in drafting regulations include the following:
   • A local authority, responding to public opinion, must first assess fluoridation itself. Then, it can apply to the Department of National Health and Population Development for approval.
   • Having received an application from a local authority, the Department may permit fluoridation under specified conditions, but it will not be compulsory.
4. The government neither promotes nor discourages other fluoride vehicles. Fluoride toothpastes and tablets are available for purchase.

Source: A letter from the Director-General, Department of National Health and Population Development, Private Bag X63, 0001 Pretoria, Republic of South Africa, dated 27 July 1987.

Sweden

Population, 8.4 million.

1. No drinking waters contain added fluoride.
2. In 1977, about 750,000 or 9 percent drank water naturally containing 0.8 ppm fluoride or more.
3. The Water Fluoridation Act of 1962 made it possible for municipalities to seek permission for local fluoridation. Of the nine towns and several rural districts that were granted permission, none had yet implemented fluoridation before

the Water Fluoridation Act was withdrawn in 1971. In 1977, a parliamentary committee, the Fluoride Commission, was appointed to consider the issue. The Fluoride Commission opposed legislation permitting fluoridation, on the grounds that tooth decay had declined due to other measures and further preventive effects could be obtained voluntarily. The Commission noted that many people consider fluoridation to be an encroachment on the individual's freedom of choice and noted that long-term environmental effects of fluoride are not well-enough understood. The Minister of Health in 1985 declared that the government did not intend to raise the issue of fluoridation again.

4. Fluoride toothpastes with fluoride concentrations of less than 0.15 percent are available without prescription and constitute more than 80 percent of the market. Fluoride mouth rinses require a prescription if they contain more than 0.025 percent sodium fluoride. Fluoride tablets, which contain 0.25 mg fluoride, can be obtained only with a dentist's prescription.

Sources: Statens Offentliga Utredningar, *Fluor i Karies-förebyggande Syfte.* Including English summary. Stockholm, 1981.

Sundberg, H. "The Legal Aspects Related to Caries Prevention in Sweden." Frank, R. M., and S. O'Hickey, eds. *Strategy for Dental Caries Prevention in European Countries According to their Laws and Regulations.* Oxford: IRL Press, 1987: 139–144.

Burt, Brian A., and Elof O. Petterson. "Fluoridation: Developments in Sweden." *British Dental Journal.* Vol. 133 (18 July 1972): 57–59.

Petterson, Elof O. "Attitudes Concerning Water Fluroidation Among Graduating Swedish Dentists." *Community Dentistry and Oral Epidemiology.* Vol. 7 (April 1979): 69–74.

Switzerland

Population, 6.5 million.

1. Only the people in Canton Basel-City (population about 200,000 or 3 percent) drink water with added fluoride.
2. There are only rare cases (2,000 to 3,000 people or 0.03 to 0.046 percent) where the drinking water naturally contains fluoride at 1 ppm or more.

3. Decisions about fluoridation are made by local authorities. There are two main reasons for decisions against water fluoridation in a number of cities: economic costs associated with fluoridating complex water supply systems; and the promise of salt fluoridation, in the light of the effectiveness of iodized salt.
4. Except in Canton Basel-City, table salt containing 0.025 percent fluoride is available for purchase. There is also unfluoridated table salt available. In 1982, fluoridated salt made up 72 percent of sales. Fluoride toothpastes (up to 0.15 percent) are available for purchase. Fluoride tablets (0.25 mg) and gels (1.0 to 1.3 percent) are sold only in pharmacies and drugstores.

Sources: A letter from: E. Tremp, Swiss Federal Office of Public Health, Bollwerk 27, 3001 Bern, Switzerland, dated 2 July 1987. *See also:*

Hefti, A. F. "The Experience of Water Fluoridation in Switzerland." *Experience on Water Fluoridation in Europe.* Copenhagen: World Health Organization Regional Office for Europe, 1987: 76–83.

Tremp, E. "Dental Caries Prevention, Laws and Regulations in Switzerland." Frank, R. M. and S. O'Hickey, eds. *Strategy for Dental Caries Prevention in European Countries According to Their Laws and Regulations.* Oxford: IRL Press, 1987: 173–179.

Thailand

Population, 48.85 million in 1982.

1. No drinking water contains added fluoride.
2. About 3.95 million or 8.1 percent either live in an area containing fluoride deposits according to the Department of Mineral Resources, or drink water naturally containing fluoride at an optimum level or greater from 0.70 to 3.01 ppm.
3. The government currently has no policy on fluoridation.
4. The government provides fluoride mouth rinses (0.2 percent sodium fluoride) for all primary schools. It also requires every registered brand of toothpaste to contain fluoride (0.11 percent or less), and it produces fluoride tablets. Dentists individually may provide fluoride tablets, syrup, and topical treatments.

Source: A letter from Tirdpong Jayanandana, Minister of Public Health, Devaves Palace, Bangkok, Thailand, dated 11 August 1987.

Turkey

Population, 51.8 million.

1. No drinking waters contain added fluoride.
2. Of 66 provinces, 15 contain at least some water supplies with fluoride at a level of 1 ppm or greater.
4. No foods contain added fluoride. The Ministry of Health encourages the use of fluoride toothpastes. Dental treatment centers and dental health programs give topical fluoride treatments.

Source: A letter from Yucel Ayasli, Counsellor, Turkish Embassy, 60 Mugga Way, Red Hill ACT 2603, Australia, dated 20 April 1987.

Union of Soviet Socialist Republics

Population, 275.6 million.

1. About 41.34 million or 15 percent drink water with added fluoride, according to World Health Organization figures. Independent testing of water samples in Leningrad and Moscow suggests that fluoridation may be less pervasive or reliable than these figures indicate.
3. The Council of Ministers of the USSR authorized fluoridation throughout the country in 1964. Local decisions are made by the Chief State Sanitary Inspectors of Soviet Republics, taking into account a number of specific factors. The two most important indicators of the need for fluoridation are a fluoride level of less than 0.5 ppm and a high level of tooth decay in children.

Sources:
Pakhomov, G. N. "The Experience of Water Fluoridation in USSR." *Experience on Water Fluoridation in Europe.* Copenhagen: World Health Organization Regional Office for Europe, 1987: 84–92.

Table 1 in Ibid: 5.

Abrams, Richard A. "Community Water Fluoridation in Leningrad and Moscow." *Community Dentistry and Oral Epidemiology.* Vol. 16, 1988: 129–130.

United Kingdom

Population, 56.5 million.

1. Approximately 5 million or 9 percent drink water with added fluoride.
2. Approximately half a million or 0.9 percent drink water which naturally contains fluoride near 1 ppm.
3. The government supports fluoridation, believing it to be safe and effective. Nevertheless, the government is also aware of public concern about fluoridation and, as a result, believes that decisions should be taken at a local level rather than nationally. The Water (Fluoridation) Act, which came into effect in 1985, requires local health authorities to undertake extensive public consultations prior to any decision to implement fluoridation.
4. The government supports the use of fluoride toothpastes and, in unfluoridated areas, fluoride tablets and gels. Fluoride in table salt is not supported.

Sources: A letter from M. Houghton, Department of Health and Social Security, Hannibal House, Elephant and Castle, London SE1 6TE, UK, dated 30 June 1987. *See also:*

Downer, M. C. "Dental Caries Prevention in the United Kingdom and its Statutory Basis. Frank, R. M. and S. O'Hickey, eds. *Strategy for Dental Caries Prevention in European Countries According to Their Laws and Regulations.* Oxford: IRL Press, 1987: 37–49.

James, P. M. C. "The Experience of Water Fluoridation in the United Kingdom." *Experience on Water Fluoridation in Europe.* Copenhagen: World Health Organization Regional Office for Europe, 1987: 93–101.

Royal College of Physicians. *Fluoride, Teeth and Health.* Tunbridge Wells, Kent: Pitman Medical, 1976.

United States

Population, 243 million in 1985.

1. Approximately 121 million or 50 percent drink water with added fluoride.
2. Approximately 9 million of the 212 million served by public water supplies drink water whose natural fluoride content is at optimal or higher levels.
3. The federal government actively promotes fluoridation, encouraging all communities to adopt it. Decisions are made by local governments. Some states have laws requiring local fluoridation.
4. Fluoride tablets are distributed through school programs and dental clinics. School water fluoridation is encouraged where community water supplies are not fluoridated. Fluoride toothpastes, mouthwashes, gels, and bottled water are widely available. Topical fluoride treatments by dentists are available at the dentist's discretion, and there are government-supported programs of topical treatments in schools.

Sources: *Fluoridation Census 1985.* Atlanta: U.S. Department of Health and Human Services, July 1988; and a letter from Edward Groth III, dated 3 January 1989. *See also:*

McClure, Frank J. *Water Fluoridation: The Search and the Victory.* Washington, D.C. U.S. Department of Health, Education, and Welfare, 1970.

McNeil, Donald R. *The Fight for Fluoridation.* New York: Oxford University Press, 1957.

Waldbott, George L. in collaboration with Albert W. Burgstahler, and H. Lewis McKinney. *Fluoridation: The Great Dilemma.* Lawrence, Kans.: Coronado Press, 1978.

Zimbabwe

Population, 9.0 million.

1. No drinking water contains added fluoride.
2. Projections indicate that perhaps 362,000 or 4.0 percent drink water with natural fluoride equal to or above the optimal level.
3. The government supports fluoridation. Local authorities have responsibility for implementation.
4. The government promotes several fluoride vehicles, aided by the dental association and fluoride toothpaste companies.

Source: A letter from W. Dandato Sithole, Chief Government Dental Officer, P.O. Box 8559, Causeway, Harare, Zimbabwe, dated 30 June 1987.

Miscellaneous

In addition to European countries which I have already listed, the World Health Organization, in *Experience on Water Fluoridation in Europe*, Copenhagen: World Health Organization Regional Office for Europe, 1987, gives the following figures on page 5 for the fraction of the population in Europe which is served by fluoridated drinking water. No sources are given for this data.

- Albania: Population 3.0 million, 0 percent.
- Bulgaria: Population 9.0 million, 0 percent.
- Hungary: Population 10.6 million, 0 percent.
- Italy: Population 57.3 million, 0 percent.
- Spain: Population 38.9 million, 0 percent.

Information Sought But Not Received

Letters were sent to health departments with a detailed address in the following countries, with no reply: Bulgaria, Burma, France, India, Indonesia, Italy, Japan, South Korea, Malaysia, Nigeria, Pakistan, Sri Lanka, USSR, United States, and Yugoslavia.

Letters were sent to the Australian embassies of the following countries, with no reply: Bangladesh, People's Republic of China, Cyprus, Egypt, Iraq, Jordon, Mexico, Peru, Spain, Uruguay, Vietnam, and Zambia. The embassies of Argentina, German Democratic Republic, and Kenya replied saying they had requested information from relevant authorities, but no information was received.

Letters were also sent to "The Department of Health" in the capital cities of the following countries, with no reply: Albania, Hungary, North Korea, and Uganda.

NOTES

CHAPTER 1

1. Bette Hileman, "Fluoridation of Water," *Chemical & Engineering News*, vol. 66, no. 31 (1 August 1988): 26–42.

2. Stated in each issue of *Chemical & Engineering News* is the disclaimer that the American Chemical Society "assumes no responsibility for the statements and opinions advanced by the contributors to its publications." Nevertheless, the views expressed are given considerable legitimacy by their very publication.

3. In a special issue of the *Journal of the American Dental Association* on fluoridation, the introduction likened antifluoridationists to those who opposed fire and the wheel, who believed the earth is flat, who opposed the automobile, who opposed anesthesia, and who opposed blood transfusions, vaccination, immunization, Pasteurization, and chlorination. "Fluoridation is Here to Stay," *Journal of the American Dental Association*, vol. 65, no. 5 (November 1962): 578–580.

4. Kai Hunstadbraten, "Fluoride in Caries Prophylaxis at the Turn of the Century," *Bulletin of the History of Dentistry*, vol. 30, no. 2 (October 1982): 117–120.

5. One part per million fluoride means one milligram of fluoride in each liter of water.

6. Michael Wollan, "Controlling the Potential Hazards of Government-Sponsored Technology," *George Washington Law Review*, vol. 36, no. 5 (July 1968): 1105–1137, at 1128.

7. This figure understates the extent of fluoridation of public water supplies, because many of the 50 percent who drink unfluoridated water do not use public water supplies but instead obtain water from wells and other sources. Furthermore, some waters are naturally fluoridated and do not count as having added fluoride.

8. The appendix contains information on the extent of fluoridation and government policies in a range of countries.

9. In referring to leading supporters or opponents of fluoridation who are scientists, I use the term scientists loosely to include doctors and dentists who are familiar with scientific research on fluoridation.

10. Notably, Donald R. McNeil, *The Fight for Fluoridation*, New York: Oxford University Press (1957).

11. My approach to the fluoridation controversy is elaborated and placed in context in chapter 8.

12. John Colquhoun, *Education and Fluoridation in New Zealand: An Historical Study*, Ph.D. thesis, University of Auckland (1987); Edward Groth III, *Two Issues of Science and Public Policy: Air Pollution Control in the San Francisco Bay Area and Fluoridation of Community Water Supplies*, Ph.D. dissertation, Stanford University (1973); Edward Groth III, "Science and the Fluoridation Controversy," *Chemistry*, vol. 49, no. 4 (May 1976): 5–9; Allan Mazur, *The Dynamics of Technical Controversy*, Washington, D.C.: Communications Press (1981); Wendy Varney, *Fluoride in Australia: A Case to Answer*, Sydney: Hale and Iremonger (1986); and Wollan, op. cit. Some of the explicitly antifluoridation literature is also valuable here, notably George L. Waldbott in collaboration with Albert W. Burgstahler and H. Lewis McKinney, *Fluoridation: The Great Dilemma*, Lawrence, Kans.: Coronado Press (1978).

13. Chapter 8 was written after Groth's commentary was completed, hence my remarks in chapter 8 on his contribution. Groth gave me comments on a draft of chapter 8, but preferred to leave his own essay unaltered.

CHAPTER 2

1. John J. Murray and Andrew J. Rugg-Gunn, *Fluorides in Caries Prevention*, Bristol: Wright PSG, second edition (1982): 16.

2. Ibid., 67.

3. Ernest Newbrun, "Water Fluoridation and Dietary Fluoride," in Ernest Newbrun (ed.), *Fluorides and Dental Caries*, Springfield, Ill.: Charles C. Thomas (Third edition, 1986): 3–32, at 14.

4. Wesley O. Young, David F. Striffler, and Brian A. Burt, "The Prevention and Control of Dental Caries: Fluoridation," in David F. Striffler, Wesley O. Young, and Brian A. Burt, *Dentistry, Dental Prac-*

tice, and the Community, Philadelphia: W. B. Saunders (Third edition, 1983): 155–200, at 179.

5. Alan M. Slutsky, Sheldon Rovin, and Norma A. Kaplis, "Fluoridation: 100 Questions and Answers," Stephen Barrett and Sheldon Rovin, eds., *The Tooth Robbers: A Pro-Fluoridation Handbook*, Phildelphia: George F. Stickley (1980): 44–65, at 48.

6. Philip R. N. Sutton, *Fluoridation: Errors and Omissions in Experimental Trials*, Melbourne: Melbourne University Press (Second edition, 1960): 5.

7. Ibid., "Part Three: Criticisms and Comments," 73–129, including reviews by Donald Galagan, by J. R. Blayney and I. N. Hill, by R. M. Grainger (all from the *Australian Dental Journal*, February 1960), and by J. Ferris Fuller (from the *New Zealand Dental Journal*, January 1960), with replies from Sutton. *See also* James M. Dunning, "Biased Criticism of Fluoridation," *Nutrition Reviews*, vol. 18, no. 6 (June 1960): 161–165.

8. Sutton, op. cit. (note 6), 45.

9. Ibid., 97.

10. Ibid., 106.

11. Ibid., 75 (emphasis in the original).

12. Ibid., 1.

13. Ibid., 77–78.

14. Sutton's book is not cited by: P. Adler, "Fluorides and Dental Health," in *Fluorides and Human Health*, Geneva: World Health Organization (1970):323–354; Murray and Rugg-Gunn, op. cit. (note 1); Newbrun, op. cit. (note 3); Royal College of Physicians of London, *Fluoride, Teeth and Health*, Tunbridge Wells, Kent: Pitman Medical (1976); Young et al., op. cit. (note 4).

James Morse Dunning, *Principles of Dental Public Health*, Cambridge, Mass.: Harvard University Press (1962), appears not to give any reference to Sutton although he had reviewed Sutton's book not long before (Dunning, 1960, op. cit. (note 7)).

A partial exception is Frank J. McClure, *Water Fluoridation: The Search and the Victory*, Bethesda, Md.: U.S. Department of Health, Education, and Welfare; National Institutes of Health; National Institute of Dental Research (1970): 288, who lists Sutton's monograph in a list of fluoridation literature but does not discuss it in the text.

15. Mark Diesendorf, "The Mystery of Declining Tooth Decay," *Nature*, vol. 322, (10 July 1986): 125–129; Mark Diesendorf, "A Re-

examination of Australian Fluoridation Trials," *Search*, vol. 17, nos. 10–12, (October–December 1986): 256–262.

16. John Colquhoun, "Influence of Social Class and Fluoridation on Child Dental Health," *Community Dentistry and Oral Epidemiology*, vol. 13 (1985): 37–41; J. Colquhoun, "Fluoridation in New Zealand: New Evidence," *American Laboratory*, vol. 17, no. 5, (May 1985): 66–72, and vol. 17, no. 6 (June 1985): 98–109; John Colquhoun and Robert Mann, "The Hastings Fluoridation Experiment: Science or Swindle?," *Ecologist*, vol. 16, no. 6 (1986): 243–248, and letter (postscript), vol. 17, no. 2/3 (1987): 125–126; John Colquhoun, "Child Dental Health Differences in New Zealand," *Community Health Studies*, vol. 11, no. 2 (1987): 85–90; John Colquhoun, "Decline in Primary Tooth Decay in New Zealand," *Community Health Studies*, vol. 12, no. 2 (1988): 187-191. Colquhoun's work includes comparison of dental decay in fluoridated and nonfluoridated areas as well as a critique of earlier studies.

17. F. B. Exner and G. L. Waldbott (James Rorty, ed.), *The American Fluoridation Experiment*, New York: Devin-Adair (1957): 113–116.

18. R. Ziegelbecker, "Fluoridated Water and Teeth," *Fluoride*, vol. 14, no. 3 (July 1981): 123–128.

19. H. Busse, E. Bergmann, and K. Bergmann, "Fluoride and Dental Caries: Two Different Statistical Approaches to the Same Data Source," *Statistics in Medicine*, vol. 6 (1987): 823–842.

20. I thank Mark Diesendorf for this point.

21. Alfred Aslander, "The Theory of Complete Tooth Nutrition as a Natural and Effective Dental Caries Prophylaxis," *Journal of Applied Nutrition*, vol. 17 (1964): 190–204. I thank Albert Burgstahler for bringing this point to my attention. A survey of the effect of minerals on tooth decay is given by M. E. J. Curzon and T. W. Cutress (eds.), *Trace Elements and Dental Disease*, Boston: Wright/PSG (1983).

22. A less colloquial phrasing is the following from J. J. Murray (ed.) *Appropriate Use of Fluorides for Human Health*, Geneva: World Health Organization (1986): 116. "The two other principal means of preventing dental caries [besides fluoride] are dietary control and oral hygiene. However, the role and applicability of these two measures in public health are connected with complex behavioural and cultural problems. For this reason, they are not conducive to a rapid improvement in dental health."

23. Exner and Waldbott, op. cit.

24. Key accounts of a general nature include Albert W. Burgstahler, "Dental and Medical Aspects of Fluoridated Drinking

Water," *Transactions of the Kansas Academy of Science,* vol. 68, no. 2, (1965): 223–243, and "Corrigenda and Addenda," vol. 68, no. 3 (1965): 418; Exner and Waldbott, op. cit.; George L. Waldbott in collaboration with Albert W. Burgstahler and H. Lewis McKinney, *Fluoridation: The Great Dilemma,* Lawrence, Kans.: Coronado Press (1978); John Yiamouyiannis, *Fluoride: The Aging Factor,* Delaware, Ohio: Health Action Press (Second edition, 1986).

25. Murray and Rugg-Gunn, op. cit., chapter 13; Waldbott et al., op. cit., chapter 7.

26. National Health and Medical Research Council, *Report of the Working Party on Fluorides in the Control of Dental Caries,* Canberra: Australian Government Publishing Service (1985): 4. For a similar statement, *see* Royal College of Physicians of London, op. cit., 38.

27. Waldbott et al., chapter 8.

28. Newbrun, op. cit., 15. As noted by some critics, there *were* significant differences between the Newburgh and Kingston children on some tests; these have been ignored by proponents such as Newbrun.

29. Murray and Rugg-Gunn, op. cit., 241.

30. Waldbott et al., op. cit., and many references therein, dating from the 1950s.

31. For scientifically sensitive counters to Waldbott's work (and to other scientific claims of hazards from fluoridation), *see* Safe Drinking Water Committee, Advisory Center on Toxicology, Assembly of Life Sciences, National Research Council, *Drinking Water and Health,* Washington, D.C.: National Academy of Sciences (1977): 369–400; Donald R. Taves, "Claims of Harm from Fluoridation," in Erling Johansen, Donald R. Taves, and Thor O. Olsen (eds.), *Continuing Evaluation of the Use of Fluorides,* Boulder, Colo.: Westview Press (1979): 295–321.

32. Harold C. Hodge, "Evaluation of some Objections to Water Fluoridation," in Newbrun, op. cit., 221–255, at 239. For a similarly brief dismissal of Waldbott's work, *see* Dunning (1962) op. cit., 347. The report of the Royal College of Physicians of London, op. cit., 62–64, gives more detail on Waldbott's work, but ends by dismissing it with reference to the same American Academy of Allergy statement.

33. Murray and Rugg-Gunn, op. cit.

34. For example, Ernest Newbrun, "The Safety of Water Fluoridation," *Journal of the American Dental Association,* vol. 94, no. 2 (February 1977): 301–304; Frank A. Smith, "Safety of Water Fluorida-

tion," *Journal of the American Dental Association*, vol. 65, no. 5 (November 1962): 598–602; and Young et al., op. cit.

35. For example, Royal College of Physicians of London, op. cit. Hodge, op. cit., 239, by contrast, says "Such anecdotal reports by others have also been presented."

36. Walbott's reluctance here may have been due to his bad experience with Hornung, described in chapter 4.

37. G. W. Grimbergen, "A Double Blind Test for Determination of Intolerance to Fluoridated Water," *Fluoride*, vol. 7, no. 3 (July 1974): 146–152.

See also Reuben Feltman and George Kosel, "Prenatal and Postnatal Ingestion of Fluorides—Fourteen Years of Investigation—Final Report," *Journal of Dental Medicine*, vol. 16, no. 4 (October 1961): 190–198; H. T. Petraborg, "Chronic Fluoride Intoxication from Drinking Water," *Fluoride*, vol. 7, no. 1 (January 1974): 47–52; H. T. Petraborg, "Hydrofluorosis in the Fluoridated Milwaukee Area," *Fluoride*, vol. 10, no. 4 (October 1977): 165–169.

See also Lois I. Juncos and James V. Donadio, Jr., "Renal Failure and Fluorosis," *Journal of the American Medical Association*, vol. 222, no. 7 (13 November 1972): 783–785; John Lee, "Gilbert's Disease and Fluoride Intake," *Fluoride*, vol. 16, no. 3 (July 1983): 139–145.

38. One exception is Taves, op. cit.

39. Evelleen Richards, "The Politics of Therapeutic Evaluation: The Vitamin C and Cancer Controversy," *Social Studies of Science*, vol. 18 (1988): 653–701.

40. For a full account and further references, see Yiamouyiannis, op. cit. See also J. B. Bundock, D. Burk, J. R. Graham, and P. J. Morin, "Fluorides, Water Fluoridation, Cancer and Genetic Diseases," *Science and Public Policy*, vol. 12, no. 1 (February 1985): 36–46.

41. Richard Doll and Leo Kinlen, "Fluoridation of Water and Cancer Mortality in the U.S.A.," *Lancet* (18 June 1977): 1300–1302; J. David Erickson, "Mortality in Selected Cities with Fluoridated and Non-Fluoridated Water Supplies," *New England Journal of Medicine*, vol. 298 (18 May 1978): 1112–1116; Robert N. Hoover, Frank W. McKay, and Joseph F. Fraumeni, Jr., "Fluoridated Drinking Water and the Occurrence of Cancer," *Journal of the National Cancer Institute*, vol. 57, no. 4 (October 1976): 757–768; Leo Kinlen and Richard Doll, "Fluoridation of Water Supplies and Cancer Mortality. III: A Re-Examination of Mortality in Cities in the USA," *Journal of Epidemiology and Community Health*, vol. 35 (1981): 239–244; P. D. Oldham and D. J. Newell, "Fluoridation of Water Supplies and Cancer—A Possible Association?"

Applied Statistics, vol. 26, no. 2 (1977): 125–135, and letter, vol. 28, no. 2 (1979): 184; Eugene Rogot, A. Richey Sharrett, Manning Feinleib, and Richard R. Fabsitz, "Trends in Urban Mortality in Relation to Fluoridation Status," *American Journal of Epidemiology*, vol. 107, no. 2 (1978): 104–112.

42. Mark Diesendorf, "International Symposium on Fluoridation," *Social Science and Medicine*, vol. 27, no. 9, (1988): 1003–1005.

43. "Water throughout history has been perceived as the stuff which radiates purity." Ivan Illich, *H₂O and the Waters of Forgetfulness*, London: Marion Boyars (1986): 75–76. Illich deals with the complex cultural role of water.

44. Dunning (1962) op. cit., 372.

45. A concise exposition of this view is given by Lee A. Krimmer in a letter, *Journal of the American Dental Association*, vol. 88, no. 6 (June 1974): 1241–1242. "For millions of years, man's water supply was that of running streams, lakes, rivers, wells, and cisterns. All of these forms were soil leaching, enriched with the minerals from the soil they contacted. As cities grew, man established the reservoir water supply. Reservoirs are essentially rain water collected from short runoffs and devoid of minerals. . . . God put fluoride into the water and man inadvertently took it out."

46. For example, P. Jean Frazier, "Priorities to Preserve Fluoride Uses; Rationales and Strategies," *Journal of Public Health Dentistry*, vol. 45, no. 3 (Summer 1985): 149–165, at 162–163; Ruth Roemer, "Water Fluoridation: Public Health Responsibility and the Democratic Process," *American Journal of Public Health and the Nation's Health*, vol. 55, no. 7 (July 1965): 1337–1348, at 1344–1346.

47. The uses of rhetorical devices in technical arguments on fluoridation and nuclear power are discerningly treated by Allan Mazur, "Disputes Between Experts," *Minerva*, vol. 11, no. 2 (April 1973): 243–262, reproduced in Allan Mazur, *The Dynamics of Technical Controversy*, Washington, D.C.: Communications Press (1981).

CHAPTER 3

Most of the material in this chapter is adapted from Brian Martin, "Coherency of Viewpoints Among Fluoridation Partisans," *Metascience*, vol. 6, no. 1 (1988): 2–19.

1. Commonwealth Department of Health, *Fluoridation of Water*, Canberra: Australian Government Publishing Service (1985): 34–41.

2. An excellent account of the politics of fluoridation in Victoria is given by Brian W. Head in "The Fluoridation Controversy in Victoria: Public Policy and Group Politics," *Australian Journal of Public Administration*, vol. 37, no. 3 (September 1978): 257–273. For other states, there are no equivalent accounts although Wendy Varney provides considerable documentation, especially for New South Wales, in *Fluoride in Australia: A Case to Answer*, Sydney: Hale and Iremonger (1986).

Carr described the introduction of fluoridation in Canberra as a process in which the four relevant Commonwealth ministers—Health, Australian Capital Territory, Works, and Attorney-General who are elected parliamentarians with briefs similar to American members of the cabinet—each took advice from their departments which, in turn, consulted their experts. After discussion in cabinet, the government took a decision.

Traynor described the Canberra decision in this way: Traynor was the dentist who treated Harold Holt, the federal Treasurer. The federal president of the Australian Dental Association suggested to Traynor that he raise the question of fluoridation for Canberra with Holt. Via Holt, a visit was arranged between the Minister of Health and Traynor along with Peter Lazar, director of the Dental Health Education and Research Foundation. Later, Lazar and Traynor met with Prime Minister Robert Menzies, who was favorable. (Earlier, they had approached the opposition Australian Labor Party's spokesperson on health, who was also agreeable.) Shortly afterward, Menzies put the motion for fluoridation in parliament.

A somewhat different sequence is given by James Killen in *Killen: Inside Australian Politics*, Sydney: Methuen Haynes, (1985): 89–90. *See also* Penelope Layland, "What Happened in 1964 . . ." *Canberra Times*, (29 September 1989): 9.

3. *See*, for example, Geoffrey E. Smith, "Is Fluoride a Mutagen?" *Science of the Total Environment*, vol. 68 (1988): 79–96, at 79. "The success of water fluoridation in combating tooth decay would appear to be well-established." Since my interview with him, Smith seems to have reevaluated his position on the benefits of fluoridation in the light of recently published critiques. *See* Geoffrey E. Smith, "Is Fluoridation a Fraud?" *Science of the Total Environment*, vol. 76 (1988): 167–184.

4. H. M. Collins and T. J. Pinch, "The Construction of the Paranormal: Nothing Unscientific Is Happening," Roy Wallis (ed.), *On the Margins of Science: The Social Construction of Rejected Knowledge*, Keele: University of Keele (1979): 237–269; G. Nigel Gilbert and Michael Mulkay, "Warranting Scientific Belief," *Social Studies of Science*, vol. 12 (1982): 383–408; Michael Mulkay and G. Nigel Gilbert, "Accounting for Error: How Scientists Construct Their Social World When They Account for Correct and Incorrect Belief," *Sociology*, vol. 16 (1982): 165–183.

5. A proponent whom I didn't interview told me he had heard it said that Amies was more likely to obtain ego gratification from opposing fluoridation than from scientific work, at which he was mediocre.

6. This account is presented in "Fluoridation: The Cancer Scare," *Consumer Reports*, vol. 43, no. 7 (July 1978): 392–396.

7. Patricia Speller, *Regional Progress*, Melbourne (15 October 1986): 8.

8. E. Storey, letter, *The Age*, Melbourne (27 September 1986): 12.

9. Malcolm Peter Crisp, *Report of the Royal Commissioner into the Fluoridation of Public Water Supplies*, Hobart: Government Printer (1968).

10. D. M. Myers, V. D. Plueckhahn, and A. L. G. Rees, *Report of the Committee of Inquiry into the Fluoridation of Victorian Water Supplies*, Melbourne: Government Printer (1980).

11. Smith, whose comments concerned the role of scientists, is a possible exception.

12. Concerning the Tasmanian and Victorian inquiries, Varney, op. cit., 23, states along this line that "Judging from the circumstances and conduct of both of these inquiries, it is doubtful that their chief purpose was to probe into, and weigh up, the conflicting evidence. Rather they were to convey an image of neutrality and open-mindedness on the part of the respective governments and so to allay public fears by supposedly having thoroughly investigated the matter prior to government's final decision."

13. Leon Festinger, *A Theory of Cognitive Dissonance*, Stanford: Stanford University Press (1957).

14. The polarization that results from the intense controversies over nuclear power and fluoridation is raised by Allan Mazur, "Disputes Between Experts," *Minerva*, vol. 11, no. 2, (April 1973): 243–262, at 258–260, reproduced in Allan Mazur, *The Dynamics of Technical Controversy*, Washington, D.C.: Communications Press (1981).

15. Books which give a good feel for fluoridation campaigning are from the proponents' perspective, Paul Castle, *The Politics of Fluoridation: The Campaign for Fluoridation in the West Midlands of England*, London: John Libbey (1987); and from the opponents' perspective, Hans Moolenburgh, *Fluoride: The Freedom Fight*, Edinburgh: Mainstream (1987).

16. Varney, op. cit., points out that the proponents in Australia are backed by the dental and medical professions, the federal and most state governments, and several major industries. But, from the point of

view of profluoridation partisans, this does not translate into volunteers to carry out the day-to-day "legwork" on the issue.

17. The argument here is compatible with standard ideas in social psychology. *See*, for example, George Cvetkovich, Steve R. Baumgardner, and Joseph E. Trimble, *Social Psychology*, New York: Holt, Rinehart and Winston (1984): 176–209; and Kenneth J. Gergen and Mary M. Gergen, *Social Psychology*, New York: Springer Verlag (Second edition, 1986): 158–191. Attitudes which are based on direct experience (such as attending meetings, speaking, or writing letters in the fluoridation debate) are more likely to be salient and central to attitude structures, and more likely to cause a reduction in dissonance with related but peripheral attitudes.

18. Edward Groth III, "The Fluoridation Controversy: Some Implications for Science and Public Policy," unpublished seminar paper presented to the Dental Public Health Program, School of Public Health, University of Michigan (28 March 1980): 65. *See also* his sections on personalities (57–58) and lack of a clientele for a middle-of-the-road position (65–66).

19. To my knowledge, Geoffrey Smith is the only one of those interviewed who has been criticized by both proponents and opponents.

20. John Colquhoun has developed this perspective in "Professional Education and the Fluoridation Paradigm," *New Zealand Journal of Educational Studies*, vol. 24, no. 2 (1989): 159–173.

21. Thomas S. Kuhn, *The Structure of Scientific Revolutions*, Chicago: University of Chicago Press (Second edition, 1970).

CHAPTER 4

1. Donald R. McNeil, *The Fight for Fluoridation*, New York: Oxford University Press (1957): 65.

2. Ibid., 61–62.

3. Frank J. McClure, *Water Fluoridation: The Search and the Victory*, Bethesda, Md: U.S. Department of Health, Education, and Welfare; National Institutes of Health; National Institute of Dental Research (1970): 249.

4. Ibid., 249–255.

5. Edward Groth III, *Two Issues of Science and Public Policy: Air Pollution Control in the San Francisco Bay Area and Fluoridation of Community Water Supplies*, Ph.D. dissertation, Stanford University (1973): 162.

6. F. B. Exner and G. L. Waldbott (James Rorty, ed.), *The American Fluoridation Experiment*, New York: Devin-Adair (1957):179–181.

7. George L. Waldbott, in collaboration with Albert W. Burgstahler and H. Lewis McKinney, *Fluoridation: The Great Dilemma*, Lawrence, Kans.: Coronado Press (1978): 285.

8. Brian A. Burt and Elof O. Petterson, "Fluoridation: Developments in Sweden," *British Dental Journal*, vol. 133 (18 July 1972): 57–59.

9. Conrad A. Naleway, letter, *Chemical and Engineering News*, vol. 66, no. 41 (10 October 1988): 2–3.

10. "Six Ways to Mislead the Public," *Consumer Reports*, vol. 43, no. 8 (August 1978): 480–482, at 482.

11. Charles Eliot Perkins, *The Truth About Water Fluoridation*, Washington, D.C.: Fluoridation Educational Society (1952): 7.

12. Peter Cooper, letter, *Canberra Times* (30 August 1979): 2; Peter Cooper, "Fluoride and Cancer: No Link and a Non-issue," *Canberra Times* (30 August 1979): 18; Peter Cooper, letter, *Canberra Times* (11 March 1980): 12.

13. Mark Diesendorf, letter, *ANU Reporter*, vol. 11, no. 2 (21 March 1980): 4; Mark Diesendorf, letter, *Canberra Times* (10 April 1980): 19; Peter Cooper, *ANU Reporter*, vol. 11, no. 3 (11 April 1980): 4.

14. Robert Isman, "Fluoridation: Strategies for Success," *American Journal of Public Health*, vol. 71, no. 7 (July 1981): 717–721, at 721.

15. Ernest Newbrun, "The Public's Oral Health and the Dental Research Community—Participant or Observer?" *Journal of Public Health Dentistry*, vol. 45, no. 4 (Fall 1985): 208–212, at 210.

16. Michael W. Easley, "The New Antifluoridationists: Who Are They and How Do They Operate?" *Journal of Public Health Dentistry*, vol. 45, no. 3 (summer 1985): 133–141, at 138.

17. Ibid., 140. This view has much support among proponents. *See*, for example, Donald R. McNeil, "Time to Walk Boldly," *Journal of the American Dental Association*, vol. 63, no. 3 (September 1961): 333–343.

18. For other examples or recommendations of a refusal to debate, see Eric M. Bishop, "Publicity During a Fluoridation Campaign," *Journal of the American Dental Association*, vol. 65, no. 5 (November 1962): 663–667, at 666; John Colquhoun, *Education and Fluoridation in New Zealand: An Historical Study*, Ph.D. thesis, University of Auckland

(1987): 245–246; Groth, op. cit., 182–183; Harry M. Raulet, "The Health Professional and the Fluoridation Issue: A Case of Role Conflict," *Journal of Social Issues*, vol. 17, no. 4 (1961): 45–54, at 49–51; Wendy Varney, *Fluoride in Australia: A Case to Answer*, Sydney: Hale and Iremonger (1986): 88–89; Michael Wollan, "Controlling the Potential Hazards of Government-Sponsored Technology," *George Washington Law Review*, vol. 36, no. 5 (July 1968): 1105–1137, at 1133.

19. Newbrun, op. cit., 211.

20. Raulet, op. cit. Donald R. McNeil, in *Fluoridation: For Your Community and Your State*, American Dental Association (1969): 16, describes the problem from the point of view of proponents. "As for debates, the question of whether to debate a scientifically proven measure such as fluoridation has plagued citizens' committees for years. Experience has shown that only if proper ground rules are established should a citizens' committee agree to debate. Too many debates degenerate into wide-open affairs surrounded by a carnival atmosphere, with intelligent reason falling by the wayside."

21. F. A. Bull, "Promotion and Application of Water Fluoridation," *Proceedings of the Fourth Annual Conference of State Dental Directors with the Public Health Service and the Children's Bureau*, Washington, D.C., (6–8 June 1951): 9–23 (as distributed by Robert J. H. Mick, 915 Stone Road, Laurel Springs N.J. 08021). For Bull's views in a form prepared for distribution, *see* F. A. Bull, "A Public Health Dentist's Viewpoint," *Journal of the American Dental Association*, vol. 44, no. 2, (February 1952): 147–151.

22. For example, Exner and Waldbott, op. cit., 148–149, 177–178. For a proponent's assessment, *see* McNeil (1961) op. cit.

23. Bull, op. cit., 11.

24. Waldbott et al., op. cit., 264–265. Waldbott is wrong on this last statement, according to Brian Burt, who says the experience of dental researchers is that very mildly mottled teeth do not get worse over time.

25. Bull, op. cit., 10.

26. Ibid., 11.

27. Ibid., 12.

28. Ibid.

29. Ibid., 17.

30. Annabelle Bender Motz, "The Fluoridation Issue as Studied by Social Scientists," N. David Richards and Lois K. Cohen (eds.), *Social Sciences and Dentistry: A Critical Bibliography*, The Hague: A. Sijthoff (1971): 347–364, at 357–359.

31. Ibid., 358.

32. Perkins, op. cit., 45.

33. Exner and Waldbott, op. cit., 126.

34. Ibid., 118.

35. Ibid., 119.

36. Gladys Caldwell and Philip E. Zanfagna, *Fluoridation and Truth Decay*, Reseda, Calif.: Top-Ecol Press (1974): 258.

37. Ibid., 3.

38. Glen S. R. Walker, *Fluoridation: Poison on Tap*, Melbourne: Glen Walker, G.P.O. Box 935G, Melbourne, Victoria 3001, Australia (1982): 323.

39. Robert J. H. Mick, "Slavery—20th Century," typescript, 915 Stone Road, Laurel Springs, N.J. 08021. Mick's views are reported, for example, in "Fluoridation Called 'Criminal Conspiracy,'" *Morning Star*, Allentown, Pa. (12 April 1988).

40. Sheldon Rovin, "Reaction Paper," *Journal of Public Health Dentistry*, vol. 45, no. 3 (Summer 1985): 146–148, at 146.

41. Ibid.

42. A few proponents, such as Donald R. Taves, have treated the opponents' arguments more seriously. See Edward Groth III's comments on reviews of the scientific literature in his commentary in this book.

43. I thank Edward Groth III for useful comments on this point.

44. Russell B. Scobie, "Water Fluoridation: A Survey of the International Picture," *Alabama Journal of Medical Science*, vol. 12, no. 3 (1975): 225–229, at 225.

45. McNeil, 1969, op. cit., 14.

46. H. S. Horowitz, "Established Methods of Prevention," *British Dental Journal*, vol. 149 (2 December 1980): 311–318, at 312.

47. Ronald J. Hunt, "Community Characteristics, Opinion Leadership, and Fluoridation Outcome in Small Iowa Communities," *Journal of Public Health Dentistry*, vol. 43, no. 2 (spring 1983): 152–160, at 154.

48. J. J. Murray (ed.), *Appropriate Use of Fluorides for Human Health*, Geneva: World Health Organization (1986): v.

49. Kenneth R. Elwell and Kenneth A. Easlick, *Classification and Appraisal of Objections to Fluoridation*, Ann Arbor, Mich.: University of Michigan (n.d. [1960]): 1, 9. Their response to Waldbott relies heavily on the Hornung episode, described later in this chapter.

50. Groth, op. cit., 331–332.

51. For example: "Fluoridation—As Evidence of its Safety Mounts, the Position of the Antifluoridationist Declines," *Journal of the American Dental Association*, vol. 49, no. 3 (September 1954): 364–365; Bureau of Public Information, "Cabinet Official Challenges Fluoridation Opponents," *Journal of the American Dental Association*, vol. 58, no. 4 (April 1959): 129–131; "Secretary Flemming of Health, Education, and Welfare Urges Speed-up of Fluoridation," *Journal of the American Dental Association*, vol. 60, no. 2 (February 1960): 230–231; "More Supporting Evidence for Fluoridation," *Journal of the American Dental Association*, vol. 61, no. 1 (July 1960): 84–85; "Dentistry: Foremost Champion of Fluoridation," *Journal of the American Dental Association*, vol. 65, no. 5 (November 1962): 716–717; Stephen Barrett, "Fluoridation: Poison-Mongers Delaying Health for Millions?" *Journal of the American Dental Association*, vol. 93, no. 5 (November 1976): 880; [Daniel McCann,] "Fluoride and Oral Health: A Story of Achievements and Challenges," *Journal of the American Dental Association*, vol. 118, no. 5 (May 1989): 529–540.

52. Mark Diesendorf, "The Mystery of Declining Tooth Decay," *Nature*, vol. 322 (10 July 1986): 125–129.

53. Craig's critique is mentioned in Mark Diesendorf, letter, *Chemical & Engineering News*, vol. 67, no. 5 (30 January 1989): 2–3.

54. Graham G. Craig, unpublished letter to the editor of *Nature*, dated 15 August 1986.

55. J. J. Murray and Andrew Rugg-Gunn, "Fluoridation and Declining Decay: A Reply to Diesendorf," British Fluoridation Society, 63 Wimpole Street, London W1M 8AL (December 1987).

56. J. Colquhoun, "Fluoridation in New Zealand: New Evidence," *American Laboratory*, vol. 17, no. 5 (May 1985): 66–72; and vol. 17, no. 6 (June 1985): 98–109.

57. Frederick J. Scott, Jr., "Fluoridation Won't Rest in Peace or Turmoil," *American Laboratory* (September 1986): 8, 10.

58. John Colquhoun and Robert Mann, "The Hastings Fluoridation Experiment: Science or Swindle?" *The Ecologist*, vol. 16, no. 6 (1986): 243–248 and letter (postscript), *The Ecologist*, vol. 17, no. 2/3 (1987): 125–126.

59. John Colquhoun and Robert Mann, "Hastings Fluoridation: Reply to Health Department" (February 1988).

60. Groth, op. cit., 295.

61. Edward Groth III, letter to Brian Martin, dated 8 December 1988.

62. See the next chapter. One dental journal which has published a number of antifluoridation articles is the *Pakistan Dental Review*, hardly a prestigious publication.

63. David B. Ast, comment, in *Proceedings of the Fourth Annual Conference of State Dental Directors with the Public Health Service and the Children's Bureau*, Washington, D.C. (6–8 June 1951): 27 (as distributed by Robert J. H. Mick, 915 Stone Road, Laurel Springs, N.J. 08021).

64. See chapter 2, note 41.

65. Brian A. Burt and Eugenio D. Beltran, "Water Fluoridation: A Response to Critics in Australia and New Zealand," *Journal of Public Health Dentistry*, vol. 48, no. 4 (Fall 1988): 214–219. *See also* the letters in reply by Colquhoun and Diesendorf and the further response by Burt and Beltran in *Journal of Public Health Dentistry*, vol. 49, no. 3 (summer 1989): 131–137.

66. R. Harvey Brown, "Fluoride and the Prevention of Dental Caries. Part I: The Role of Fluoride in the Decline of Caries," *New Zealand Dental Journal*, vol. 84 (October 1988): 103–108. *See also* the letters in reply by Colquhoun, Mann, and Diesendorf, *New Zealand Dental Journal*, vol. 85 (April 1989): 63–65.

67. One curious consequence of this is that the published responses may make use of the unpublished critiques, as in Burt and Beltran's (op. cit., 214) use of Graham Craig's unpublished critique of Diesendorf's *Nature* paper.

68. Geoffrey E. Smith, "Toxicity of Fluoride-Containing Dental Preparations: A Review," *Science of the Total Environment*, vol. 43 (1985): 41–61; "A Surfeit of Fluoride?" *Science Progress, Oxford*, vol. 69 (1985): 429–442; "Fluoride and Bone: An Unusual Hypothesis," *Xenobiotica*, vol. 15, no. 3 (1985): 177–186; Geoffrey E. Smith, "Fluoride, the Environment, and Human Health," *Perspectives in Biology and Medicine*, vol. 29, no. 4, (summer 1986): 560–572; "Can a

Vaccine Prevent Cavities?" *Trends in Pharmacological Sciences*, vol. 7, no. 3 (March 1986): 108–112; "Fluoride and Fluoridation," *Social Science and Medicine*, vol. 26, no. 4, (1988): 451–462; "Is Fluoride a Mutagen?" *Science of the Total Environment*, vol. 68 (1988): 79–96; and "Tooth Decay in the Developing World: Could a Vaccine Help Prevent Cavities?" *Perspectives in Biology and Medicine*, vol. 31, no. 3 (spring 1988): 440–453.

69. Deborah Smith, "Scandal in Academe," *National Times*, Sydney (25–31 October 1985): 3–4, 26–27.

70. Ian I. Mitroff, *The Subjective Side of Science: A Philosophical Inquiry into the Psychology of the Apollo Moon Scientists*, Amsterdam: Elsevier (1974).

71. Groth (1973), op. cit.: 172–177, gives examples on both sides.

72. Donald Galagan, in Philip R. N. Sutton, *Fluoridation: Errors and Omissions in Experimental Trials*, Melbourne: Melbourne University Press, (Second edition, 1960): 74–76.

73. McNeil (1957), op. cit.: 50.

74. "Reprints of Articles on Antifluoridationists Ready," *Journal of the American Dental Association*, vol. 49, no. 4 (October 1954): 482–483; "Expand Material on Antifluoridationists," *Journal of the American Dental Association*, vol. 51, no. 1 (July 1955): 97. Material on opponents similar to that found in the dossier appeared in editorials in the *Journal of the American Dental Association* even earlier. For example, "Verdict on Seattle: Referendum on Fluoridation," *Journal of the American Dental Association*, vol. 44, no. 4 (April 1952): 457–459, gives damaging information on Royal L. Lee; and "Ten Cent Arguments Against Fluoridation," *Journal of the American Dental Association*, vol. 44, no. 5 (May 1952): 563–564, attacks W. D. Herrstrom.

75. Bureau of Public Information, American Dental Association, "Comments on Opponents of Fluoridation," *Journal of the American Dental Association*, vol. 65, no. 5 (November 1962): 694–710, at 694; and vol. 71, no. 5 (November 1965): 1155–1183, at 1155.

76. Ibid., 701, 1172.

77. Ibid., 1171.

78. Ibid., 708–709 and 1180–1181.

79. Ibid., 709, 1181.

80. Ibid., 710, 1182.

81. Ibid.

82. Ibid., 710, 1182 (emphasis in the original). Walbott responded to an earlier, unpublished version of the dossier in George L. Waldbott, letter, *Journal of the American Dental Association*, vol. 55, no. 6 (December 1957): 873.

83. G. L. Waldbott, *A Struggle with Titans*, New York: Carlton Press (1965): 66.

84. McClure, op. cit., 264.

85. Ibid.

86. Ibid., 265; the original is Heinrich Hornung, "Fluoridation: Observations of a German Professor and Public Health Officer," *Journal of the American Dental Association*, vol. 53, no. 3 (September 1956): 325–326, at 326.

87. Waldbott (1965), op. cit.: 229.

88. Hornung, op. cit., 325; Waldbott (1965), op. cit., 230.

89. Waldbott (1965), op. cit.: 231.

90. Ibid., 232.

91. Ibid.

92. McClure, op. cit., 265.

93. Ibid.

94. *See also* Groth (1973), op. cit., 310–321, for an account of the treatment of Waldbott.

95. "Fluoridation: The Cancer Scare," *Consumer Reports*, vol. 43, no. 7 (July 1978): 392–396.

96. For the perspective of a leading Dutch antifluoridationist on this episode, see Hans Moolenburgh, *Fluoride: The Freedom Fight*, Edinburgh: Mainstream (1987): 176–189.

97. *Consumer Reports*, op. cit., 394.

98. Ibid., 395. This passage has been quoted frequently in proponent literature.

99. I thank Edward Groth III for this information.

100. *Consumer Reports*, op. cit., 395.

101. Ibid.

102. Ibid.

103. Mary Bernhardt and Bob Sprague, "The Poisonmongers," Stephen Barrett (ed.), *The Health Robbers*, Philadelphia: George F.

Stickley (Second edition, 1980): 208–219, at 217, 219; reprinted in Stephen Barrett and Sheldon Rovin (eds), *The Tooth Robbers: A Profluoridation Handbook*, Philadelphia: George F. Stickley (1980): 1–8.

104. On the controversy over laetrile, *see* Gerald E. Markle and James C. Petersen (eds.), *Politics, Science and Cancer: The Laetrile Phenomenon*, Boulder: Westview (1980).

105. Ralph W. Moss, *The Cancer Syndrome*, New York: Grove Press (1980).

106. Berhardt and Sprague, op. cit., 219 (emphasis in the original).

107. Ibid., 217.

108. John Yiamouyiannis, *Fluoride: The Aging Factor*, Delaware, Ohio: Health Action Press (Second edition, 1986): 149.

109. Bernhardt and Sprague, op. cit., 212 (emphasis in the original).

110. *See also* Mary Bernhardt, "Fluoridation: How Far in 20 Years?" *Journal of the American Dental Association*, vol. 71, no. 5 (November 1965): 1115–1120.

111. Richard Doll and Leo Kinlen, letter, *The Lancet*, vol. 1 (21 January 1978): 150.

112. The treatment of scientists such as Alfred Taylor, who did studies on fluoride and cancer in mice, and Ionel Rapaport, who examined links between fluoridation and mongoloid births, illustrates all the points made in this chapter. See the excellent account in Groth (1973), op. cit.: 279–296.

CHAPTER 5

A small portion of the material in this chapter is adapted from Brian Martin, "Analyzing the Fluoridation Controversy: Resources and Structures," *Social Studies of Science*, vol. 18 (1988): 331–363.

1. An attempt to have a person barred from practicing dentistry normally involves rhetoric, too, as the following examples illustrate. The point I am trying to make here could be described as a distinction between rhetoric used to threaten a person's credibility (chapter 4) and rhetoric used to threaten a person's physical practices, including publications, research work, and job (this chapter). Even this distinction contains some conceptual messiness. My aim is less to establish a conceptual classification of the exercise of power than to demonstrate the power dynamics of the fluoridation controversy.

2. Brian Martin, "The Scientific Straightjacket: The Power Structure of Science and the Suppression of Environmental Scholarship," *The Ecologist*, vol. 11, no. 1 (January/February 1981): 33–43; "Suppression of Dissident Experts: Ideological Struggle in Australia," *Crime and Social Justice*, no. 19 (summer 1983): 91–99; "Science Policy: Dissent and Its Difficulties," *Philosophy and Social Action*, vol. 12, no. 1 (January–March 1986): 5–23; and Brian Martin, C. M. Ann Baker, Clyde Manwell, and Cedric Pugh (eds.), *Intellectual Suppression: Australian Case Histories, Analysis and Responses*, Sydney: Angus and Robertson (1986).

See also, for example, David W. Ewing, *Freedom Inside the Organization: Bringing Civil Liberties to the Workplace*, New York: Dutton (1977); Myron Peretz Glazer and Penina Migdal Glazer, *The Whistleblowers: Exposing Corruption in Government and Industry*, New York: Basic Books (1989); Ralph Nader, Peter J. Petkas, and Kate Blackwell (eds.), *Whistle Blowing: The Report of the Conference on Professional Responsibility*, New York: Grossman (1972); Charles Peters and Taylor Branch (writers and editors), *Blowing the Whistle: Dissent in the Public Interest*, New York: Praeger (1972); Deena Weinstein, *Bureaucratic Opposition: Challenging Abuses at the Workplace*, New York: Pergamon (1979); and Alan F. Westin, with Henry I. Kurtz and Albert Robbins (eds.), *Whistle Blowing! Loyalty and Dissent in the Corporation*, New York: McGraw-Hill (1981).

3. John B. Neilands, letter, *Chemical and Engineering News* (31 October 1988): 3; and John Yiamouyiannis, *Fluoride: The Aging Factor*, Delaware, Ohio: Health Action Press (Second edition, 1986): 149–150.

4. Ivan H. Northfield, notarized statement, dated 5 August 1969.

5. G. L. Waldbott, *A Struggle with Titans*, New York: Carlton Press (1965): 237.

6. Edward Groth III, letter to Brian Martin, dated 8 December 1988.

7. Yiamouyiannis, op. cit.: 158–159.

8. Virginia Crawford, text of tape of statement, Flint, Mich., dated February 1964.

9. Waldbott, op. cit., 43.

10. Ibid., 201.

11. Ibid., 341–342. See also George L. Waldbott, in collaboration with Albert W. Burgstahler and H. Lewis McKinney, *Fluoridation: The Great Dilemma*, Lawrence, Kans.: Coronado Press (1978): 323.

12. H. William Gross, Committee for the Betterment of Oral Health, letter, dated 6 October 1961. See also Waldbott, op. cit., 277.

13. Waldbott, op. cit., 140–141. *See also* Harry M. Raulet, "The Health Professional and the Fluoridation Issue: A Case of Role Conflict," *Journal of Social Issues*, vol. 17, no. 4 (1961): 45–54, at 46. "In neither city did a local physician or dentist work actively and openly against the fluoridation proposal, but the proponents, very much concerned with professional solidarity in the matter, were quite bitter toward their few colleagues who refused to sign the endorsement."

14. For example, Carol S. Farkas and Edward J. Farkas, "Potential Effect of Food Processing on the Fluoride Content of Infant Foods," *Science of the Total Environment*, vol. 2 (1974): 399–405.

15. Carol Farkas, letter to Brian Martin, dated 6 April 1986.

16. Roger J. Berry and W. Trillwood, "Sodium Fluoride and Cell Growth," *British Medical Journal* (26 October 1963): 1064. Note that Berry and Trillwood's results at lower fluoride concentrations have not been reproduced by other investigators: *See* Royal College of Physicians of London, *Fluoride, Teeth and Health*, Tunbridge Wells, Kent: Pitman Medical (1976): 57.

17. Waldbott, op cit., 249.

18. Hans Moolenburgh, *Fluoride: The Freedom Fight*, Edinburgh: Mainstream (1987): 24–25, 47.

19. Ibid., 107.

20. Wendy Varney, *Fluoride in Australia: A Case to Answer*, Sydney: Hale and Iremonger (1986): 95; Anne-Lise Gotzsche, *The Fluoride Question*, London: Davis-Poynter (1975): 17; and John Polya, personal communication. For Polya's arguments on fluoridation, see John Polya, *Are We Safe? A Layman's Guide to Controversy in Public Health*, Melbourne: Cheshire (1964).

21. Glen S. R. Walker, *Fluoridation: Poison on Tap*, Melbourne: Glen Walker (1982): 196–204; and Geoffrey E. Smith, "Fluoride: The Frightening Facts," *Simply Living*, vol. 2, no. 1 (1983): 29–36, at 34.

22. S. G. Kings, Federal President, Australian Dental Association, letter to The Chairman, CSIRO, dated 14 February 1984; Colin H. Wall, Executive Director, Australian Dental Association, letter to J. P. Wild, Chairman, CSIRO, dated 21 August 1985; and N. L. Henry, Federal President, Australian Dental Association, letter to Barry O. Jones, Minister for Science and Technology, dated 28 August 1985. This case is described in Mark Diesendorf, letter, *Chemical and Engineering News*, vol. 67, no. 5 (30 January 1989): 2–3; and Varney, op. cit., 89.

23. Mark Donohoe, letter, *Central Coast Express*, (18 June 1986): 6; M. Walsh, Acting Secretary, Medical Board of New South Wales, letter to M. Donohoe (9 September 1986).

24. John Colquhoun, *Education and Fluoridation in New Zealand: An Historical Study*, Ph.D. thesis, University of Auckland (1987): 231–232.

25. Ibid., 232.

26. Ibid.

27. Ibid., 311–312. This incident is also reported by John Colquhoun and Robert Mann in "The Hastings Fluoridation Experiment: Science or Swindle?" *The Ecologist*, vol. 16, no. 6 (1986): 243–248, at 247.

28. This highly important point is amply documented in Edward Groth III, in his review of the scientific literature, *Two Issues of Science and Public Policy: Air Pollution Control in the San Francisco Bay Area and Fluoridation of Community Water Supplies*, Ph.D. dissertation, Stanford University (1973), chapter 5. Groth states on page 276, that "A consistent, serious, flaw in this body of research, and one which is probably closely related to the quality of the studies, is commitment to predetermined conclusions on the part of the investigators."

29. Mark Diesendorf, letter, *New Doctor*, no. 19 (April 1981): 2.

30. Bette Hileman, "Fluoridation of Water," *Chemical & Engineering News*, vol. 66, no. 31 (1 August 1988): 26–42, at 36. A copy of the reviewers' comments was provided to me by Harold Warner. The paper was later published as Sohan L. Manocha, Harold Warner, and Zbigniew L. Olkowski, "Cytochemical Response of Kidney, Liver and Nervous System to Fluoride Ions in Drinking Water," *Histochemical Journal*, vol. 7 (1975): 343–355.

31. R. S. Scorer, "Teething Troubles," *New Ecologist*, vol. 9, no. 2, (March–April 1979): 70–71, at p. 71.

32. Waldbott, op. cit., 323.

33. Waldbott et al., op. cit., 334–335; Walker, op. cit., 145–146.

34. Albert Schatz, "Some Comments on Two Books Dealing with the Toxicology of Fluorine Compounds," *Pakistan Dental Review*, vol. 15, no. 2 (April 1965): 68–71; Waldbott, op. cit., 276–285.

35. Philip R. N. Sutton, *Fluoridation, 1979: Scientific Criticisms and Fluoride Dangers*, Melbourne: Philip R. N. Sutton (1980): 32–33; and a letter, *Chemical and Engineering News*, vol. 67, no. 4 (23 January 1989): 3.

36. Sutton (1980), op. cit., 33; and (1989), op. cit.

37. Sutton (1980), op. cit., 33.

38. "Editors Say Press is Free on Fluoridation Reporting," *Journal of th~ American Dental Association*, vol. 54, no. 4 (April 1957): ɔ42–543.

39. *See* the numerous cases in Gladys Caldwell and Philip E. Zanfagna, *Fluoridation and Truth Decay*, Reseda, Calif.: Top-Ecol Press (1974): 15–16, 39–40, and 53–72; F. B. Exner and G. L. Waldbott (James Rorty, ed.), *The American Fluoridation Experiment*, New York: Devin-Adair (1957): 184–191; Sutton, op. cit., 23–33; Waldbott et al., op. cit., 318–352; and Yiamouyiannis, op. cit. Allan Mazur, "Disputes Between Experts," *Minerva*, vol. 11, no. 2 (April 1973): 243–262, reproduced in-Allan Mazur, *The Dynamics of Technical Controversy*, Washington, D.C.: Communications Press (1981), at page 261, implies that one approach used by proponents has been to "suppress, discredit or ignore the criticism" but gives no examples.

40. Robert Swan, editor, *Simply Living*, letter to Gordon Medcalf, dated 20 January 1984.

41. A possible exception is the more neutral analysis of Groth, op. cit., who lists a number of cases on pages 179–185. However, many proponents would consider Groth to be a de facto opponent, partly *because* he documents attacks on opponents.

42. I thank Edward Groth III for emphasizing this point to me.

43. The fluoridation debate is not the only scientific debate where these sorts of attacks have been documented. There are numerous examples from around the world in which scientists critical of nuclear power have been transferred, censored, lost research funds, and been sacked from jobs. *See* Leslie J. Freeman, *Nuclear Witnesses*, New York: Norton (1981); and Brian Martin, "Nuclear Suppression," *Science and Public Policy*, vol. 13, no. 6, (December 1986): 312–320. The characteristic of cases of "suppression of dissent" is that the target has done research or spoken out critically of nuclear power, while others with equivalent work records have not been attacked in the same way.

Nuclear scientists and engineers working in government research organizations or corporations can be attacked directly by management who support nuclear power. Critics in universities are harder to attack, since university administrations usually have no direct commitment to nuclear power. University scientists are vulnerable to having research grants cut off, and, in some cases, to the blocking of tenure or promotion. This may occur as a result of outside pressure, usually operating through connections between powerful figures inside the university and pronuclear groups outside. Nevertheless, opponents who are scientists in universities are much more protected from attack than those in government or industry.

Another area where these sorts of attacks on scientists who are critics have been well documented is pesticides. Rachel Carson, author of the immensely influential *Silent Spring*, was subject to vicious attacks, although her independent position provided protection. *See* Frank Graham, Jr., *Since Silent Spring*, Boston: Houghton Mifflin (1970). University critics have suffered the same gamut of attacks as have critics of nuclear power, while few inside government—not to mention the chemical industry—have had the inclination or temerity to speak up critically. *See* Samuel S. Epstein, *The Politics of Cancer*, San Francisco: Sierra Club Books (1978); and Robert van den Bosch, *The Pesticide Conspiracy*, Garden City, N.Y.: Doubleday (1978).

44. Randall Collins, *The Credential Society: An Historical Sociology of Education and Stratification*, New York: Academic Press (1979); Eliot Freidson, *Professional Dominance: The Social Structure of Medical Care*, New York: Atherton (1970); Terence J. Johnson, *Professions and Power*, London: Macmillan (1972); Magali Sarfatti Larson, *The Rise of Professionalism: A Sociological Analysis*, Berkeley, Calif.: University of California Press (1977); and Evan Willis, *Medical Dominance: The Division of Labour in Australian Health Care*, Sydney: Allen and Unwin (1983). For a critical discussion, *see* Mike Saks, "Removing the Blinkers? A Critique of Recent Contributions to the Sociology of Professions," *Sociological Review*, vol. 31, no. 1 (1983): 1–21. For an excellent treatment of dentistry from this perspective, *see* Peter Davis, *The Social Context of Dentistry*, London: Croom Helm (1980).

45. I thank Edward Groth III for emphasizing this point to me.

46. Students in one of my classes interviewed local dentists on their views about fluoridation. While neither a complete nor a random sample was involved, the results were striking. Eighteen of twenty dentists interviewed were graduates of Sydney University, and every one of the eighteen supported fluoridation. Without exception, they thought the dental school had presented them with strongly profluoridation views, and some mentioned that contrary views were excluded or denigrated.

47. Elof O. Petterson, "Attitudes Concerning Water Fluoridation among Graduating Swedish Dentists," *Community Dentistry and Oral Epidemiology*, vol. 7 (April 1979): 69–74.

48. Lesley Doyal with Imogen Pennell, *The Political Economy of Health*, London: Pluto (1979); and Ivan Illich, *Medical Nemesis: The Expropriation of Health*, London: Calder and Boyars (1975).

49. Davis, op. cit., 120.

50. Working Group on Preventive Dental Services, *Preventive Dental Services: Practices, Guidelines and Recommendations*, Canada: Minister of National Health and Welfare (1979): 173.

51. Commonwealth Department of Health, *Fluoridation of Water: A Collection of Reports and Statements*, Canberra: Australian Government Publishing Service (1985): 2.

52. Colquhoun, op. cit. Also, John Colquhoun, "Decline in Primary Tooth Decay in New Zealand," *Community Health Studies*, vol. 12, no. 2 (1988): 187–191. For speculations about a similar long-term decline in tooth decay in the United States, see Brian A. Burt, "The Future of the Caries Decline," *Journal of Public Health Dentistry*, vol. 45, no. 4 (Fall 1985): 261–269.

53. Gilles Dussault and Aubrey Sheiham, "Medical Theories and Professional Development: The Theory of Focal Sepsis and Dentistry in Early Twentieth Century Britain," *Social Science and Medicine*, vol. 16, (1982): 1405–1412. See also Davis, op. cit., 103–106.

54. Frank Parkin, *Marxism and Class Theory: A Bourgeois Critique*, London: Tavistock (1979), chapters 4–6.

55. Jethro K. Lieberman, *The Tyranny of the Experts: How Professionals are Closing the Open Society*, New York: Walker (1970).

56. Davis, op. cit.

57. Ibid., 126–129.

58. My argument here is greatly indebted to Varney, op. cit.

59. Douglas O. deShazer, "Knowledge and Opinions of Dental Students on Fluoridation," *Journal of Dental Education*, vol. 31, no. 1 (March 1967): 28–33, at 32.

60. Bruce L. Douglas, Donald A. Wallace, Monroe Lerner, and Sylvia B. Coppersmith, "Impact of Water Fluoridation on Dental Practice and Dental Manpower," *Journal of the American Dental Association*, vol. 84, no. 2 (February 1972): 355–367, at 355. See also Bruce L. Douglas, Donald A. Wallace, Monroe Lerner, and Sylvia B. Coppersmith, "The Impact of Fluoridation on Patterns of Dental Treatment," *Journal of Public Health Dentistry*, vol. 31, no. 4 (fall 1971): 225–240.

61. Sutton (1980), op. cit.: 47–53.

62. I thank Albert Burgstahler and Edward Groth III for emphasizing this point about ethics.

63. Dennis H. Leverett, "Fluorides and the Changing Prevalence of Dental Caries," *Science*, vol. 217 (2 July 1982): 26–30, at 30. Note that Leverett's article appeared in *Science*, not a dental journal.

64. Edward Groth III, in a letter to Brian Martin, dated 8 December 1988, said that "Leverett was not being innovative . . . he was just saying openly what all of his fellow pros were saying whenever the

issue of total fluoride intake came up." But there has been no move to do the research to see if total fluoride dosage is so high that water fluoride levels should be lowered.

65. Leverett's career apparently has not suffered as a result of his *Science* paper.

66. A. S. Gray, "Fluoridation: Time for a New Base Line?" *Journal of the Canadian Dental Association*, vol. 53, no. 10 (October 1987): 763–765, at 764.

67. Albert Burgstahler provided me with copies of a letter from Dennis H. Leverett to David Werdegar, Health Director, San Francisco Health Department, dated 17 July 1985; and a letter from A. S. Gray to John Osterman, Lakeshore General Hospital, Quebec, dated 7 March 1988, in which they both appear to "renounce" any deviation from the standard profluoridation line. This again suggests the powerful pressures to maintain set positions.

68. Edward Groth III points out in a letter to Brian Martin, dated 8 December 1988, that the sides are not perfectly symmetrical, since the antifluoridationists have only one means to prevent the health risks and coercion they see to be associated with fluoridation; whereas the proponents have other options to promote dental public health. Evidence for and against the view that opponents, given the chance, would suppress proponents remains to be collected. Evidence in some other areas—such as the plight of left-wing and right-wing critics under regimes of the opposite orientation—supports the symmetry thesis.

CHAPTER 6

1. Eugene Garfield, "Fluoridation, 'Texas Teeth,' and the Great Conspiracy. Part 1. The Issues," *Current Contents*, vol. 17, no. 12 (24 March 1986): 3–9, at 6.

2. Ibid.

3. It might be argued that antifluoridationists have an interest in freedom of choice and in opposing the coercion of compulsory mass medication. Here, I set this aside and concentrate on interests such as money, power, and prestige. One difficulty is that noble values, such as freedom, often serve as legitimations for more sordid interests, in the same way that "freedom" in capitalist societies is often a mask for corporate power and "peace" in Communist societies involves support for government military policies. Beliefs in values such as peace and freedom may be quite sincere and influential, but analysis of interests concentrates on material factors influencing people's actions.

4. Phillip Finch's *God, Guts, and Guns,* New York: Seaview/Putnam (1983), a discussion of the radical right in the United States in the 1980s, does not mention fluoridation.

5. *See,* for example, articles reprinted in *Cancer Control Journal,* vol. 5, nos. 1 and 2 (1978): 75–80.

6. G. L. Waldbott, *A Struggle with Titans,* New York: Carlton Press (1965): 101.

7. Expositions of the view that corporate interests have been behind the promotion of fluoridation are given by many authors, including P. Clavell Blount, *Compulsory Mass Medication,* London: The Clair Press (1964); Gladys Caldwell and Philip E. Zanfagna, *Fluoridation and Truth Decay,* Reseda, Calif.: Top-Ecol Press (1974); F. B. Exner, "Economic Motives Behind Fluoridation," *Aqua Pura,* vol. 3, no. 8 (January 1966): 1–4; F. B. Exner and G. L. Waldbott, (James Rorty, ed.), *The American Fluoridation Experiment,* New York: Devin-Adair (1957); Anne-Lise Gotzsche, *The Fluoride Question,* London: Davis-Poynter (1975); Wendy Varney, *Fluoride in Australia: A Case to Answer,* Sydney: Hale and Iremonger (1986); Waldbott, op. cit.; and George L. Waldbott, in collaboration with Albert W. Burgstahler and H. Lewis McKinney, *Fluoridation: The Great Dilemma,* Lawrence, Kans.: Coronado Press (1978). I am especially indebeted to the accounts by Varney and by Waldbott et al. In addition, Edward Groth III and John Small offered valuable cautionary comments.

8. Waldbott et al., op. cit., 305.

9. Ibid., 312; and Varney, op. cit., 59.

10. John Small, letter to Brian Martin, dated November 1988.

11. Rebecca Hanmer, deputy assistant administrator for Water, United States Environmental Protection Agency, letter to Leslie A. Russell, dated 30 March 1983. Copies of this letter have been circulated around antifluoridation networks.

12. I thank Mark Diesendorf and Edward Groth III for comments in relation to this point.

13. Statement by Dr. Charles T. Betts, in *Fluoridation of Water,* Hearings before the Committee on Interstate and Foreign Commerce, House of Representatives, Eighty-Third Congress, Second Session, on H.R. 2341, A Bill to Protect the Public Health from the Dangers of Fluorination of Water (25–27 May 1954): 86–95, at 93.

14. Waldbott et al., op. cit., 313.

15. Varney, op. cit., 72.

16. *Fluoridation*, New York: American Council on Science and Health (June 1983). I thank Edward Groth III for information on ACSH.

17. A general perspective on this, though not in relation to fluoridation, is given by Peter Davis, *The Social Context of Dentistry*, London: Croom Helm (1980): 58–59.

18. Another path not taken is the promotion of "complete tooth nutrition," which involves ingesting a variety of key minerals and vitamins during childhood. *See* Alfred Aslander, "The Theory of Complete Tooth Nutrition as a Natural and Effective Dental Caries Prophylaxis," *Journal of Applied Nutrition*, vol. 17 (1964): 190–204. I thank Albert Burgstahler for making this point.

19. Robert L. Crain, Elihu Katz, and Donald B. Rosenthal, *The Politics of Community Conflict: The Fluoridation Decision*, Indianapolis: Bobbs–Merrill (1969); and Varney, op. cit., chapter 4.

20. The key debate here has been whether fluoridation is legal, especially under the United States Constitution, rather than an examination of the role of the legal system in the struggle over fluoridation. *See*, for example: Lester E. Block, "Antifluoridationists Persist: The Constitutional Basis for Fluoridation," *Journal of Public Health Dentistry*, vol. 46, no. 4, (fall 1986): 188–198; Bernard J. Conway, "Legal Aspects of Municipal Fluoridation," *Journal of the American Water Works Association* (October 1958): 1330–1336; Arthur Selwyn Miller, "Fluoridation vs. the Constitution," *Saturday Review*, vol. 48, no. 14 (3 April 1965): 49–53; Ruth Roemer, "Water Fluoridation: Public Health Responsibility and the Democratic Process," *American Journal of Public Health and the Nation's Health*, vol. 55, no. 7 (July 1965): 1337–1348; Ruth Roemer, "Legislation on Fluorides and Dental Health," *International Digest of Health Legislation*, vol. 34, no. 1 (1983): 1–31; and George A. Strong, "Liberty, Religion and Fluoridation," *Santa Clara Lawyer*, vol. 8 (1967): 37–58.

21. There is little comparative analysis on any issue involving the effect of social and political structures on issues involving technical expertise. See Brendan Gillespie, Dave Eva, and Ron Johnston, "Carcinogenic Risk Assessment in the United States and Great Britain: The Case of Aldrin/Dieldrin," *Social Studies of Science*, vol. 9 (1979): 265–301; Alan Irwin, *Risk and the Control of Technology: Public Policies for Road Traffic Safety in Britain and the United States*, Manchester: Manchester University Press (1985); and Sheila Jasanoff, *Risk Management and Political Culture: A Comparative Study of Science in the Policy Context*, New York: Russell Sage Foundation (1986). I thank Sheila Jasanoff for helpful comments about the literature in this area.

CHAPTER 7

1. Harvey M. Sapolsky, "Science, Voters, and the Fluoridation Controversy," *Science*, vol. 162 (25 October 1968): 427–433, at 432.

2. Donald R. McNeil, "Political Aspects of Fluoridation," *Journal of the American Dental Association*, vol. 65, no. 5 (November 1962): 659–662, at 659.

3. Donald R. McNeil, "America's Longest War: The Fight over Fluoridation, 1950–," *Wilson Quarterly*, vol. 9 (summer 1985): 140–153, at 153.

4. Russell B. Scobie, "Water Fluoridation: A Survey of the International Picture," *Alabama Journal of Medical Sciences*, vol. 12, no. 3 (1975): 225–229, at 229.

5. *See*, for example, Malcolm L. Goggin (ed.), *Governing Science and Technology in a Democracy*, Knoxville: University of Tennessee Press (1986); and James C. Petersen (ed.), *Citizen Participation in Science Policy*, Amherst: University of Massachusetts Press (1984).

6. *See* especially Robert L. Crain, Elihu Katz, and Donald B. Rosenthal, *The Politics of Community Conflict: The Fluoridation Decision*, Indianapolis: Bobbs-Merrill, (1969).

7. Deena Weinstein, *Bureaucratic Opposition: Challenging Abuses at the Workplace*, New York: Pergamon (1979).

8. Jane J. Mansbridge, *Beyond Adversary Democracy*, New York: Basic Books (1980).

9. In a letter to Brian Martin, dated 8 December 1988, Edward Groth III comments that such a compromise is usually opposed both by antifluoridationists—who say people would not go to the trouble of obtaining the unfluoridated water—and by profluoridationists—who do not want to admit there are any legitimate objections to fluoridated water.

10. Rita Arditti, Pat Brennan and Steve Cavrak (eds.), *Science and Liberation*, Boston: South End Press (1980); David Dickson, *Alternative Technology and the Politics of Technical Change*, London: Fontana (1974); Brian Martin, *The Bias of Science*, Canberra: Society for Social Responsibility in Science (ACT) (1979); Hilary Rose and Steven Rose (eds.), *The Political Economy of Science* and *The Radicalisation of Science*, London: Macmillan (1976); and the journals *Radical Science Journal*, *Science for People*, and *Science for the People*. Excellent case studies which illustrate the role of values in science include Phillip M.

Boffey, *The Brain Bank of America: An Inquiry into the Politics of Science*, New York: McGraw-Hill (1975); David Dickson, *The New Politics of Science*, New York: Pantheon (1984); Samuel S. Epstein, *The Politics of Cancer*, San Francisco: Sierra Club Books (1978); Ian I. Mitroff, *The Subjective Side of Science: A Philosophical Inquiry into the Psychology of the Apollo Moon Scientists*, Amsterdam: Elsevier (1974); and Joel Primack and Frank von Hippel, *Advice and Dissent: Scientists in the Political Arena*, New York: Basic Books (1974).

11. *See*, for example, Leonard A. Cole, "Resolving Science Controversies: From Science Court to Science Hearings Panel," in Goggin, op. cit., 244–261.

12. Ned Crosby, Janet M. Kelly, and Paul Schaefer, "Citizens Panels: A New Approach to Citizen Participation," *Public Administration Review*, vol. 46 (March/April 1986): 170–178. Their term "citizens panels" has since been changed to "policy juries." For more information contact the Jefferson Center, Plymouth Building, 12 S. Sixth Street, Minneapolis, Minn. 55042.

13. P. C. Dienel, *Die Planungszelle*, Opladen: Westdeutscher Verlag (1978); Peter C. Dienel, "Contributing to Social Decision Methodology: Citizen Reports on Technological Projects," C. Vlek and G. Cvetkovich (eds.), *Social Decision Methodology for Technological Projects*, Dordrecht: Kluwer (1989): 133–151; Detlef Garbe, "Planning Cell and Citizen Report: A Report on German Experiences with New Participation Instruments," *European Journal of Political Research*, vol. 14 (1986): 221–236; and O. Renn, H. U. Stegelmann, G. Albrecht, U. Kotte, and H. P. Peters, "An Empirical Investigation of Citizens' Preferences Among Four Energy Scenarios," *Technological Forecasting and Social Change*, vol. 26 (1984): 11–46.

14. Closure is the principal focus of the important collection by H. Tristram Engelhardt, Jr., and Arthur L. Caplan (eds.), *Scientific Controversies: Case Studies in the Resolution and Closure of Disputes in Science and Technology*, Cambridge: Cambridge University Press (1987).

15. John Colquhoun reports the conclusions of his world tour in "New Evidence on Fluoridation," *Social Science and Medicine*, vol. 19, no. 11 (1984): 1239–1246.

16. K. Tennakone and S. Wickramanayake, "Aluminium Leaching from Cooking Utensils," *Nature*, vol. 325 (15 January 1987): 202.

17. The clinical status of Alzheimer's disease is questionable. *See* Jaber F. Gubrium, "Structuring and Deconstructing the Course of Illness: The Alzheimer's Disease Experience," *Sociology of Health and Illness*, vol. 9 (1987): 1–24.

18. J. Savory, J. R. Nicholson, and M. R. Wills, "Is Aluminium Leaching Enhanced by Fluoride?" *Nature*, vol. 327 (14 May 1987): 107–108; K. Tennakone and S. Wickramanayaka, "Aluminium and Cooking," *Nature*, vol. 329 (1 October 1987): 398; and S. Watanabe and C. Dawes, "The Effect of pH and Fluoride on Leaching of Aluminum from Kitchen Utensils," *Fluoride*, vol. 21, (April 1988): 58–59.

19. *See*, for example, Olli Simonen and Ossi Laitinen, "Does Fluoridation of Drinking-Water Prevent Bone Fragility and Osteoporosis?" *Lancet*, vol. 2 (24 August 1985): 432–434.

20. *See*, for example, Ilkka Arnala, Esko M. Alhava, Reijo Kivivuori, and Pentti Kauranen, "Hip Fracture Incidence Not Affected by Fluoridation," *Acta Orthopaedica Scandinavica*, vol. 57 (1986): 344–348.

21. Edward Groth III, letter to Brian Martin, dated 8 December 1988. I thank him also for valuable comments in relation to the previous two paragraphs.

22. R. L. Glass (ed.), First International Conference on the Declining Prevalence of Dental Caries, Boston (25–26 June 1982) published in *Journal of Dental Research*, vol. 61 (November 1982): 1301–1383.

23. *See*, for example, E. C. Reynolds, and A. del Rio, "Effect of Casein and Whey-Protein Solutions on Caries Experience and Feeding Patterns of the Rat," *Archives of Oral Biology*, vol. 29, no. 11 (1984): 927–933.

24. Geoffrey E. Smith, "Can a Vaccine Prevent Cavities?" *Trends in Pharmacological Sciences*, vol. 7, no. 3 (March 1986): 108–112.

25. A good feel for profluoride strategy is given by P. Jean Frazier in "Priorities to Preserve Fluoride Uses: Rationales and Strategies," *Journal of Public Health Dentistry*, vol. 45, no. 3 (summer 1985): 149–165, and the following reaction papers and discussion on pages 166–179.

26. I thank Edward Groth III for emphasizing this point.

27. H. M. Collins, *Changing Order: Replication and Induction in Scientific Practice*, London: Sage (1985); Andrew Pickering, *Constructing Quarks: A Sociological History of Particle Physics*, Edinburgh: Edinburgh University Press (1984); and Evelleen Richards, "The Politics of Therapeutic Evaluation: The Vitamin C and Cancer Controversy," *Social Studies of Science*, vol. 18 (1988): 653–701.

28. On Tiel-Culemborg, *see* Hans Moolenburgh, *Fluoridation: The Freedom Fight*, Edinburgh: Mainstream (1987): 34–35, 114–115, and 128–129. On Anglesey-Mon, *see* Mark Diesendorf, "Anglesey Fluoridation Trials Re-examined," *Fluoride*, vol. 22, no. 2 (April 1989): 53–58.

29. Some fluoridation opponents have also attacked fluoride toothpastes and other fluoride products.

30. Moolenburgh, op. cit.

31. See chapter 4.

CHAPTER 8

Portions of this chapter are adapted from Brian Martin, "The Sociology of the Fluoridation Controversy: A Reexamination," *Sociological Quarterly*, vol. 30, no. 1 (1989): 59-76.

1. Good reviews of social science research include P. Jean Frazier, "Fluoridation: A Review of Social Research," *Journal of Public Health Dentistry*, vol. 40, no. 3 (summer 1980): 214-233; P. Jean Frazier, "Public and Professional Adoption of Selected Methods to Prevent Dental Decay," L. K. Cohen and P. S. Bryant (eds.), *Social Sciences and Dentistry: A Critical Bibliography. Volume II*, London: Quintessence (1984): 84-144; and Annabelle Bender Motz, "The Fluoridation Issue as Studied by Social Scientists," N. David Richards and Lois K. Cohen (eds.), *Social Sciences and Dentistry: A Critical Bibliography*, The Hague: A. Sijthoff (1971): 347-364. For a critique, *see* Brian Martin, "The Sociology of the Fluoridation Controversy: A Reexamination," *Sociological Quarterly*, vol. 30, no. 1 (1989): 59-76.

2. Bernard Mausner and Judith Mausner, "A Study of the Antiscientific Attitude," *Scientific American*, vol. 192 (February 1955): 35-39.

3. A. Stafford Metz, "An Analysis of Some Determinants of Attitude Toward Fluoridation," *Social Forces*, vol. 44 (1966): 477-484.

4. Thomas F. A. Plaut, "Analysis of Voting Behavior on a Fluoridation Referendum," *Public Opinion Quarterly*, vol. 23 (1959): 213-222.

5. William A. Gamson, "Public Information in a Fluoridation Referendum," *Health Education Journal*, vol. 19 (March 1961): 47-54; and William A. Gamson and Peter H. Irons, "Community Characteristics and Fluoridation Outcome," *Journal of Social Issues*, vol. 17, no. 4 (1961): 66-74.

6. John M. Frankel and Myron Allukian, "Sixteen Referenda on Fluoridation in Massachusetts: An Analysis," *Journal of Public Health Dentistry*, vol. 33, no. 2 (spring 1973): 96-103.

7. Harvey M. Sapolsky, "Science, Voters, and the Fluoridation Controversy," *Science*, vol. 162 (25 October 1968): 427-433.

8. William A. Gamson, "The Fluoridation Dialogue: Is It an Ideological Conflict?" *Public Opinion Quarterly*, vol. 25 (1961): 526–537; Arnold L. Green, "The Ideology of Anti-fluoridation Leaders," *Journal of Social Issues*, vol. 17, no. 4 (1961): 13–25; Erwin L. Linn, "An Appraisal of Sociological Research on the Public's Attitudes Toward Fluoridation," *Journal of Public Health Dentistry*, vol. 29 (1969): 36–45; and Arnold Simmel, "A Signpost for Research on Fluoridation Conflicts: The Concept of Relative Deprivation," *Journal of Social Issues*, vol. 17, no. 4 (1961): 26–36.

9. Robert L. Crain, Elihu Katz, and Donald B. Rosenthal, *The Politics of Community Conflict: The Fluoridation Decision*, Indianapolis: Bobbs-Merrill (1969): 6–9, 31–51, and 215–222.

10. Crain et al., op. cit., 58–70; Sapolsky, op. cit.; and Harvey M. Sapolsky, "The Fluoridation Controversy: An Alternative Explanation," *Public Opinion Quarterly*, vol. 33, (1969): 240–248.

11. Mausner and Mausner, op. cit.

12. S. Stephen Kegeles, "Some Unanswered Questions and Action Implications of Social Research in Fluoridation," *Journal of Social Issues*, vol. 17, no. 4 (1961): 75–81, at 81.

13. William A. Gamson, "Community Issues and Their Outcome: How to Lose a Fluoridation Referendum," Alvin W. Gouldner and S. Michael Miller (eds.), *Applied Sociology: Opportunities and Problems*, New York: Free Press (1965): 350–357.

14. Motz, op. cit., 359–360.

15. Henry Frankel, "The Continental Drift Debate," H. Tristram Engelhardt, Jr., and Arthur L. Caplan (eds.), *Scientific Controversies: Case Studies in the Resolution and Closure of Disputes in Science and Technology*, Cambridge: Cambridge University Press (1987): 203–248.

16. James S. Coleman, *Community Conflict*, New York: Free Press (1957); Crain et al., op. cit.; Brian W. Head, "The Fluoridation Controversy in Victoria: Public Policy and Group Politics," *Australian Journal of Public Administration*, vol. 37 (1978): 257–273; Austin Mitchell, "Fluoridation in Dunedin: A Study of Pressure Groups and Public Opinion," *Political Science*, vol. 12 (1960): 71–93; and Maurice Pinard, "Structural Attachments and Political Support in Urban Politics: The Case of Fluoridation Referendums," *American Journal of Sociology*, vol. 68 (1963): 513–526.

17. Characteristic examples are Dorothy Nelkin, *Nuclear Power and its Critics: The Cayuga Lake Controversy*, Ithaca, N.Y.: Cornell University Press (1971); and Dorothy Nelkin, "The Political Impact of Technical Expertise," *Social Studies of Science*, vol. 5 (1975): 35–54.

Studies of a similar orientation are represented in Engelhardt and Caplan, op. cit.; and Dorothy Nelkin (ed.), *Controversy: Politics of Technical Decisions*, Beverly Hills: Sage (1979). *See also* Phillip M. Boffey, *The Brain Bank of America: An Inquiry into the Politics of Science*, New York: McGraw-Hill (1975); David Dickson, *The New Politics of Science*, New York: Pantheon (1984); Daniel S. Greenberg, *The Politics of Pure Science*, New York: New American Library (1967); and Joel Primack and Frank von Hippel, *Advice and Dissent: Scientists in the Political Arena*, New York: Basic Books (1974).

18. This is explicit in the mammoth volume edited by Engelhardt and Caplan, op. cit., for example at p. 5: "A scientific controversy with a heavy political and ethical overlay is not, then, one controversy but a scientific controversy (or controversies) plus a controversy (or controversies) concerning social and political theories and viewpoints."

19. See, for example, Richard J. Hastreiter, "Fluoridation Conflict: A History and Conceptual Synthesis," *Journal of the American Dental Association*, vol. 106, no. 4 (April 1983): 486–490. A more successful attempt of this general type, explaining public attitudes to nuclear power, is by James M. Jasper in "The Political Life Cycle of Technological Controversies," *Social Forces*, vol. 67, no. 2 (December 1988): 357–377.

20. The major example is Wendy Varney, *Fluoride in Australia: A Case to Answer*, Sydney: Hale and Iremonger (1986).

21. The only left-wing analysis of fluoridation of which I am aware, prior to Varney's, is by M. Klerer in "The Fluoridation Experiment," *Contemporary Issues*, vol. 7 (1956): 119–167. Incidentally, I have never seen a citation to this paper. I thank Allen Hunter for drawing it to my attention.

22. George L. Waldbott, in collaboration with Albert W. Burgstahler and H. Lewis McKinney, *Fluoridation: The Great Dilemma*, Lawrence, Kans.: Coronado Press (1978); and Michael Wollan, "Controlling the Potential Hazards of Government-Sponsored Technology," *George Washington Law Review*, vol. 36, no. 5 (July 1968): 1105–1137.

23. The work of Allan Mazur deserves separate mention here. In "Disputes Between Experts," *Minerva*, vol. 11, no. 2 (April 1973): 243–262, later incorporated in *The Dynamics of Technical Controversy*, Washington, D.C.: Communications Press (1981), he analyzes the rhetoric over scientific knowledge on both sides of the controversies over fluoridation and low-level ionizing radiation, but only hints at more than rhetorical confrontation. Underlying Mazur's apparently symmetrical analysis is a positivist conception of scientific knowledge, which he clarified for me in correspondence. In a later study, "Opposition to Technological Innovation," *Minerva*, vol. 13, no. 1 (spring 1975): 58–81, Mazur focuses on the opponents. (For the limitations of his model of

media influence, *see* Jasper, op. cit.) To my knowledge, he has never carried out a study of the promotion of fluoridation, possibly reflecting a post-1973 assessment of the weakness of the scientific case against fluoridation.

24. Barry Barnes, *Scientific Knowledge and Sociological Theory*, London: Routledge and Kegan Paul (1974); and Michael Mulkay, *Science and the Sociology of Knowledge*, London: Allen and Unwin (1979).

25. David Bloor, *Knowledge and Social Imagery*, London: Routledge and Kegan Paul (1976).

26. *See*, for example, H. M. Collins, "The Seven Sexes: A Study in the Sociology of a Phenomenon, or the Replication of Experiments in Physics," *Sociology*, vol. 9 (1975): 205–224; H. M. Collins, "Son of Seven Sexes: The Social Destruction of a Physical Phenonemon," *Social Studies of Science*, vol. 11 (1981): 33–62; G. Nigel Gilbert and Michael Mulkay, *Opening Pandora's Box: A Sociological Analysis of Scientists' Discourse*, Cambridge: Cambridge University Press (1984); Bill Harvey, "The Effects of Social Context on the Process of Scientific Investigation: Experimental Tests of Quantum Mechanics," Karin D. Knorr, Roger Krohn, and Richard Whitley (eds.), *The Social Process of Scientific Investigation*, Dordrecht: D. Reidel (1980): 139–163; Bruno Latour and Stephen Woolgar, *Laboratory Life: The Social Construction of Scientific Facts*, London: Sage (1979); Michael Mulkay and G. Nigel Gilbert, "Putting Philosophy to Work: Karl Popper's Influence on Scientific Practice," *Philosophy of the Social Sciences*, vol. 11 (1981): 389–407; and Trevor J. Pinch, "The Sun-set: The Presentation of Certainty in Scientific Life," *Social Studies of Science*, vol. 11 (1981): 131–158.

There is also a considerable literature on resources used in social struggles, for example, by social movements. *See*, for example, J. Craig Jenkins, "Resource Mobilization Theory and the Study of Social Movements," *Annual Review of Sociology*, vol. 9 (1983): 527–553.

I do not discuss this literature further since my focus is on struggles over scientific knowledge. Note that applying resource mobilization theory to the fluoridation controversy would mean focusing on the opponents. A more symmetrical approach would examine both the proponents and the opponents as contending movements, with differential access to resources associated with the state, corporations, professions, and other areas of society.

27. *See*, for example, Barnes, op. cit.; Barry Barnes, *Interests and the Growth of Knowledge*, London: Routledge and Kegan Paul (1977); Barry Barnes, *T. S. Kuhn and Social Science*, London: Macmillan (1982); Bloor, op. cit.; Michel Callon and John Law, "On Interests and their Transformation: Enrolment and Counter-enrolment," *Social Studies of Science*, vol. 12 (1982): 615–625; Paul Forman, "Weimar Culture,

Causality, and Quantum Theory, 1918–1927: Adaptation by German Physicists and Mathematicians to a Hostile Intellectual Environment," *Historical Studies in the Physical Sciences*, vol. 3 (1971): 1–115; Jonathan Harwood, "The Race-intelligence Controversy: A Sociological Approach," *Social Studies of Science*, vol. 6 (1976): 369–394, and vol. 7 (1977): 1–30; Donald MacKenzie, "Statistical Theory and Social Interests: A Case-study," *Social Studies of Science*, vol. 8 (1978): 35–83; Steven Shapin, "The Politics of Observation: Cerebral Anatomy and Social Interests in the Edinburgh Phrenology Disputes," Roy Wallis (ed.), *On the Margins of Science: The Social Construction of Rejected Knowledge*, Keele: University of Keele (1979): 139–178; and Robert M. Young, "The Historiographic and Ideological Contexts of the Nineteenth-Century Debate on Man's Place in Nature," Mikuláš Teich and Robert M. Young (eds.), *Changing Perspectives in the History of Science*, London: Heinemann (1973): 344–438.

For criticisms of interests analysis, *see* Steve Woolgar, "Interests and Explanation in the Social Study of Science," *Social Studies of Science*, vol. 11 (1981): 365–394; and Steven Yearley, "The Relationship Between Epistemological and Sociological Cognitive Interests: Some Ambiguities Underlying the Use of Interest Theory in the Study of Scientific Knowledge," *Studies in History and Philosophy of Science*, vol. 13, no. 4 (December 1982): 353–388.

See also the replies by Barry Barnes, "On the 'Hows' and 'Whys' of Cultural Change (Response to Woolgar)," *Social Studies of Science*, vol. 11 (1981): 481–498; Donald MacKenzie, "Interests, Positivism, and History," *Social Studies of Science*, vol. 11 (1981): 498–504; and Donald MacKenzie, "Reply to Steven Yearley," *Studies in History and Philosophy of Science*, vol. 15, no. 3 (September 1984): 251–259.

28. *See*, for example, David Bloor, "The Strengths of the Strong Programme," *Philosophy of the Social Sciences*, vol. 11 (1981): 199–213; and Larry Laudan, "The Pseudo-Science of Science?" *Philosophy of the Social Sciences*, vol. 11 (1981): 173–198.

29. I am indebted in this section to discussions with Evelleen Richards and Pam Scott which are part of our ongoing collaboration on the role of the researcher in contemporary controversies.

30. Crain et al., op. cit., v and vii.

31. James Morse Dunning, *Principles of Dental Public Health*, Cambridge, Mass.: Harvard University Press (1962): 176.

32. Donald R. McNeil, "Political Aspects of Fluoridaton," *Journal of the American Dental Association*, vol. 65, no. 5 (November 1962): 659–662; *Fluoridation: For Your Community and Your State*, American Dental Association, (1969); and "America's Longest War: The Fight over Fluoridation, 1950–," *Wilson Quarterly*, vol. 9 (summer 1985): 140–153.

33. Wollan, op. cit.

34. Waldbott et al., op. cit.

35. Varney, op. cit.

36. Mark Diesendorf and Wendy Varney, "Fluoridation: Politics and Strategies," *Social Alternatives*, vol. 5, no. 2 (April 1986): 48–53.

37. John Colquhoun, *Education and Fluoridation in New Zealand: An Historical Study*, Ph.D. thesis, University of Auckland (1987).

38. The published form of this paper is Brian Martin "Science Policy: Dissent and Its Difficulties," *Philosophy and Social Action*, vol. 12, no. 1 (January–March 1986): 5–23.

39. I did mention Storey's views as presented in a letter to a newspaper.

40. I have received significant criticisms from, among others, P. C. Blount, Albert Burgstahler, Robert Mick, and John Yiamouyiannis.

41. Edward Groth III, one of the few to attempt to avoid taking sides, commented on his difficulties in a letter to me dated 22 September 1988: ". . . my work became known to the anti-fluoridationists very early on (since I had contacted them for a lot of my research materials). They immediately did try to use me and my ideas to advance their own goals, and that led to a series of attacks on me, some rather vicious, from the pro-fluoridation forces. There was indeed enormous pressure to choose a side, or withdraw. I didn't, because I never saw myself as interested in the *outcome* of fluoridation decisions. I was interested in the *process*, and I was convinced that society needed to find better ways to deal with this issue. I managed to maintain the integrity of that posture pretty well, to my own satisfaction. But the proponents still regarded me as an 'anti,' because as we both know, neutral or symmetrical critical approaches help the antis by legitimizing the controversy. Efforts were made, therefore, to discredit me personally and to portray my dissertation as an antifluoridation tract."

For Groth, the intimidating climate from the proponents was a fairly small negative factor, but it was still sufficient to keep him from publishing further in the field, given that his position did not require publication for career purposes.

INDEX